BIOGRAPHY
OF THE GODS

A. EUSTACE HAYDON

FREDERICK UNGAR PUBLISHING CO.
NEW YORK

TO

CYRUS S. EATON

PREFACE

The gods are a splendid company. It is a pity that they are not better known. This book tells the story of the gods who lingered long enough in the light of history to leave a record of their birth and their development as the companions of man. Most of the gods who began the pilgrimage with their earthly companions died young. Excavations are continually revealing previously unknown deities, some of them bragging in stone of their greatness and power. Man made his appearance in history before any of the gods. The mighty deities of the ancient empires died long ago, leaving their records in the dust and debris of their ruined cities. None of the gods to whom men still make appeal is very old. The oldest among them, Shiva of India, can be traced only some five thousand years into the past.

The gods are not only colorful, but each one has a distinct personal character whose history and marks of origin are closely related to some special human group. The effort to unify the great gods in some abstract, impersonal absolute, or cosmic ultimate, falsifies each one of them and robs him of his historic meaning and usefulness. To talk of a "God" behind the vast variety of ceaselessly changing deities of the religions is to talk the language of agnosticism. If there be such a God, we do not know him. All we have is the idea of God.

The earliest gods were real, tangible, visible phases of nature. Man gave them personality and human qualities by his emotional response and his use of language to describe and address them. Once man had learned to understand the natural world it would seem, in retrospect, that none of these early deities could survive.

vii

However, they were saved by what Andrew Lang called "a primitive blunder." When early man imagined a ghost or a separable soul that could exist apart from the body, the way was opened to the creation of a spiritual world. The gods could now become spirits dwelling in a supernatural realm. There they could continue to grow without limit, feeding on the rich food of man's desires, dreams, hopes, and ideals. The creation of a spiritual world beyond the everyday realm of living made possible heavens and hells, elaborate theologies, philosophies, and the intricate architectonic systems of metaphysics. All this from a "primitive blunder"!

With increasing knowledge of nature and of human nature, men of intellect began to question the existence of a personal god. As long as twenty-five centuries ago, the philosophers of large areas of the Orient had given up the idea. In the Western world, Immanuel Kant and David Hume, at the close of the eighteenth century, examined all the proofs of the existence of God and decided that they were not valid. Concerning the problem of God's existence, Professor Edward Scribner Ames said "God is as real as Uncle Sam or Alma Mater." In response, Professor George Burman Foster wrote in a letter a half-century ago, "I agree with you, Ames, we do have to give up God." "To ask 'Does God exist?' is to ask the wrong question," Professor James Hayden Tufts said long ago; "The question should be 'Does the Universe give support to man's hopes and ideals?'" To this, only scientific humanism can give an adequate answer.

If the remaining gods take the twilight path to oblivion, it will not be because they have been destroyed by reason or because their existence cannot be proved. A wise theologian, Professor Cornell, has said, "I cannot prove that there is a God, but I need him and I keep him by faith." The gods were born of and nurtured by human need, and they will live as long as they are needed. Only one thing is fatal to the gods—uselessness. Such superfluousness has swept away many thousands of them.

Here then are the life stories of the great gods who still hold a place in the heart of their devotees, and short sketches of many who died with their empires thousands of years ago. A continuous survey of the research in this area during the last twenty years has not demanded any significant changes in the text. For this history of the gods to the present time we may hopefully and gratefully accept Professor Max Otto's statement that the work is "definitive."

A. EUSTACE HAYDON

Pacific Palisades
California

September 1966

ACKNOWLEDGMENTS

Acknowledgment is gratefully made to the following publishers and individuals for the use of quotations from the works listed below:

G. Bell and Sons: R. A. Nicholson, The Mystics of Islam.

Benziger Brothers: Matthew Britt, The Hymns of the Breviary and Missal.

The Buddhist Lodge, London: Ch'u Ta-Kao, trans. Tao-Te-King.

Cambridge University Press: E. B. Cowell, The Jataka; A. J. Arberry, The Doctrine of the Sufis; R. A. Nicholson, Islamic Mysticism.

Doubleday, Doran and Company: Don Marquis, Dreams and Dust.

E. P. Dutton and Company, Everyman's Library: J. M. Rodwell, trans. The Koran; W. G. Aston, trans. Nihongi.

The Eastern Buddhist Society: D. T. Suzuki, Manual of Zen Buddhism.

Ginn and Company: A. Kaegi, The Rigveda.

Harper and Brothers: Philip Schaff, The Creeds of Christendom.

The President and Fellows of Harvard College, Harvard University Press: Lord Chalmers, Buddha's Teachings.

E. J. Lazarus and Company: Ralph T. H. Griffith, trans. The Hymns of the Rigveda.

Luzac and Company: D. T. Suzuki, Outlines of Mahayana Buddhism.

The Macmillan Company: R. Tagore, Songs of Kabir; R. Tagore, Gitanjali.

Oxford University Press: R. P. Masani, The Conference of the Birds; The Sacred Books of the East; The Sacred Books of the Buddhists; M. N. Dhalla, Our Perfecting World.

Charles Scribner's Sons: George Foot Moore, History of Religions; James H. Breasted, The Development of Religion and Thought in Ancient Egypt.

The Society for Promoting Christian Knowledge: Mrs. Rundle Charles, Te Deum Laudamus.

The University of Chicago Press: J. M. P. Smith, editor, The Bible, an American Translation; Moses Buttenwieser, The Psalms.

Williams and Norgate: J. Estlin Carpenter, Theism in Medieval India.

CONTENTS

BIOGRAPHY OF THE GODS

CHAPTER I

THE BIRTH OF THE GODS

Celebrate the holy race of the deathless gods who are forever,
Those that were born of Earth and starry Heaven
And gloomy Night and them that briny Sea did rear.[1]

HE gods are the real aristocrats of history. Even the lost and forgotten ones had their day of glory, and the great gods have lived in honor through thousands of years. Exalted and beneficent friends, they have shared the triumphs and tragedies of man's long labor as he strove to mold a world to his will, and to build cultures to fulfill his heart's desires. Man knew so little and feared so much, the flame of intelligence burned so feebly and hope so far outran attainment, that the gods became indispensable. They were mightier than man, masters of human destiny, to be called upon in every time of need. Man gladly acclaimed them supreme in power and wisdom and goodness because of his own helplessness. They crowded the airways and earthways in forms innumerable, every one playing a significant part in the drama of time, and every one with a life history entangled in the fate and fortune of the lowly human actors in the play. All the gods were born far down on this side of man's beginning and each has his life story recorded in terms of the social experience of some human group.

The search for the origins of the gods began long ago—but with reservations. Rarely did an investigator expect to uncover the place, time and manner of birth of his own god. It was

usually assumed by religious philosophers that the *real* gods
were beginningless. Christian scholars speculated for centuries
on the origin of "heathen" deities without even a shadow of
suspicion as to possible implications for their own unchallenged, eternal god. When the early scientists began their quest
for the simplest and most primitive form of the idea of the
supernatural, they rarely seem to have been aware that they
were dealing with the ultimate stuff of which all the gods were
made; rather they treated the "crude" and "superstitious" concepts of preliterate peoples as blundering gropings toward the
"true" idea of God. Thus the search for divine origins was
clouded by a misunderstanding. It took long to realize that
when thought pushed beyond the folk gods it faced the blank
unknown, that all the reality there was to the gods was embodied in the ideas of them, that the only real and practically
effective gods were those embedded in the experience and
thought of the people who depended upon them, and that an
unknown god, behind and beyond the god-idea, was empty of
meaning for religion.

There has been no lack of theories as to how the gods began. Popular folklore from Egypt, Babylonia, India, China
and Japan abounds with tales of their birth, creation or miraculous appearance. Speculation played with the problem in ancient Greece. One thinker suggested that the earliest gods were
beneficent powers of nature which won a place in human devotion through their helpfulness,[2] another that they were
originally men who were lifted to divine rank after their death
because of their great services to mankind,[3] and still another
that a clever ruler invented the gods to help the government
control the moral behavior of the people.[4] A favorite theory of
the early Christian writers was that the pagan deities had their
origin in the fallen angels or demons.[5] Some later scholars found
the originals of the gods of classical antiquity in Old Testament characters.[6]

When the western world became more intelligently aware of the non-Christian religions, both cultural and preliterate, theories of divine origins were less naïve and more abundant. To some writers the fetish, any object infused with mysterious potency, seemed the crudest and therefore the earliest idea of the supernatural.[7] Others found the rudimentary form of the god-idea in souls of the dead or in spirits.[8] The relationship of the great gods to heaven, sun, moon and storm was so evident that the theory of their birth from favorable phases of nature was repeatedly defended in ancient and modern times.[9]

Before the close of the eighteenth century scholars had begun to suspect that the many diverse deities may not have arisen from a single source, but this tendency to look for multiple origins was checked in the middle of the nineteenth century when scientists began their search for the universal law of the evolution of religions. Since they understood religion to mean man's relation to divine beings, it was necessary to find the simplest and earliest idea of the supernatural as the starting point of their evolutionary series. Then the quest for a single, ultimate origin of the gods began again.

The peculiar stress upon theology, characteristic of Christianity, kept the attention of the pioneer students of religious origins focused upon the birth of the gods. No other phase of early religions has been so carefully studied by so many competent scholars. Their researches yielded many theories but little agreement. Guesses of earlier centuries, that the gods grew from the fetish, or from worship of the souls of the dead or spirits, were revived by writers who knew how to put their findings into attractive scientific form.[10] The great importance of nature deities in preliterate cultures and in the early stages of the great religions led some to support the ancient opinion that the first gods were forces of the natural environment.[11] Some found in the social attitude toward the totem, as the symbol of a group, the source of the earliest gods.[12] When the

creative rôle of emotion in religions was given adequate recognition, other scholars sought the origin of the gods in reac-
tions below the intellectual level—in the projection of human
qualities into actual and imagined objects of the external
world or in emotional responses to super-usual, startling, awe-
inspiring situations, when mystery came crowding in upon the
familiar flow of everyday custom.[13] It was agreed that all these
factors entered into the making of the gods, but there was little
agreement as to the nature of the ultimate beginning. While
theories jostled each other in increasing profusion, a few orthodox thinkers defended the oldest Christian theory, that in the
beginning of human history there was the idea of One Supreme
God, which except in Judaism and Christianity, was gradually obscured or lost in the drift of the ages.[14] In this way
they could account for their own pure conception of God and
the crude, debased or false ideas of other religions. At last, out
of the confusion and conflict of theories two conclusions
emerged—that there was no single origin for all the gods and
that every god had his own individual and distinctive development.

Over the era of ultimate beginnings is drawn the veil of
oblivion. We may never know the story of man's adventurous
climb to humanity from the level of the sub-human, nor
through what ways of travail and terror he toiled to learn the
rudimentary rules of the art of living. The record of nature's
discipline of earliest man is buried beneath the débris of ages.
Earth yields to the spade of the excavator mute evidence of
his wanderings over the land surfaces of the prehistoric world.
While the material remains reveal clearly the story of the
physical struggle for life, we have no method of entry into the
thought of these pioneers of mankind. The experience of thousands of years of culture has built between them and us a bar-
rier of new meanings.

Fortunately it is unnecessary to pry into the minds of the

men who lived in the morning of history to understand the origin of their divine friends. Emotion, not intellect, mothered the earliest gods. Primitive man did not think his way through to them; he met them face to face as beneficent helpers in his quest for the goods of existence. For him life was an adventure in an untamed and precarious world. He stood at the first frontier. The empires of thought and of material mastery were still beyond the horizon. Men of the dawn age lived because experience, rooted in the sub-human, taught them the ways of adjustment to the cosmic environment. The first test of their survival as human beings was passed when they learned the practical methods of control over nature and the art of social co-operation which guaranteed them the essential goods of existence and the security of comradeship. Within the enfolding safety of tried, tribal customs the members of a group could feel confident. Yet in those far-off, early days, when man was making his first challenge for the right to live on the planet, there must have been many times when he stood bewildered, watching the world with troubled eyes. Nature had many moods. She could be indifferent, surly, hostile and terrifying, but in many of her phases she was beneficent and kind. In the presence of the friendly forms of nature man felt a glow of satisfaction, a simple reaction scarcely above the level of the physical, yet in that response he took his first faltering step toward the making of his gods.

The glow of emotional warmth touched a multitude of things in the early life of man. Every object and event that had a bearing upon the fulfillment of his desires acquired value. His immediate surroundings were a part of his life—the family fire, the door, the tools by which he won a livelihood, his weapons of defense, springs of fresh water, fruit-bearing trees, the hills, the fields, the rivers, the dawn light, sun, rain, cooling winds, the fertile earth—all these and many other phases of his environment were enmeshed in the web of his daily behavior and suffused with emotion. The multitude of gods of the religions of primitive ages arose from this non-rational response of feeling. Not all the candidates for divine rank were able to rise to a significant place in history. Some of them were too familiar and too tangible. They lost the element of mystery and were merged in the matter-of-fact world under man's control. But some, even of the everyday objects, were so charged with emotion, so clothed with memories, and so closely identified with the interests of a group, that they grew into important deities. Thus the hearth-fire was more than fire. In many cultures it became a beneficent goddess presiding over the welfare of the home.

A host of objects touched by the glow of emotion in the earliest ages never passed the first stage of grateful recognition; many flourished as gods until they lost their value with the changing times; a goodly number continued to grow in importance as they weathered, with man, the storms of the centuries in the slow advance to higher culture. The testing of the gods was severe. Only those survived, as candidates for a cultural career, who were of significant service to man, who were at the center of interest of a social group and were associated with the fulfillment of socially approved desires.

When the early culture peoples first emerge from the obscurity of pre-history their most important gods clearly reveal the stamp of their nature origin. It would be strange if this bond between man and his environment did not appear. A child of earth, he lived by nature's sufferance. To her beneficence and helpfulness he responded in attitudes of gratitude, dependence and devotion. Although these early divinities were simply phases of nature, as gods they drew their distinctive meaning from the life interests of their people. There is one sun, but the Sun-gods are as varied in character as the cultures which created them. Every group gave its own peculiar overtones to each of the beneficent powers of the environment. The needs of a people determined their relative importance. As real gods of visible presence they kept their places because of their usefulness. Consequently, a divine Heaven-power who had the highest rank in one group might have an insignificant place in another. People in northern climates have always found in the sun a valuable friend, but in regions of intense heat there is no attitude of appreciation for this blazing ruler of the day. In some of his phases he may even be classed with the enemies of man. Rain was almost everywhere a beneficent deity, but in areas where it is never lacking, Rain-gods do not appear. Sometimes a god, originally all-important, lost all significance for his own people owing to migration to a new environment or a change in the nature of their needs.

Differences of climate, varied tribal ways of winning the goods of life, manifold mutations of geographic setting and divergent experiences in meeting problems led to endless variety of meaning and importance of the nature powers for the many families of men. But the differences serve only to confirm the origin of these gods in man's outflow of feeling toward his friends in nature for valuable help received. We are not so far removed in imagination from the world of early man, and nature is not so greatly changed, that we are unable to put ourselves emotionally into the situations which he confronted as he strove to find physical well-being in those dangerous days of the beginning of culture. The significant thing is that man responded with grateful feeling to all phases of nature which were helpful to him and that the particular forces which were his special friends, as givers of the goods of life, rose to positions of commanding importance and were recognized as indispensable aids in the realization of his values. They were still no more than nature powers, but they were so suffused with the warmth of his emotion and so weighted with his desires that he depended upon them as super-human helpers in the fulfillment of his hopes.

How man expressed his appreciation of these real and visible gods in the hidden deeps of prehistory we cannot know. When the earliest records reveal the relationship he has caught them in the net of language and established social relations with them by communication. His gratitude, pouring out to them in words, clothed them with human qualities and projected into them the same interests and desires he recognized in himself. When the welcome rain-storm was greeted as a boisterous warrior, shouting his thunderous battle-cry and brandishing his flame-tipped weapon against the destructive drought, the storm was inevitably made manlike by verbal imagery. The dawn, hailed as "Child of heaven, the young maid, flushing in her shining raiment," [15] could not but take her place among living beings. The homely, helpful nature powers were humanized by the magic of language. They came alive, acquired personality and were ready to play their historic rôle as divine companions of a human group in the climb toward intellectual and material maturity of culture.

The importance of emotion as an original element in the making of the gods cannot be overemphasized. In situations of need and frustration it has continued to be a fundamental force in shaping and maintaining them. Through all the ages, desire and hope have outweighed reason in molding the historic ideas of deity. If man had been able to win his way to complete security and happiness as he advanced in knowledge and culture, he might have developed his feeling-response to nature into a poetic mysticism. Then the gods of his childhood would have faded from the earthly scene or remained as merely poetic symbols. But desire drove him ever toward new horizons and failure followed his footsteps through all the centuries. Man's need for help preserved and magnified the gods.

While the emotional response to helpful natural forces was certainly the original source from which the gods arose, it alone would not have been sufficient to preserve them when increased experience brought the functioning of natural phenomena within the sphere of human understanding. Other factors were also involved in the making of the gods as we know them in the drama of history.

The most momentous event in the intellectual history of the pre-scientific age was the achievement of the twin ideas of soul and spirit. Early man knew well the stark fact of death but often in dreams the long-dead appeared to the sleeper or he himself made journeys while his body slept. These vivid experiences were as real to him as the happenings of the waking hours. He came to believe that the vital part of a person could abandon the body at times and even continue to live in separate form after death. Favorite words for this vague, intangible self were "shadow," "breath" or "life"—words of primitive times which remain as the soul-words in many cultural languages. When the idea of a separable soul was attained, it flowed over from men and animals to the objects of nature until they were all ensouled and the whole world peopled with myriads of invisible spirits. In time, this concept split the universe into two parts —the unseen, intangible, spiritual realm and the material, actual world—and created the classical dualisms of body-soul, material-spiritual, this world-other world. It built a spiritual world to become a safe harbor for ideal values unattainable on earth, the dwelling place of spiritual beings, including the gods.

Born in the imagination of primitive man this idea of spirit, rationalized and refined by countless generations, has dominated religious and philosophic thought until modern times. Its first great service was the spiritualizing of the gods. Instead of real beings of visible form they became invisible spirits behind the actual and tangible world. Severed from direct connection with sun or wind or earth, they were able to grow in power and grandeur without restraint. As dwellers in the unseen, spiritual realm they escaped the local limitations of their earlier history and at the same time were free to adapt their characters to every change in intellectual and cultural climate. Limitless possibilities were open to them. As the unseen helpers of men their dominion could be expanded to the utmost imaginative reach of human desires. The powers of nature might fade as gods, but the gods as spirits were only at the morning of their life. The concept of spirit was not essential to the birth of the gods but very significant for their preservation. Alone it could not have produced them; without it the death rate of the deities of the early world would have been greatly increased.

Another phase of the experience of early man helped to give depth and mystery to his emerging god-ideas. He was continuously confronted by unusual and startling happenings, uncanny and bewildering events which were still beyond his power of understanding, for which he had no learned, traditional response. In such situations he could only stand in awe or wonder or admiration. He was face to face with the unknown. The familiar horizon of fact took on a new dimension. The face of the commonplace world assumed for the moment a mask of mystery. Ecstatic experiences in the dance or in highly emotional ceremonies, in intoxication or in mystic trance were touched by the same strange quality beyond anything in the routine of daily life. This feeling of the presence of mystery, crowding in upon the boundaries of safe tribal ways gave a deeper meaning to the idea of a spiritual realm of unseen powers. The gods as spirits belonged to the vastness of the unknown. There they could be clothed with all imaginable majesty and endued with endless potentiality and power, while at the same time they were close to the call of earth-bound man.

The early peoples, driven by hungerings far beyond their feeble grasp of fulfillment, found in their friendly gods a source of hope and courage. In situations of need, when knowledge faltered, when tools were futile and earthly companions of no avail, these unseen helpers could gracefully grow, in the mysterious, spiritual realm, into ever more beneficent beings in response to insistent human desires.

Not only gods but also devils were born in the emotional response of early man to nature. The dangerous phases of the outer environment were just as real to him as those which gave him help. In the far-off days of the dawn of culture, when the human thrust of life was proving its right to exist amid the welter of other animal forms, when even the finding of food was a precarious adventure, it is easy to understand man's feeling of friendliness and gratitude toward the powers that gave him help. His response of withdrawal and apprehension in relation to hostile and terrifying powers was also natural. Both good and evil forces were equally visible and tangible in the early days. Nature had a double face. Her mood of menace was as real as her smile of encouragement. The refreshing rain, so gladly welcomed after drought, might come as the fearful and destructive storm. The sun, so often the source of comfort and stimulation, could also be an evil force, parching the pastureland, killing the crops, destroying the food supply. Rivers which were familiar friends could rise in angry fury to overwhelm the land and threaten the life of man. All the friendly gods were sometimes angry, but since their dominant mood was kindly, man learned the art of warding off their wrath so as to enjoy not only their bounty but the added security of protection under the shelter of their terrible power. Only rarely did the fearful phase of a god acquire a separate identity. It did sometimes happen as, for example, when the destructive storm of wind and lightning was personalized by the Vedic Aryans as the dangerous Rudra, while the beneficent storm became the beloved Indra, wielding the lightning to destroy the demon of drought and bring food and fertility.

When dawn opened the eastern portals for the sun, the light of day made the world a friendly place, but night brought in its train a host of real and imagined dangers lurking under the cover of darkness. The deeps of the forests and jungles, desert lands, the fantastic rocks, echoing clefts and caverns of high mountains, drought and killing cold, dangerous river falls and passes retained in historic times the memory of their menace to early man. These dangerous forces of nature were given human qualities and personified by the use of language in the same manner as the gods and, like the gods, they passed through the process of spiritualization. As evil beings of the spiritual realm all the attributes of mystery and limitless vastness which belonged to the unseen world applied to them. They could be made to carry responsibility for all the unhappy experiences which afflicted man. As the gods grew by being loaded with attributes for the fulfillment of human wishes, so the evil powers attained vast proportions as the sources of human suffering and frustration. Out of this process came the splendid devils who, in some cultures, achieved rôles of such universal scope and cosmic grandeur that they challenged the dominion of the gods over the earthly scene.

Between devils and gods, however, there was a great difference in life span, dictated by the nature of their origins. The gods could live on and grow continuously, because, as beloved friends, they were fed by man's desires. All the radiance of increasing knowledge barely touched these good beings of the unseen world. Needy man clung to them as guarantors of his unfulfilled hopes. The spiritual powers of evil were on a different basis. They lacked the rich soil of human wishes in which to thrive. With every step of advance in human knowledge the doomsday of the demons drew nearer. When critical thought began to dissipate the spirit population of the early world, the devils were the first to go. Man kept his gods because he wanted them.

While many of the great gods of culture history may be traced back to a simple origin in man's emotional response to beneficent phases of the natural environment, not all of the galaxy of early gods were born in that way. Some were originally men who attained divine status in the after-life. Persons of special ability and power, wise leaders, creators of culture, great heroes who had proved their worth as benefactors of the group could not be surrendered to the empty oblivion of death. The living still needed their help. When the soul-idea was established in early thought, these great individuals could live on in the invisible world to work for the welfare of their people. Family affection and loyalty could save even ordinary men from being swallowed in the abyss of death. The ancient cults of the dead grew out of the natural desire to feed them, to announce important events to them and to consult them in times of crisis. Common men, however dear to their immediate friends, lived only as long as they were remembered—after three generations at most the shadows closed over them and they joined the ranks of the nameless and forgotten dead—but great souls, whose services extended beyond the family to the larger social group, were not lost. Through the elaboration of tradition and folk tale they were kept vividly in memory and continued to grow until they held a place in the company of the high gods as the helpers of men. Yet they could never escape the restrictions of their human origin. Purely spiritual beings could be lifted to infinite heights by human wishes, but these gods were touched by the quality of humanity and associated with special earthly functions which set bounds to their development. Their nearness to man, however, sometimes qualified them as mediators between the high gods and the earth. They were also limited by their relation to a particular tribal lineage or an ethnic stock. Any disturbance in the social life which reduced their people to a lowly status, or broke the continuity of a dynasty, threatened the life of such gods, while deities of non-human origin could transcend these dangers and live on through all the vicissitudes of internal change in the culture of a group.

The mold that shaped the gods had many faces. Most important of the blended influences were man's emotional reaction to beneficent phases of his environment, the humanizing and personalizing effect of language, the idea of spirit, the feeling of mystery, and the eager outreach of human need for help. Not all these elements were present in the making of all the gods nor were all equally important everywhere. The essential thing was that man made a working alliance with the forces that affected his life and satisfied his desires. In the beginning most of these forces belonged to the realm of nature, but when the divine pattern had been established, the process of enlarging the company of the gods could go on indefinitely. When gods became unseen, spiritual beings they could be multiplied to the limit of the heart's desire.

Religions have differed greatly in their willingness to welcome new gods. After they had attained to the idea of one supreme deity, Judaism, Christianity and especially Islam were always carefully on guard against the rise of younger candidates for divine rank. There was no such inhibition in the earlier religions of the Mediterranean world; and in the cultures of the Far East the making of new gods has continued until modern times.

The later and lowlier members of the divine hierarchy are made on the master model of the older gods. Important nature powers are sometimes surrounded by thousands of lesser beings representing minor phases of the natural world. The greatest Storm-god of Japan gave birth to nine deities who were the various modes of his activity. In Roman religion twelve lesser gods arose to supervise each stage of the farming process from ploughing to harvest. Values of social relations, such as Harmony, Peace, Love, Piety, Justice, were ranked as divinities. They fitted into the pattern as desirable and beneficent potencies making for human happiness. Sometimes the attributes of great gods—their creative word, or wisdom, or holy spirit, became separated from them to go off on an independent divine career. Righteousness, Power, Grace, Pity, Mercy, Wisdom, Providence have always been divine qualities—attributes of the one God in monotheism, but giving rise to separate deities in Buddhism. The early gods furnished the pattern. Those who were later born were only a more detailed recognition by men of dynamic natural and social forces valuable as aids in winning the goods of life.

The creator gods came late. Man and his celestial friends had travelled far along the winding ways of history before any thinker was troubled about how the world began. When the problem emerged and it was necessary to choose between a beginningless universe and a beginningless god, most of the ancient peoples said, "In the beginning, God." Then some one of the many divine figures was honored as the creator. The earliest efforts to describe the origin of the world followed the patterns of human creative activities. God molded the earth on a potter's wheel, or wove it on a loom, or spoke it into existence by words of magic power. Many cultures traced the beginning to a divine pair—Father-Heaven and Mother-Earth—from whom sprang the family of gods and all the manifold earthly existences. An ancient myth, well-known in India and Europe taught that the Creator was born from a cosmic egg which floated on the abyss of primeval waters. India had several candidates for the creative rôle when a bold thinker invented a god specialized for the task, Viśvekarman, the "All-maker." In Babylonia, several gods in succession were honored as creators as the presidency of the divine hierarchy changed with the passing dynasties. Only in Zoroastrianism were there two creators, one of good, the other of evil. In the great monotheisms the one God was at once beginningless and the author of the universe. In the more metaphysical systems, thought pushed aside supreme personal deities to seek the ultimate origin in an impersonal unity of spirit or matter or both. Then philosophy was forced to choose between a beginningless universe with both gods and men on this side of the origin, or a beginningless god, the source of all. Neither could be proved by reason. Choice of one rather than the other depended upon the cultural heritage. All this philosophic speculation about origins was far removed from the age of the birth of the gods. None of the divine figures of the early world was beginningless. The Eternal One of the philosopher had no relation to the historic deities of the primeval ages. It is relatively modern, born like a wraith from the restless fires of intellect, less than three thousand years ago.

The early gods were very near to man, companions of his nights and days, in tangible and visible form. They took their character from the earthly scene and grew in grandeur, nobility and power as man won his way to higher culture. Man accepted them and used them with little interest in understanding them. They were taken for granted as old friends. As far back as the memory of the fathers ran, they had been kindly helpers of the human family. Although the gods took up their residence in the unseen realm of spirits, they retained their intimate relationship with the life of their people. This connection was the source of their vitality. When, by some unhappy accident of time, the bond was broken, the gods died and were forgotten. Those who lived, grew and changed through the centuries because the roots of their being were in the soil of social history. The biography of a god can be written only as a phase of the life process of a people.

CHAPTER II

HOW THE GODS CHANGE

As the forehead of Man grows broader, so do his creeds;
And his gods they are shaped in his image, and mirror his needs;
And he clothes them with thunders and beauty, he clothes them with
    music and fire;
Seeing not, as he bows by their altars, that he worships his own desire.[1]

HE vitality of the gods is most clearly manifest in their ability to change. They draw their qualities from roots struck deep into the social lives of their peoples. As the most exalted members of the community, higher than chief or king, they bear heavy responsibility for the welfare of the folk. So intimately are gods bound to the men they serve, that each group puts its own individual stamp of cultural coloring upon its gods. Line after line, their characters are etched in as they share the joys and sorrows, triumphs and defeats, dreams and frustrations of those who trust them. All significant changes in the restless human scene are reflected in the lives of the gods. As long as they are alive they take on new forms, with this advantage over their mortal devotees that they belong to the unseen world and are able to develop without restraint in the forcing soil of human need.

Gods who have won a secure place in the gratitude of their worshippers for services rendered, grow most easily by enlarging their powers in response to still unsatisfied desires. The unattained always calls to man from beyond the horizon; his hope always outruns his powers of realization. From the earliest ages he has loaded responsibility upon his heavenly friends to do for him what he could not do for himself, and the gods have graciously bowed to bear the burden. The Storm-god of Vedic India, the mighty Indra, brought the rains after long drought and was honored as the bounteous giver of fertility to the fields. He was not allowed to rest on his laurels. The desires of his people urged him to new tasks until he became the giver of fertility to the herds, of strong sons in the family, the source of wealth and prosperity. Since he was a god with a terrifying voice, who wielded the lightning sword, he could be an effective War-god, a giver of victory and rich plunder. Thus desire lured many of the early gods to expand their powers.

Sometimes a god was compelled to assume new duties or to take over the functions of other gods in order to hold his place in popular devotion. When Yahweh of Israel assumed lordship over the land of Palestine, he was a god of power, mighty and terrible in battle. There he met old deities, the Ba'alim, who knew how to give crops and fertility. They threatened to win his people away from him for he had no experience in farming. Yahweh met the situation by assuming responsibility for agricultural prosperity, adding to his own great powers the functions of the gods of the land. He made the transition and won mastery only after a long, agonized struggle. The Egyptian gods found a simpler method of growth. When the functions of two gods were blended in one the names of both deities remained, joined by a hyphen, to make the name of the new god who combined in himself their joint responsibilities and powers.

Changes in political fortune also affected the gods. They sometimes grew swiftly in power with the triumphant advance of their peoples. Fortunate tribal gods followed the march of conquest or confederation to become national gods. Yahweh of Israel walked in this path. Jupiter of the city of Rome became first, Jupiter, head of the Latin League, crowding Diana from her throne, and, at last, Jupiter Optimus Maximus, the world-striding god of Imperial Rome. When Thutmose III of Egypt expanded his empire to the borders of the Near Eastern world, Amon could claim the glory of a cosmic ruler, supreme over all the gods of the earth. Thus the splendor and might of the earthly monarchs was reflected in the heavenly court. In both Egypt and Babylonia, the gods rose and fell with the changing fortunes of their cities. The supreme deity for any period was the god of the capital city. He took over not only the throne of heaven but also the legendary exploits of the gods who preceded him.

The great personal gods have grown in moral character through the centuries following the development of the ever-nobler social ideals of their peoples. No god could hold his place for long if he were less moral than the ethical standard of his worshippers. Rarely do deities die, however, because men outgrow them in morality. They adjust themselves to the ideals of each new age. There is often a striking transformation in the character of a god at different periods of his history. All the supreme, personal deities must grow to perfection in justice and moral goodness. The youthful Zeus, forced to mingle with the goddesses of an older Mediterranean fertility religion, was too boisterous, too reckless in his love life, to meet the high standards of a Plato and the great dramatists of cultured Athens. They lifted him above his earlier limitations to become a divine power, guiding all human beings the righteous way. The development of Yahweh had an entirely different setting. He attained to his magnificent moral heights in a time of social distress. As an efficient War-god in his earlier days he had qualities which seemed hard and ruthless to men of later generations. Yet when the eighth-century prophets, champions of the people's cause in a period of injustice and social maladjustment, needed a god not only of power but of justice, righteousness, mercy and love, Yahweh responded to the need. He assumed all these qualities and reinforced with his will the prophetic vision of the social ideal.

Morality is as old as the gods, and in some cultures neither seeks nor receives support from them. Usually, however, the highest god of a group gives divine sanction to the moral code. Then he, himself, must embody it and change as it changes. Dwelling in the spirit world, he may assume gracefully the virtues of the higher life of which men dream but rarely realize perfectly in practice.

Successful prophets are the great artists in the transformation of their gods. They come in times of social disorder, when the old securities are crumbling and the well-worn ways of thought and behavior become useless in the presence of new problems. Then these great sages point out the path to salvation, and the gods, accustomed to bear the burdens of their devotees, take on the character necessary for the new task. Allied with Zarathustra in his struggle against the wrongs of a local community, Ahura Mazda became a world champion of the good in a cosmic battle with the powers of evil. Answering the call of Mohammed, Allah broke the bonds which bound him to Arabia, assumed the qualities necessary for his prophet's work, and entered upon his career as a god of the world. The saving of man from trouble, from tragedy, from final frustration was the cause in which all the great gods served. They were guarantors of the good life for man and had to become adequate to meet all conditions, intellectual and social. The demands made upon them were as varied as the cultural experiences of the far-flung families of men. Each god walked in the midst of his people and followed the path of change in the light of their needs. In each culture, seer, thinker, prophet or dreamer guided his god from change to change in the shifting scenes of the drama of time.

Some gods grew to their greatest splendor in response to the human call for help in times of cultural disaster. Almost all religions have known an age of frustration when men were affected by a failure of nerve and lost hope of building a good world. Amid the ruins of hard-won civilizations they lamented the frailty of human nature and the futility of man's best efforts. Then desire outsoared despair by a flight to the gods. To become adequate to guarantee the certain realization of human hopes, they could be no less than omniscient, omnipotent, all-beneficent, eternal. It was not arrogance nor conscious egotism that made man chain the gods to his unrealized ideal. It was rather his passionate hunger for life, a longing for days made perfect in beauty and joy, the lure of a dream he would not surrender. So the gods, already great, grew to majestic proportions and in some religions men learned to yield entire responsibility for salvation to their omni-competent hands.

For more than two thousand years, the personal gods who claimed to be all-powerful as well as all-good, have been worried by the nagging presence of the problem of evil. A god who assumed the title of creator of the world, was in an especially difficult position. Why did he create evil? If he willingly allowed evil to exist, how could he be good? If it came into existence and flourished in spite of him, how could he be almighty? Power and goodness were essential qualities in a god whom men must trust for the fulfillment of their hopes. Neither of them could be surrendered, although the cruel pack of physical and social evils raised discordant clamorings against the faith. Behind a subtly woven shield of theological defenses such great deities as Yahweh, Allah and the Christian God preserved their attributes of omnipotence and goodness unchanged for a score of centuries. In modern times, however, the defense grows feeble. Evil is too real, too terrible to be excused as a servant of an unknown divine purpose. The great gods are yielding to change once more, surrendering omnipotence to preserve their goodness without which no god could live. So they become finite gods of perfect goodness, sharing with man the battle against evil. One of the supreme personal gods, Ahura Mazda, through all his early career, was not troubled by this problem. From the beginning he was a finite god, forced to fight a cosmic battle of nine thousand years against the evil creations of a dark spirit as eternal as himself.

Sometimes the forces of change were so disconcerting that the gods found it impossible to meet the new conditions successfully. Then they dragged out a feeble existence, using up their capital of past glory. Slowly starved by a grudging environment, their vitality sapped by neglect, they loitered reluctantly along the descending path to oblivion. Lesser deities of the early world often suffered this fate when their tribes moved or were driven to a new geographic environment and learned a new manner of making a living. Gods of the forest and jungle who had made their reputation as helpers in the hunt were lost when their people became keepers of cattle. The several specialized forms of the Sun-god which the Aryans brought with them to India were devitalized in their new home. In the torrid climate of the Indus Valley, heat was the least welcome gift of the gods. They lived on, however, transformed into abstract figures of light. In the north temperate zone, the dawn earned the gratitude and devotion of many nomadic groups of the ancient days. She was a lovely goddess, full-breasted and radiant, who daily drove out the darkness and freed men from the anxiety, cold and danger of the long, night hours. Wandering peoples, living close to nature, praised her radiant beauty and gave thanks for her daily comforting care. With settled life and the greater security of culture, man's direct dependence upon her grew less. Her ancient splendor faded. In later ages she remained only as a symbol for poet and artist.

There were times when man's confidence in his techniques for securing values reduced the prestige of the gods. The sacrificial ceremony in Vedic India was a means of enlisting divine help in fulfilling many forms of desire. As the ritual grew more

elaborate and the priesthood more powerful, the correctly performed ceremony became a force controlling the gods. Instead
of bending graciously to answer a cry for aid, they were commanded by the priests and compelled to dance like puppets to
the magic music of the sacrificial spells. The priests praised
them extravagantly, but no halo of laudatory words could hide
the loss of prestige and dignity of gods who must needs bow
before the words of a priestly master. They were being gently
prepared for retirement.

Gods of rain, fertility, war and healing were very important
in the religions of ancient times. Their great gifts, food, health,
wealth and victory, are as anxiously sought by modern man as
by his primeval ancestors. Yet these gods have lost their prestige
almost everywhere. In some parts of the world, intolerant
supreme gods, jealous of all rivals, crowded them out and assumed their duties. They have lived on in the tolerant climate
of the Far East until the modern era. Now they are being challenged even there by the more effective methods of science.
Irrigation, scientific agriculture, modern medicine, and the
marvelous results of science applied to warfare have freed men
from dependence upon gods for these services. They linger on
with little honor except in times of dire distress when nature
in niggardly mood, or impending death, defies man's best wisdom. All the exploits of the old War-gods appear pathetic before man's mastery of the art of destruction. Even the great
solitary gods who long ago took over the tasks of the specialized warrior deities are embarrassed in this age of world
conflict, either because their peoples have robbed them of their
old-time lust for battle or because, as universal gods, they belong to both sides of the warring hosts. All the lesser deities
who have been meeting the practical needs of countless millions
for thousands of years are inevitably doomed by the law that
a god dies when he is no longer needed. Goods man can get for
himself by practical means he needs no god to guarantee.

Sometimes, in the past, the gods of a people have had their vitality drained away by the sudden shock of new ideas. The brilliant Aryan gods of India three thousand years ago were checked in mid-career by the emergence of the twin ideas of endless immortality on the wheel of rebirth, and karma, the law of the deed, which fixed man's fate on the wheel. The old gods had no power to grant salvation through release from the eternal round of reincarnation. They, themselves, became entangled in the karma coils. One group of seekers after salvation created a new god to guarantee it. Others found the way without the help of gods. The ancient deities lived on. They could still do all that they had ever done, and the priests knew how to command their services, but their former grandeur was gone. All their best gifts were not good enough for men in quest of the new ideal.

The gods of conquered states suffered varied changes of fortune as ambitious rulers played the age-old game of war for empire. Sometimes deities who could not defend their land and sovereignty died and were forgotten. More often they clung to their followers and were permitted to continue their work in a subservient rank. Occasionally the defeated gods belonged to a high culture which over-awed their barbarian conquerors. Then the victorious deities gradually absorbed the functions and qualities of their predecessors and the old gods continued to rule in reality, if not in name, through their successors.

Peaceful interaction of cultures was as influential in developing and changing the gods as the sharp shock of conquest. The prestige of great deities standing on the frontier reached into Arabia to mold Allah for his cultural career. None of the gods who laid claim to world dominion after the passing of the glory of Greece could escape the effects of the climate of Hellenism nor evade the challenge of Greek thought. Some of the essential traits of the Christian God were assumed in this cultural environment; both Yahweh and Allah were refined in its undying fires. The meeting of cultures sometimes brought great gods face to face, to vie with each other for supremacy. Then their characters tended to take on the same pattern, for neither of them was willing to be less than the other in any valuable quality. In modern times the swift advance of the western world, over which the Christian God holds sway, has given him enough prestige to lure some Oriental deities into imitation of him.

Long continued rivalry between states may transform gods into devils, for gods who fight for the enemy can only be evil powers. Some quarrel of thousands of years ago between the two branches of the Indo-Iranians probably explains why god for one is devil for the other. The struggle for mastery in Egypt, between north and south at the dawn of history, resulted in changing the celestial Set, of the south, into a dangerous demon after Horus of the north won supremacy.

The close bond between the royal power and the chief god of the state caused continuous changes for the gods, from honor to dishonor, as dynasties rose and fell. In Egypt the god of the capital city might rise from a nobody to be loaded with the highest divine honors, only to sink back into the crowd of lesser deities when the scepter fell from the hand of his patron.

The gods have shared sometimes in the rivalry between rulers and priests. Nabonnedos of Babylon gave the prestige of royal favor to Shamash of Sippar, long renowned for wisdom and justice. The priests of Marduk were furious that their god, who claimed the highest rank, should be so insulted. They became a treacherous "fifth column" and opened the gates of the city to the armies of Cyrus. The Persian conquerors restored Marduk to his place of honor, but under the shadow of the great Ahura Mazda all the Babylonian gods gradually declined. Another such struggle was staged in Egypt, in the fourteenth century B.C., between the brilliant dreamer Akhnaton and the priests of Amon. The young Pharaoh had found a new god, Aton, the sole ruler of the universe, creator, preserver and light of the world. In his zeal, he tried to suppress all other gods and obliterate their names and memories. The disgrace fell especially upon Amon, god of the imperial city, who had led the Pharaohs to empire, who had weighted down his priests with riches. While Akhnaton lived, the priests protested in vain. Amon of Thebes remained in eclipse for seventeen years. But the young Pharaoh's god died with him, and Amon gathered up the reins of divine power once more.

It is no new thing for gods to suffer from rulers who are unsympathetic or too sophisticated. The divinities of Chinese popular religion had grown heavy with honorary titles heaped upon them through the centuries by successive sovereigns. In the fourteenth century, a Ming Emperor, steeped in naturalistic philosophy, took all their titles away. They had no priests to defend them but even without names of honor and in spite of the cold neglect of the intellectuals, they were still safe for centuries in the affections of the folk.

The gods were touched with a slow sickness when they were illuminated by the probing searchlight of philosophy. Born in the days of earth's cultural childhood, haloed by emotion, they were personal, limited, lovable, weighted with human qualities, molded in character by man's desires. Their altars were enshrined in the heart of man, not in his head. When thinkers began the intellectual quest for the ultimate meaning of the universe, the personal gods of the priests and people became an embarrassment. For different reasons in each of the ancient cultures, philosophers pushed beyond them to an impersonal unity—an Absolute, a Cosmic Order, Fate, or a First Cause. There was scant resemblance between these characterless deities made in the mind, without emotional warmth, and the friendly, lovable gods who had grown old in the service of men. The folk deities might soon have been reduced to mere shadows but for the fact that even the philosopher treated his abstract divinity as though it had all the qualities of the traditional gods, while the people, untouched by philosophy, were unaware that anything had happened to their heavenly friends. Nevertheless, a process of change was started which would not stop until it had drained all vitality from the personal gods. The timeless and changeless Absolutes, beyond good and evil, retained meaning for religion only because mystical experience gave them an emotional glow. The empty face of god as First Cause acquired a familiar expression only because faith smuggled into it the qualities of the traditional deity. A Cosmic Order, Law or Fate, deaf to the call of human need, was a sorry substitute for the lavish deities of popular religion. These philosophic gods were only the last wraith-like appearances of the old divinities before they dissolved in the light of new knowledge of the universe.

So long as a god lives, he changes. Only a being so vague and colorless, so far removed and transcendent as to have no relationship with the earthly affairs of men, can remain untroubled by the tides of change. The great deities who have breasted the storms of centuries to stand on the horizon of the modern world, have lived on because they knew how to adjust their characters to the altered intellectual and social climate of each new era. Theologians, seeking an anchorage in a storm-swept world, have called them changeless, "the same, yesterday, today and forever," but history records their changing modes. Because they were sensitive to the varying needs of the human scene, they achieved glory and long-enduring dominion. Untold multitudes of gods fell by the wayside. Death took its toll of the gods as of men. Many of them have left not even a grave-stone on the highways of history to record their passing. Some have returned to us from the ruins of buried cities to boast in stone of their former grandeur. A goodly company of ancient deities ruled in splendor over a longer time span than some of the living gods have yet attained. Before the last great change overtook them, several families of gods now dead, wove their lives into the great cultures inherited by the deities of the modern world. They deserve to be remembered.

CHAPTER III

THE GODS WHO DIED

And into what night have the Orient deities strayed?
Swart gods of the Nile, in dusk splendors arrayed,
   Brooding Isis and somber Osiris,
   You were gone ere the fragile papyrus,
(That bragged you eternal!) decayed.[1]

OST of the gods died long ago. The myriads who lived long enough to leave their names recorded on the tablets of time are few in comparison with the vast, nameless multitudes who were buried with their devotees in the deep oblivion of the lost past. Only a fragment of the million years of man's climb to culture can be reconstructed. Who can tell what the men who wandered, wondering and hungering, through the Miocene, Pliocene and Pleistocene periods thought of the powers that favored them in the fight for existence? Even Neanderthal man, who left remains of his many thousand years of culture over Europe and the Near East vanished without revealing to us a glimpse of the gropings of his mind and heart. The Cro-Magnon artists tell us something of their desires in their cave paintings but no hint of their divine friends. A vast time span separates the earliest ancestors of mankind from those ethnic groups who first emerged from the darkness of the unknown to greet us on the horizon of history. During those unrecorded ages, there was time for countless tribes of men in widely separated areas of the world to establish distinctive attitudes toward the striking elements of nature encountered in their struggle for survival—sky and sun and moon, wind and rain and storm, springs and mountains and rivers, cold and heat, animals, plants, and human leaders of unusual power. Some of these environmental forces were helpful, some dangerous, and some might be both, but none could be ignored by men who lived by nature's sufferance. That the lost gods of these lost peoples were nature forces, humanized by emotion to meet their special needs, may be taken for granted since the chief deities of every one of the ancient cultures we know at the dawn of history were nature powers. But Sky-gods, Sun-gods, Rain-gods, Storm-gods were not the same everywhere. Variations of geography, climate, problems and experience molded the personality of each of them with distinctive qualities of character to make him peculiarly useful to his own human group. All of these primeval gods are lost beyond recall in the dark, sealed recesses of antiquity.

Vital statistics for even the greatest of the ancient gods are dubious. The time and place of their births are often shrouded in veils of mystery. When historic records begin to shed their grudging light, gods are already old and bear the marks of long development. Those who first appear are the proud and arrogant patrons of the successful builders of cities and civilizations who strode to their thrones over defeated peoples and lesser gods. When death came to them in turn they died lingeringly, anchored to life by their great prestige. Very rarely was the end sudden and absolute. Only the total destruction of a city or a people, by war or other catastrophe could bring about an abrupt and datable termination of their gods' life stories. Usually they lived on for centuries with altered characteristics and diminishing powers as the interests of their worshippers changed, and other gods usurped their places to give more lavishly the material and social goods they had been fashioned to provide.

A host of deities shared the adventures of the many peoples

seeking land, power or plunder in the Near East during the three thousand years of restless movement and warfare before the Christian era. Very few stamped their characters clearly upon the pages of history before they died. Only two, Yahweh and Ahura Mazda are alive today, and they were young, or unknown, certainly unimportant in the time of these ancient deities. Most of them appear only as names, and there must be many more among the nameless dead. Household gods, gods of cities, tribal gods and the inner circle of great deities belonging to each of the peoples jostling each other in the melting pot of mingled cultures from Asia Minor to the borders of India, from Egypt to the Zagros Mountains and beyond, make up an impressive array. The bare lists of their names recovered from temple and court records are tantalizing in their lack of information regarding the nature of those who bore them. A little light breaks through sometimes when the unknown figures are equated in the lists with deities of renown in the Babylonian, Semitic and Indo-European areas. Usually only the great gods are so identified. Then there is monotony in the constant appearance of these important deities as humanized phases of nature—heaven, sun, storm, rain and the fertile mother earth. Their powers were expanded to bear the burden of the ambitions and hopes of their peoples. They failed the folk who trusted them and perished in their defeat.

The fortunes of war, and the rise and fall of political powers were the important factors shaping the destinies of the Near Eastern gods known to history. This celestial company was not intolerant, and no god would have thought of denying existence to another, but victory or superior cultural achievement demanded its toll of prestige and homage. A triumphant deity not only reduced his neighbors in rank but felt no qualms about claiming as his own the legends of prowess or even the titles of those who had been vanquished.

When the Sumerian civilization in the lower valley of the

Tigris and Euphrates Rivers began to feel the impact of the Semites in the third millennium B.C., Enlil, the Storm-god of Nippur, was recognized as the greatest deity of the region.[2] The Moon-god, Sin of Ur, Ea, Eridu's god of the waters, Ningirsu of Lagash, Nergal of Cuthah, Shamash of Sippar— all Sun-gods—held local sovereignty in their respective cities and were feeding their power by absorbing the lesser nature deities of their territories, but Enlil towered above them all as "King of the lands and father of the gods." His divine "word" had given to the world's oldest known conquerors the right to rule the alluvium plains.

Enlil's city of Nippur once belonged to Ninib, a Sun-god, whose early history has not been recovered. When the Sumerian conquerors entered the valley, Enlil took control, assumed Ninib's attributes as a fertility giver and finally claimed him as his son. The qualities and legends of these two gods were so completely blended that, except for the difference in rank, they were almost identical. Together they dispensed the fertilizing forces of storm-rain and sun which provided the basic goods for the life of the people. Nippur was a sacred city, with a priesthood so firmly entrenched that every dynasty rising to power in Babylonia felt the need of enlisting its support. Thus Enlil lived above the fickle changes of political fortune and enjoyed a position of unchallenged importance among the Babylonian gods for a thousand years.

Two other gods, as old as Enlil, and famous throughout the land during this early period, shared honors with him. Ea of Eridu was revered far beyond the boundaries of his city for his control of the waters and his gracious championship of man's cause even against the other gods. Anu, through a temporary supremacy of his native Uruk and his universal sway as a Heaven-god was sometimes placed at the head of the pantheon. Theologians who arranged the many gods into an ordered hierarchy put all the nature deities under the dominion of these three. Enlil assumed responsibility for earth, Anu for the sky and Ea for the waters. This majestic trinity held sway over the land, the local gods and human affairs until a new turn in mundane politics pushed them into the background before the growing splendor of Marduk of Babylon.

Marduk was originally a Sun-god, "the Shining One," "Child of the Day." Through long and friendly associatior. with Ea of Eridu, he had acquired the qualities of a fertility figure, master of water and storms. In spite of his great services he was still no more than a little, local deity until, in the time of Hammurapi, his city won the power and prestige that established him as the favorite of both gods and men. Then he was equipped by ability and authority to take over the duties of Enlil and to usurp his title, Bel, "the God." The mighty trinity of older deities had no choice but to yield gracefully to the new sovereign, as Hammurapi says they did:

When the supreme Anu, King of the Annunaki, and Enlil, the Lord of heaven and earth, who fixes the destiny of the land, had committed to Marduk, the first born of Ea, the rule of all mankind . . .[3]

Marduk was jealous of his rank. He claimed the center of the stage and demanded recognition as the greatest god, but he was generous to his divine companions so long as they kept their proper places. He even spread the mantle of his glory over them and identified them with himself as they performed their special tasks. At the same time he appropriated all powers and honors for himself. The old nature myths which for a thousand years had praised the heroic exploits of other gods were adapted to give him the central rôle. The deeds ascribed to Anu, Ninib, Enlil and Ea, in the older legends were attributed to Marduk in the Babylonian version. Thus the new ruler of the gods was able to wear the laurels of antiquity and spread his prestige to all the cities of the empire by a kind of high-handed divine plagiarism.

Across the river from Marduk's Babylon was Borsippa, an older intellectual and religious center. Its god, Nabu, was the patron of wisdom and writing and his temple schools were one of the chief sources of the astrological lore of Babylonia. When he bowed to the might of Marduk his influence was great enough to win for him a special place as the son of the great god. The two deities apparently worked together in perfect harmony but there must have been a latent antagonism between them for the Assyrian kings found it easy to stir Marduk to jealousy by exalting the greatness of Nabu.

From 2000 B.C., until the coming of the conquering Persians, Babylonia and Assyria were rivals for political supremacy. Marduk and Ashur alternated as supreme god according to the fortunes of war. Ashur was originally the heavenly master of a small ancient city which bore his name. Through military prowess he became a glorious figure, divine ruler of Assyria and god of gods. As a national deity he shared the fortunes of his people, won praise for advancement in the arts of peace and honor for victory in war. His symbol, the winged sun-disk, pointed to universal dominion.

Ashur was friendly to all the Babylonian gods but his closest companions were Adad and Shamash. Adad was a Storm-god of the west who won his greatest renown as a warrior and giver of fertility on the borders of the Mediterranean. He was really an interloper in Assyria. Shamash, in spite of his Semitic name, belonged from of old to the land. He was the ancient Sun-god of Sippar. As the far-seeing deity of light he encouraged and embodied righteousness. His daughters were Justice and Equity. Both Babylonian and Assyrian rulers honored him for thousands of years. Hammurapi revered Marduk as the chief of the gods but placed the figure of Shamash at the head of his law-code. An incorruptible judge, Shamash punished the wicked and rewarded those who cared for the oppressed:

The offspring of those who deal unjustly will not prosper.
What their mouth utters in thy presence thou wilt undo,
What issues from their mouth thou wilt annul.
Thou hearest their transgressions, the plan of the wicked thou
    rejectest.
All, whoever they be, are in thy care;
Thou undertakest their suit, those in bonds thou dost release;
Thou hearest, O Shamash, supplication, prayer and invocation.[4]

Equal to any of the great gods in universal appeal was the
goddess Ishtar or Ashtart, divine embodiment of the fertility
forces of field and family. She was born far back in the deeps of
pre-history when food and sex were central in the quest for life.
Archaeology has discovered prehistoric figurines with exag-
gerated feminine characteristics in all parts of the Near East
which may be the earliest representations of the great goddess.
It was Nana (Ishtar) of Uruk, known from the third millennium B.C., who set the pattern for the many mother goddesses of the area. She assumed responsibility for vegetation and
fertility, human love and war. As the earth-mother, she shared
with her husband and lover, the Sun or Heaven-god, under
various names, the task of perpetuating life on earth. The fire
of her passion and her earthy strength made her an invincible
warrior, especially when she was allied with the mighty Ashur.
All phases of human love belonged to her domain, yet in
strange contradiction to her normal character, she sometimes
assumed a virginal quality. Her hold upon the hearts of men
was so strong that she weathered the storms which destroyed
the ancient empires. Although the gods who knew her in her
youth had long been buried in the ruins of their conquered
cities, she continued her career, attuned to the changing times,
as a powerful goddess in the Roman empire, only to die at last
with the doomed gods of Rome.

When the might of Assyria bowed in final defeat in 606 B.C., the glory of Ashur departed. After that time the Assyrian gods were little more than a fading memory. Marduk of Babylon profited by the overthrow of his ancient rival. For a brief period under the Chaldeans he reigned as the supreme state god of the Neo-Babylonian empire. It was not long, however, until the king, Nabonnedos, aroused the anger of Marduk by giving the Sun-god, Shamash, too large a share of the royal favor. In revenge, Marduk hailed the Persian army as his champion and his priests welcomed the conquering Cyrus to Babylon. Their short-sighted policy bore bitter fruit during the following decades when all the Babylonian gods were dwarfed before a mightier rival, the great Ahura Mazda of Iran. The Persians were kind to the conquered. They and the Greeks who followed them restored temples and preserved the local priesthoods but the gods were slowly dying. After they were stripped of dominion, power and glory, the shadows of oblivion crept out to enfold them. At the end they were only local figures. World dominion passed into the hands of younger and more vigorous gods.

The gods of the cities of Elam [5] had an honorable place in history for more than two thousand years. Century after century, rulers built temples and praised the prowess of Inshushinak, "King of the Gods," and Huban, "the Mighty One," yet not a word in the record gives us any insight into their origin, nature or the special services they performed. They must have been deeply entrenched in the hearts of the people for they lived through conquest by Babylonia and four hundred years of Cassite rule. In the period of Elamite glory, after the fourteenth century B.C., they were powerful enough to carry off the great Marduk of Babylon and Nana of Uruk into captivity. In 1150 B.C. Nebuchadnezzar responded to the appeal of Marduk to be brought home on "the path of joy, the desired way to Babylon, from hostile Elam." Five centuries later Ashurbanipal rescued Nana and, to add to the glory of her triumphant return, the mighty Inshushinak and a score of the defeated gods of Elam followed in her train. They were well received in their exile homes but the hand of death was already upon them. Their rôle in history was ended.

In the Valley of the Nile another brilliant company of gods played out a drama of four thousand years and then left the stage forever.[6]

The greatest of these deities were, as elsewhere, the nature powers, but the geography of Egypt added some unique touches to their characters. Their life stories were conditioned by two main factors, the long river which provided a channel for the easy spread of culture influences, yet allowed the communities settled on its banks to maintain an autonomous, self-sufficient existence, and the various changes in the center of political power. A local god might be lifted temporarily into a prominent place in the divine hierarchy by having his home town selected as the site of the capital. Beyond the reach of civil strife, however, were always the two from whom the Nile-dwellers drew the source of their living, the sun, Re, and the Nile, whose yearly inundations provided agricultural wealth, embodied in the figure of Osiris. These gods were humanized before history began but were never dissociated from the natural elements from which they sprang.

Honored as the oldest of the nature deities was Geb, the earth. He was called the father of the gods, and even after he was superseded as the greatest of the divine company he continued to be their counsellor and spokesman. His wife was Nut, the sky. This strange reversal of the rôles of the usual original pair, Father Heaven and Mother Earth, fits the Egyptian scene where the land does not depend for its fruitfulness upon the fertilizing waters of the heavens. Between earth and sky stood Shu, the atmosphere, and his twin sister, Tefnut, the moisture of the air. Child of Geb and Nut was Re, destined for the royal throne over all the gods of Egypt. More important for the people than even the great Sun-god of the state religion was Osiris, the "heir of Geb." He was the "father and mother of men." In him were combined the fertility of the earth, the waters of the inundation and the growing vegetation. As plant life died and revived again in the season of the Nile floods, so did Osiris. Thus he became ruler of the dead and gave new life to those committed to his care. Of less importance as a nature power was the moon, the measurer, known best over all Egypt as Thoth, the god of wisdom, patron of scribes and priests.

Most of the prehistoric local deities remain in obscurity. Each district had its unifying symbol, like a flag, around which the emotions of the community gathered so that it stood for the well-being of the group life. Usually the signs of the nomes were animals—the so-called "animal gods"—but sometimes they were a tree, a flower, or inanimate objects such as arrows or carved human figures. In various ways in different localities, these signs were attached to the divine nature powers worshipped there. The result was a colorful confusion. Both the beetle and the falcon were symbols of the sun, the cow of the sky, while at Leontopolis a pair of lions represented the twins, Shu and Tefnut. When a city attained prominence in the national life its local symbol for a cosmic god spread over all the land, competing with those of the other nomes as signs of the same power. Sometimes the influence of a local deity was extended because his city fostered some phase of culture. Thus Ptah of Memphis was the patron of artisans, gold-smiths and builders; Thoth of Hermopolis was associated with the art of writing, became the special patron of scribes and priests and, at last, the private secretary of the supreme Re. A very ancient deity of the dead, Anubis, represented in the form of a jackal prowling among the graves in the desert, west of Siut, attained universal recognition in the company of Osiris when he assumed the title of the "First of the Westerners."

It may be that far back within the shadows of prehistory

there was a unity of culture along the Nile from Busiris to Abydos, under the rule of Osiris. This unity was destroyed by the city of Ombos and its god, Set. The third nome of the delta, with its local deity, Horus, then unified the north and extended its rule over all Egypt from the capital at Heliopolis. Echoes of this political struggle appear in old myths which tell of the murder of Osiris by Set, of a time when the primeval earth god, Geb, gave the rule of the north to Horus and of the south to Set and then put both under the sovereignty of Horus who became the son and avenger of Osiris. After this episode Set was excluded from the company of the gods and transformed into a demon of darkness and evil. History may be behind the myth, but it is still difficult to see clearly what gods and men were doing in Egypt six thousand years ago.

Throughout the historic period the fortunes of the gods followed the shifting scenes of politics. No changes could ever displace Re and Osiris from their anchorage in the minds of the priests and the hearts of the people, but other gods claimed a share in their glory as the standard of imperial rule moved with the changing dynasties. The success of his city made the reputation of Horus, whose sign was the falcon. He rose from a local divinity of the third nome, to be, first, the god of the delta, then of all Egypt, then a Sky-god equal to Re, and finally he was identified with the Sun-god as Re-Harackte. Since Heliopolis was the capital, the local Atum demanded recognition. He received it by being acclaimed one with Re. This relationship gave the great solar deity a new origin. Instead of being, as of old, the son of Geb and Nut, he was now a self-created being, without father or mother, who arose out of Nun, the primeval chaos of waters. The genealogy of the old gods was revised to give Atum (Re) the central place. From him sprang the twins, Shu and Tefnut, who gave birth to Geb and Nut. Their children, in turn, were the famous four, Osiris, his sister and wife, Isis, Set and Nephthys.

The disintegration of the empire of Horus brought the gods, Min of Koptos and Thoth of Hermopolis, into prominence, since their cities led the revolt. Thoth had a place in the cosmic scheme but Min was a nobody. A temporary place in the sun won him the title "King of the Gods" and a rank equal with Re and Horus.

Toward the close of the fourth millennium B.C., Menes unified Egypt once more and established his capital at Memphis, the home of Ptah, already famed as the divine artisan. Immediately Ptah became the highest deity of the land, father of the gods, and, as an expert craftsman working with the tool of truth, was credited with the creation of the world. Instead of being glorified by union with the supreme Sun-god, he received a more ancient rank through identification with Nun, the father of the Sun. Ptah was also older than Atum, of holy Heliopolis, who came into existence as a thought of his heart. Thus little local gods rose and fell as the dynasties changed.

With the passing of the Old Kingdom, Egypt had no central government for five centuries, and the little gods of the autonomous districts carried on as they had from the beginning. Each of them aspired to the highest honor, however, and almost every one of them was identified with the great god, Re. It was only necessary to join their names to his with a hyphen. At the close of the period, the invading Hyksos ruled the land for a century. Egyptian theologians expressed their opinion of the god of their conquerors by identifying him with their native devil, Set.

Many local gods had achieved renown during the centuries, but none of them could compare with the splendor of Amon of Thebes during the eighteenth dynasty. Thebes had expelled the Hyksos, established an absolute monarchy over Egypt and extended the empire north to Syria and east as far as the Euphrates. Amon shared the glory of the throne. Before the rise of Thebes he had been merely an obscure local god. Identified with Re, as Amon-Re, he acquired all his characteristics and took the supreme place among the gods. Only Ptah and Atum-Re of the old capital cities could hold up their heads in his presence. Ruler of an empire extending to the boundaries of the ancient world, Amon transcended racial and national boundaries and became a world god. Spoils of war in wealth and captives poured into his temples. His priests were loaded with power, authority and wealth, an excellent insurance for the life of any god.

When Amon-Re was at the height of his glory, Akhnaton came to the throne, his heart and mind filled with the revelation of a new god, Aton, the Sole Lord, creator and ruler of the universe. The divine symbol was the solar disk from which rays, ending in hands, reached down toward the earth and man. Egypt had long thought of Re as the divine unity embodying all the gods, and world-empire pointed to a heavenly sovereign of all mankind. The vision of Akhnaton followed through to the conclusion that there was only one god. He denied the other deities, chiseled out the name of Amon from monuments, suppressed his worship and his priests. Aton alone commanded his devotion.

Thy dawning is beautiful in the horizon of the sky,
O living Aton, beginning of life!
When thou risest in the eastern horizon,
Thou fillest every land with thy beauty.
Thou art beautiful, great, glittering, high above every land,
Thy rays, they encompass the lands, even all that thou hast made.
Thou are Re, and thou carriest them all away captive;
Thou bindest them by thy love.
Though thou art far away, thy rays are upon the earth; . . .
How manifold are thy works! . . .
O sole God, whose power no other possesseth.
Thou didst create the earth according to thy heart
While thou wast alone.[7]

While Akhnaton sang the praises of Aton, ominous rumblings of social discontent arose from the people anxious for the security of the old religion, the priests angered by the loss of wealth and prestige, and the military leaders disappointed in a king dreaming of universal love while an empire crumbled. When Akhnaton died the storm broke and the beautiful god, Aton, died with his creator. Amon returned to his throne and for centuries shared with Ptah and Re the wealth and worship of Egypt. Even when a Libyan ruler established Bast, the local deity of his capital, as the official god of the kingdom, Amon was still honored.

After the sixth century B.C., Egypt fell successively under the dominion of Persia, Greece and Rome. Subject to foreign rule, the glory of the state gods faded. Amon-Re and all the divine company, weighted with their thousands of years, turned their faces toward the west and the realm of the dead.

Meanwhile Osiris, Isis and their son, Horus, idealized by the people and ministering to their hopes of a happy after life, grew more important as the state gods failed. Osiris fitted into the pattern of other savior gods of the Near East. He died, rose again from the dead and guaranteed immortality to all who were united with him through the sacraments. Isis, the great mother, "the Mother of the Gods," was easily identified with the popular mother goddesses of the Hellenistic world, Ishtar, Cybele, Demeter, Semele and the rest. Holding the child Horus in her arms, she was a madonna figure. The cult of Isis and Osiris spread to Nubia, Greece, Italy, Sicily, Malta, Carthage, Gaul and the Danube. Isis shared with Mithra and the great mother, Cybele, a losing struggle against the Christian God. The day of doom drew near when Theodosius closed the temples in the fourth century A.D. and a Christian bishop swung an axe upon the statues of the gods. The deities of Egypt were officially dead, but Isis, the madonna, with her child

Horus, joined the Christian company identified with Mary and Christ.

The gods of Greece, too, bowed to the decree of death more than fifteen centuries ago.[8] Before their passing, they presided over a culture so brilliant and were so refined by thought that their influence has left indelible marks upon the gods who succeeded to their empire. No deities of the ancient world have been so well remembered. At critical times in the history of western culture they have reached out from their graves to shape the development of the gods of Judaism, Christianity and Islam.

Two families of gods were blended to make the company of deities appearing at the dawn of history in Greece. Beginning in the middle of the second millennium B.C., rude Aryan tribes overran in successive waves of invasion an old, established Minoan culture. It was not long until the conquerors yielded to the lure of the land and its ancient civilization. With the new way of life they inherited the local gods specialized for a thousand years to guarantee the goods of culture. They embodied the values of the fertile earth and the sea, fruit trees, vineyards and fresh spring waters, wild animals in the forested hills and flocks on sunny pasture fields; they guarded the cities and fostered the arts of peace. The gods of the invaders were celestial nature powers and had little cause to quarrel with the deities of the land who represented new interests. The two groups joined forces to form the pantheon of Greece under the leadership of Zeus, the supreme Heaven-god of the Aryan lords.

The most important divine figures in the Minoan religion were the nature goddesses. Every district had its earth mother, revered as the bounteous source of fertility. Her children, the growing grain and plants were Ploutos at Eleusis, Hyakinthos at Delphi, Erichthonios at Athens, whose nurses were Sunlight and Dew. In the Greek period, these local goddesses were absorbed in Demeter and her daughter the corn-maiden, Kore. Artemis, mistress of animals, goddess of wild nature, cared for the growth of young animals and human children. Allied with her was Eileithyia, a specialist in childbirth. Ariadne and Helen were identified with the life of the trees. Athena, the patron goddess of Greek cities in later times, was originally a Minoan deity guardian of the royal household. In warlike Mycenae she was armed to protect the palace, but her chief interest was in domestic life. She supervised the arts of weaving, embroidery, pottery, the making of shoes and metal work. When Athens was at the height of its power, she became the patron of civilization, goddess of heroes and of ordered warfare. Similar to her was the great goddess of Argos, Hera, who became the wife of Zeus. Her epithet, "cow-faced," points to an earlier interest in the productivity of cattle. As a married goddess, with a trying, tempestuous experience in her life with Zeus, she became the protector of wedded women and of women's rights.

Love in its freest form, without worry about Hera's conventions, was represented by Aphrodite. She was originally a fertility goddess and may have wandered into Greece from the East. In contrast with the virgin Artemis of the wilds, Aphrodite manifested the lovelier, milder moods of nature, flowers and springtime, the joys of peaceful dales and leafy bowers.

The Phrygian earth mother, Semele, joined the goddesses of Greece in ancient times. Her child, Dionysos, was first vegetation in general, then the fruit of the vine. As a dying and reviving god who gave, through mystic ecstasy, assurance of immortal life, he became one of the most popular deities of the folk religion.

The Minoan goddesses were strangely self-sufficient. There is hardly a hint of any male companion associated with their creative work. The primitive picture of the earth mother and her children, the various forms of vegetation, dying and resurrected to new life in the year rhythm, was the foundation, here as elsewhere, upon which the later idea of dying and rising savior gods was built.

The only goddess of certain Aryan origin was Hestia, the hearth fire. Memories and emotions of the home life gathered about her. Fire from the state hearth was carried to the colonies to preserve the home ties and loyalty to the parent city. She was a dignified and matronly goddess. The Fire-god, Hephaistos, had nothing in common with Hestia. He belonged to craftsmen, smiths and artisans.

Of all the Greek gods, Zeus was the acknowledged king. Folk memory, however, did not forget that he was a newcomer. The Titan, Prometheus, could quite properly call him an "upstart." The myth makers, peering through the shadows that shrouded the beginning of things, told of a time when the earth gave birth to heaven. Heaven and earth then produced the Titans with whom Zeus was often at war. The youngest of the Titan family, Kronos, emasculated his father and, with Rhea as wife, became the parent of the Greek deities, Hestia, Demeter, Hera, Hades, Poseidon and Zeus. The myth remembers that before Zeus there were earlier and older gods. He was the youngest, but none except the Titan brood disputed his sovereignty over gods and men.

Zeus came to Greece with the immigrant Aryans. He was the local form of the divine Heaven of the far-flung Indo-European family who molded him in different ways to meet their needs in Rome, over all Europe, in Iran and India. In his early career in Greece, Zeus combined, in his own person, the cosmic order and the thunder-storm with its fertilizing waters, phases of heaven's activity usually treated as two separate gods. He was the "cloud-gatherer," sender of the rain, hurler of thunderbolts and consequently the source of the earth's fertility, giver of wealth, protector of stores, "Zeus the Farmer." The lightning-bolt was serviceable in his rôle as guardian of social custom, justice and the moral law. In this phase of his divinity Zeus was patron of the home, of blood-relationship, protector of foreigners, fugitives and guests.

The most important gods associated with Zeus had become very complex figures before their appearance in history. Only Poseidon was still a simple nature power, deity of inland springs and waters who later assumed control of the sea. Several older gods were dispossessed and their functions assumed by Apollo. He retained some characteristics of a Sun-god, and his absorption of the lost Minoan "Master of Animals" may account for his being called the brother of Artemis. He was a shepherd's god, but extended his protection to the farmers and their grain. On the sea-coast he cared for navigation. The basis of his great career in later times was laid when he stole Delphi, seat of the oracle, from Hyakinthos, child of a prehistoric earth mother. As the oracle god, he became famous over all Greece, the final authority on all great problems of state. He guarded covenants and treaties and punished breach of faith. At the same time he was able to purge from blood guilt. By displacing Paieon, an early god of healing, he became master of the medical art and handed it down to his son, Asklepios, who lived on as a popular deity in the Mediterranean world long after the Greek gods were dead.

Another complex deity was Hermes whose name came from the stones marking graves and roads. His relation to the roads made him guide of travellers, god of traders and marketplaces, and at last the swift-footed messenger of the gods. Association with graves gave him his rôle as leader of the souls of the dead in their journey to the realm of Hades. Presiding over the activities of night and darkness, he was patron of thieves and a famous cattle stealer. Since his original home was in Arcadia, he promoted fertility of the flocks and was the favorite god of shepherds. Invention of Apollo's lyre and the pipes of Pan was also credited to him.

The overloading of the Greek gods with many responsibilities resulted from the blending into a single figure of several deities belonging to separate local areas. Fertility goddesses yielded easily to this process. They survived in Demeter. Athena became the single goddess of all Greek cities, displacing the local goddesses. As the armed maiden of "civilized" warfare, however, she could never assimilate the Thracian barbarian, Ares, god of berserk battle. Many of the moral difficulties which troubled the Greek deities in later days, came to them through these alliances with older, earthy divinities of nature.

In Homer's time the gods were completely humanized. Their heavenly home on Olympus was an ideal copy of a contemporary earthly court. Zeus ruled as king in a royal palace above the residences of the other immortals. In the great council chamber the gods met to discuss earthly strategy and to quarrel over their own problems. They lived the life of aristocrats, sitting on their thrones with the wine cup passing around. Divine servants attended them, Hebe, the cup-bearer, Themis, in charge of food, Paieon, the doctor, Hephaistos, the smith and builder, Athena, caring for the domestic arts, Iris, the messenger, later supplanted by Hermes. The Olympians had great wisdom and power but were neither all-wise nor omnipotent. They could move with amazing swiftness from place to place but not even Zeus was omnipresent. They were masters of human destiny. From their hands came well-being and misfortune, high and low estate, life and death. They were responsible for the security and prosperity of the state. To their favorites among men they gave remarkable skills, unusual mental and physical powers. Even ordinary individuals could expect them to provide health, wealth, long life, strength and all the good things of earthly existence. They had nothing to offer mortal man beyond the portals of death's dark realm.

The gods on Olympus became too completely human. In their relations with each other they were quarrelsome, deceitful, unfaithful. They roared with laughter when Hephaistos surprised his wife Aphrodite and Ares in a love tryst. Wearied by love, Zeus slept, deaf to the cries of distress from the earth. The long series of love affairs of the king of the gods became a scandal to later generations. In morality and justice the celestial company fell below the standards of human society. If they had kept their original characters as nature powers they would have been beyond reproach. No one would have found fault with the bouts of elemental forces in the processes of fertility, but when the gods were made thoroughly human, and Zeus, a good family man, acted the rôle of Heaven in relation to the many local goddesses of the earth, the result was disastrous for the Olympians.

The contribution of Hesiod to the life story of the Greek gods was not so much his sketch of their genealogies as his pathetic insistence that they watch over justice. He lived in a period of disorder and social maladjustment which could not but hope that the all-seeing Zeus would right the wrongs of the poor, the suffering and the dispossessed. Confronted by hard facts, Hesiod voiced his faith with a wry smile of skepticism.

After the sixth century the old gods lost caste with the intellectuals. Pindar did them a good turn by suppressing all the stories of their disreputable deeds. He pictured them as altogether wise, just and good. Above them all towered Zeus, perfect embodiment of justice and the moral order. By the necessities of their art the great dramatists represented the gods in human form, but beyond them, greater and more powerful than they, was the godhead, like a cosmic order, fate or inexorable destiny. For this ultimate power, Zeus seemed to be the best name. The three greatest of the tragic poets bravely believed that Zeus was on the side of justice, but at the same time they urged fearless acceptance of destiny and warned against insolence (hubris), the effort to transcend the human lot. Euripides often pictured the old gods as ridiculous and unworthy of respect, but he spoke reverently of Zeus, "whoever he may be," "whether the inexorable law of nature or the mind of mortal man who guides all human destinies according to justice."

The traditional gods never recovered from their treatment by the philosophers. Some of these thinkers explained them away as human creations; others went beyond them in quest of an ultimate natural origin of all things. Xenophanes asserted that man made the gods in his own image; Prodicus that they were elements of nature profitable to men such as the sun and moon, rivers and fountains. Thus bread was worshipped as Demeter, wine as Dionysos, fire as Hephaistos. Any useful thing might be deified. Euhemerus explained that the gods were once men who, after death, were worshipped because of their great services. Critias suggested that they were the inventions of a clever ruler to supplement the civil government in controlling the behavior of the people. Protagoras brushed aside all discussion of the nature and existence of the gods with the remark that the subject was obscure and life was short. The philosophers disagreed as to the primordial power, whether it was matter or of the nature of mind, but all agreed that the old deities were on this side of the beginning and, like man, belonged to the natural world. There was no need of the gods of religion in the new picture of the universe. The philosophers did not discover them in their researches and speculations. If they gave them a place in the cosmic scheme it was only because they were part of the cultural tradition and could not be publicly snubbed. The philosophic principles which thinkers posited to give unity to the universe had no divine qualities. When they served as gods they borrowed surreptitiously from the real deities which intellect had displaced. "The One," said Heraclitus, "is unwilling and yet is willing to be called by the name of Zeus." The "Pure Being," eternal and changeless, of Parmenides, was denied by definition the characteristics essential to a god concerned with the affairs of mortal man in time. Plato's god, the Idea of the Good, and Aristotle's first cause, the "Unmoved Mover," were vastly different from the living gods created by religions. The Olympians, involved in the problems of men, could never have lived in the rarefied atmosphere of such abstract, artificial deities. The Stoics went to the other extreme and closed the gulf between the divine and human. Their god was the immanent essence of all existing things including man.

Worried statesmen condemned this philosophic destruction of the gods because the times were troubled and the common people identified their own security with the divine protection of the state. Anaxagoras and Protagoras were early denounced as atheists. Aristotle later bore the same brand. Yet none of the philosophers was interested in destroying the gods. They deplored the disreputable characters given to them by the epic poets, myth-makers and dramatists, but were perfectly willing to find a place for them in the universe. Democritus accepted them as beings of very tenuous matter, products of natural processes, transient and subject to dissolution. Plato purified their characters, transformed them into perfect beings, calm, emotionless, but he could only give them secondary rank as creations of the supreme god. The Stoic scheme included them as varied and temporary embodiments of the divine logos, but they could be no more than secondary gods, finite and limited in power. Even the Epicureans, who had no need of gods, did not deny their existence. They pictured them dwelling in interstellar spaces in a state of such blissful happiness that it would never occur to them to interfere in the affairs of men. The philosophers were kind, but gods cannot long live on tolerance alone.

With the collapse of the Greek states the ancient deities, dependent upon the public cult, approached the close of their careers in the homeland. Some of them had already found a foothold in Italy and were able to prolong their days in association with the gods of Rome.

In contrast with the state gods, the deities who served the needs of individuals grew in popularity in times of distress and public disaster. Asklepios, the healer, a genuinely useful god, extended his domain to include the Graeco-Roman world. The very ancient gods of the Mysteries, Dionysos and Demeter, who could guarantee the great gift of immortality, met the needs of frustrated, lonely and frightened individuals in an age of lost securities and drifting landmarks. The great mother, Cybele, and Attis, shared in the work and the glory. These savior gods were not limited to national boundaries. They continued to flourish until the dark shadow of the Christian God fell upon the Mediterranean world, bringing death to a multitude of gods. Yet divine beings who have won the affection of a people are difficult to destroy. Even now, after almost two thousand years, many of the oldest gods of Greece are still alive in the form of Christian saints. Dionysos is St. Dionysius, Demeter, St. Demetrius, Artemis, St. Artemidos, Eileithyia, St. Eleutherios, and Zeus himself still dwells upon the mountain top as St. Elijah.

The Roman gods [9] did not grow from primitive origins to maturity embodying the qualities of a single, secluded culture development. They emerged from a welter of divine figures jostling each other within the narrow confines of Italy in prehistoric times. Hardly had they lifted their heads into the sunlight of history when waves of Greek influence began to break over them. From beginning to end, they were an intercultural, international family.

Earliest of the blended strains were the ancient Mediterranean mother goddesses of fertility—Tellus, Flora, Ceres, Mother Matuta—ponderous, solid figures, redolent of the soil. During the second millennium B.C., the gods of several Indo-

European groups joined them, bringing the wide-wandering Dyaus Pitar, the Heaven-god Jupiter of the Romans, counterpart of the Greek Zeus. While these two divine families were borrowing each other's powers, blending with and absorbing each other, through the harbors of the west coast came more deities from Greece and Asia Minor. Greek currents flowed in from South Italy, Etruscan from the north. Among these new pilgrim gods were old pre-Aryan deities whom the Greeks had made their own—Hephaistos, Demeter, Dionysos, Aphrodite— and the Etruscan Volcanus, the lightning, Furrina, Mother Earth, and Diva Angerona, the goddess of the dead. They ranged the sky, the air, the earth and the underworld, caring for agriculture, husbandry, war and the affairs of the dead. In them, nature had been enlisted to serve the needs of men. Out of the composite crowd came the gods who appear on the earliest Roman calendar in the sixth century B.C. Among them are the unfamiliar names of deities who had lost their hold on life before the time of the Republic. Roman scholars could not identify them. Even Varro, research student of Roman antiquities, naming Summanus, added, "whoever he is."

The most important state gods of early times were Janus, Jupiter, Mars, Quirinus and Vesta. Janus is an enigma. He had first place in the divine lists as god of beginnings. His name implies a "going" and associated him with doors and gates, but may have a deeper cosmic meaning related to the cyclic movement of the heavens. Jupiter outranked all others as the supreme Sky-god. Mars and Quirinus were the war-masters of two tribes merged in the unity of Rome. War was not Mars' earliest interest. Originally he was the storm-rain and an agricultural deity, but many peoples have found that these Storm-gods with their thunder and lightning make excellent warriors. Vesta really belonged to the family as the hearth-fire. Among the public divinities she reflected the sanctity of the home upon the affairs of the larger family.

Every Roman home had its own familiar group of divine guardians. The door, the threshold, the hearth-fire and various other parts of the house had a quality of sacredness. Each man had his Genius, each woman her Juno, the life potency peculiar to each sex. The Penates cared for the storehouse; the Lares Compitales stood guard at the boundaries of the family property. The Lares as a class were ancestral spirits and friendly, but there were also the Lemures, souls of the dead, who lingered enviously around the homes of the living. They were dangerous when not properly treated. Openly, but with mental reservations, the Romans called them "the Good Gods."

A distinctive feature of early Roman theology was the amazing multiplication of divine powers from the primitive idea of the numen. This idea probably came from an emotional reaction to any striking, startling or attractive quality in objects of the environment. The numen was a peculiar potency in things and never acquired personality. The Romans found numina everywhere and invented innumerable, active, divine potencies to supervise the activities of life. More than two score of these agencies superintended the stages of agriculture from plowing to the storing of the grain. The work of the numina may be illustrated by following the first year of the life of a little child. Alemona nourished the babe in the mother's womb, Partula, Candilefera and two Carmentes performed helpful services at childbirth. Ops protected the new-born child, Vagitanus opened the mouth at the first cry. Levana lifted the child from the earth. Cunina guarded the cradle. Rumina filled the mother's breast. Cuba lifted the child from cradle to crib. Ossipago made the bones grow firm. Statanus taught the child to stand. Fabulinus taught him to speak. Iterduca and Domiduca led him out for his first walk and back home again. When this pattern was once established it was easy to carry it to higher levels and deify virtues and other abstractions, for example, Spes, Salus, Pudicitia, Fides (Hope, Welfare, Chastity, Faith).

When Rome expanded the area of her political power, extended the lines of her commerce and became a cosmopolitan city, the new interests brought in new gods. She was kind to the gods she had conquered, preserved their cults and often gave them a place of honor in the capital. Diana of Aricia, divine patron of the Latin League, came in when Rome became its head. As the chief deity of the dominant city, however, Jupiter could not long allow Diana that much honor and crowded her from the throne. The roads were busy with commerce and travel. Tradesmen, artisans and travellers followed them to Rome. These strangers knew nothing of the Roman deities. Over the same roads, one after another, came in their foreign gods. It was not long until all the familiar divinities of Greece were worshipped in the capital city under Latin names. These newcomers were useful because they cared for interests in which the gods of Rome had had no experience. Backed by the prestige of Greek culture, however, they soon began to overshadow the native deities.

The habit of borrowing the gods of other peoples was accentuated in Rome by the awed respect paid to the Sibylline Books. This collection of cryptic, oracular sayings was consulted for advice in every time of popular distress or political emergency. On such occasions, the national deities were repeatedly snubbed and some foreign god with a far-reaching reputation called upon for help. Asklepios, famous along the Mediterranean headlands for his healing powers, received an elaborate public reception. When Hannibal was tormenting Rome during a decade marked by pestilence, crop failure and the bitterness of war, they advised an appeal to the great mother goddess, Cybele. The fortune that sometimes favors the gods attended her arrival. The dark period of disaster came to an end, and the Magna Mater could rest on her laurels, sure of her reputation in Italy.

Thus the prestige of the Roman deities was undermined. Only the supreme state god, the mighty Jupiter, Lord of Heaven, grew in power and majesty. Identified with the political fortunes of Rome, this Sky-power of the Aryan invaders rose to be the god of the city, Jupiter Optimus Maximus of the Latin League, the Genius of the Latin peoples, and at last the world-striding god of imperial Rome. Around him, the most numerous of the divine company were Greek gods parading in Roman togas. Close to the soil, however, were the little gods of the home and countryside, still safe in the hearts of the folk. Augustus tried to put new life into the old cults, but succeeded only in giving prominence to the deities closely associated with his own family and his own great name. Even the deification of the Emperor himself came largely from foreign influences.

When the Greek philosophy, which had reduced the Greek gods to shadows at home, followed them to Rome, all the personal deities, native and foreign, lost importance for the intellectuals. Cicero did not believe in them, but advised the officials to treat them as real for the sake of the people. The Stoics found a place for them as manifestations of the immanent Logos. As the old gods were dying, the divine saviors of the Mysteries, who promised a blissful immortality, grew in importance, especially Cybele and Attis, Isis and Serapis and the glorious Mithra, beloved of the Roman armies.

As in Greece, so also in the Roman Empire, the death blow to all the gods was struck by the Christian deity. None of the high-placed ones, not even Jupiter, could live in his presence. Only the little home divinities of the people evaded him by assuming the mantle of saints.

As the sway of the Christian God spread northward over Europe, hundreds of deities who, before his coming, had lived together in peace, accepted his decree of doom. The Celtic gods bowed before Roman might, but had been welcomed into the imperial pantheon. They died under the blight of Christian intolerance.

The Teutonic peoples,[10] in Pre-Christian times, had their own local families of gods who embodied the benefits of sky, sun, storm and the fertile earth. Leader of the divine company in Sweden was Frey, Thor in Norway and Odin in Germany. Before the rise of Odin, Ziu (Tyr), the old Sky-father of the Aryans, had been the greatest of the German gods. He was specialized in war. Odin supplanted him, took over the war portfolio and led his Aesir gods west and north in conquest. Under his leadership the Anglo-Saxons captured Britain. In the north, Frey, chief of the Vanir gods, was forced to yield to him. After Odin had won through to supremacy, the deities of the various groups settled down in peace to their old tasks of providing fertility, wealth and well-being for their peoples, in friendly co-operation. When the Christian God appeared upon the scene, death for the Teutonic gods followed in his wake. The mighty Odin survived, however, humbled and peaceful as St. Martin and St. Michael. Thor became St. George and St. Olaf. With the surrender of the northern deities, in the tenth century, the Christian God stood triumphant among the graves of all the gods of ancient Europe.

CHAPTER IV

AHURA MAZDA

Yathâ ahû vairyô, athâ ratus, ashâd-kîd hakâ,
Vangheus dazdâ mananghô, skyaothnanam angheus mazdâi,
Khshathremkâ ahurâi â, yim dregubyô dadad vâstârem.[1]

N the morning of man's history, when the early
peoples were taking their first faltering steps
toward culture, they gratefully acknowledged
the help which came to them from nature in
their quest for the goods of life. In the rhythmic
flow of days and seasons, the sky with its many moods had a
central place in their emotional and practical behavior. From
the heavens came the dawn, whose rosy fingers pushed back
the curtains of darkness, the all-seeing, life-giving sun, the
fertilizing rain, refreshing winds and, at night, the moonlight
and the eyes of a thousand stars. Behind all these manifest al-
lies of man was the stable order of the movement of heaven,
remaining unchanged through all the whims of weather. The
many nature powers, as bestowers of benefits, were given human qualities and treated as heavenly friends. Gratitude, hope
and desire exalted them to the status of gods. Above them,
higher than all others, was the all-covering Heaven, source and
father of the lesser gods.

When the Indo-Europeans first made their boisterous appearance on the stage of history, they had already established
Heaven as supreme among the galaxy of familiar, friendly nature powers. As the various branches of the family spread
westward over Europe, south and east over Iran and India, the

Sky-god shared their adventures and reflected their changing cultural conditions. Long after he was given personal qualities and became the all-wise, all-powerful ruler of gods and men, his name still revealed his nature origin as the shining sky. He was called Dyaus by the Indo-Aryans, Zeus by the Greeks, Jupiter by the Romans, Tyr by the Northmen, Ziu by the Teutons, names which identified him with the vault of heaven. His fate followed the fortunes of these various peoples. The turbulent Storm-god disputed the throne with him among the north Europeans and the Teutons. The Greeks and Romans remained true to him throughout the classical era of their history, but among all the peoples of Europe the old Sky-god at last yielded his throne and withdrew into oblivion before the triumphant advance of the God of Christianity, who usurped his name (Deus) as well as his dominion.

In the further east, Dyaus passed his divinity to two great figures who originated as descriptive names of his own being; then he, himself, faded back into the shining sky from which his personality had emerged. Only echoes point to the period when he was the great creator, father of gods and men, but his special title "Lord" (Asura in Sanskrit, Ahura in Avestan) identified him perpetually with the two who inherited his scepter, Varuna, "the Coverer" of India, and Ahura Mazda, "the Wise Lord" of Iran.[2]

When Varuna and Ahura Mazda are first found in religious literature they are indistinguishable in all but name and country. Because of the common origin of the two gods and the unity of cultural heritage of their peoples, we may be fairly certain that the Ahura Mazda of antiquity, as he was before the coming of the prophet Zarathustra, looks out upon us through the figure of Varuna in the Vedic poetry of ancient India.

In the Rigveda, Varuna appears as an Asura, chief of the seven Adityas, who were extolled as the guardians of heavenly light and dispensers of kindly benevolence. Asura and Deva, "shining one," were both terms descriptive of the gods, but Asura was far less generally used. It was applied most frequently to Dyaus, though Varuna, the "Asura-son" and Mitra were entitled to the rank, and other deities were occasionally honored by the same laudatory title. Mighty magical potency was associated with the Asuras, and it was generally conceded that they were older than the Devas. Before the Vedic hymns were fixed in final form, however, some conflict had occurred between Asura and Deva worshippers and the Asuras of India were gradually shorn of their glory. In the later Hindu literature they were never regarded as anything save demons, implacable enemies of the gods, though rarely antagonistic to mortals. This hostility between Asuras and Devas is reflected in the traditions of Iran with the difference that there the older Asuras retained their supremacy, and the Devas were reduced to the rank of demons.

The six Adityas, clustered around Varuna in early Vedic religion, have their parallel in the six satellites of his Iranian counterpart, Ahura Mazda. With the exception of the beloved Mitra they were vague reflections of their king. The Adityas as a whole were figures of light, "bright," "golden," "many-eyed," [3] but as the Vedic singers knew them they were divorced from sun, moon, stars and lightning, and represented light in all its manifold modes of helpfulness—friendliness, loyalty, benefaction, security and creativity. Among them Varuna towered as the great god. They seemed to be attributes of their chief, broken lights of his shining personality.

The Vedic songs were neither produced nor gathered together by theologians, and present widely divergent and contradictory pictures of the gods, their functions, characters and interrelationships. Varuna is one of many in the collection as a whole, but has a distinctive personality in the poems dedicated to him alone, or to him and his associated Adityas. [4] Had only the Varuna hymns been preserved the world would bow down before the high monotheism of the ancient Aryan singers. These devotees arrayed the all-covering, all-encompassing Lord in the attributes of a supreme god. The whole sphere of brightness was his realm. He wore the stars as a garment, created the sun, and "after his decrees o'erspread the darkness with a robe of light." [5] All good gifts came from him—rain for the pastures, glorious strength in bodies, increase of herds and families, prosperity and wealth, honor in assemblies, victory in battle and a life-span of a hundred autumns. Far-seeing, ever-vigilant, with eyes unsleeping, this "most wise god" [6] knew the processes of nature and the secret hearts of men. None could deceive him. The winkings of each mortal eye he numbered. When two men whispered and plotted together Varuna was a third in the midst of them. His spies were everywhere.[7] Though a man might flee to the highest mountain or to the remote corners of the earth he could not there escape the monarch's power.

Bounteous, compassionate, forever faithful to the good, Varuna turned a face dark with anger upon the evil-doer. His wrath burned when the holy law was broken, yet he was merciful toward the contrite heart seeking forgiveness. Against oppressors, tyrants, evil-minded enemies, liars, the human friends of demons and the forces of darkness, this terrible "hater of the false" [8] was an all-sufficient protector.

Right (rita), the natural order of the universe and moral law, was embodied in him.[9] All nature moved in regular rhythm under his command and on earth he jealously guarded the code of satisfactory, human relationships. Power and dominion belonged to him; he was the ruler of the world immortal. Gods and men alike were subject to his inexorable decree. As the "Wise Lord" his singers saluted him——

> Thou O Wise God, art Lord of all
> Thou art the King of earth and heaven.[10]

In spite of the exalted grandeur of Varuna, he was only
one of many gods in India. The adjustment of the Aryans to
the culture of their new homeland caused great changes in the
ranking of the older deities. The desperate need for rain soon
lifted Indra, the Storm-god, to a place of popularity overshad-
owing Varuna and the ancient Asuras. Within a thousand years
after their entrance into India, Varuna, the glorious, Indra, the
mighty, and all their celestial companions had fallen from their
lofty estate and slowly faded into unimportance. In Iran, on
the other hand, the Wise Lord grew steadily in power and
majesty. There too he was from the beginning surrounded by a
large company of divine associates. From being the highest
among many he became the Supreme One, in whose presence
all others were no more than angelic servants and officials of
the celestial court. Of all the brilliant galaxy of ancient Aryan
gods, Ahura Mazda alone has come striding down the centuries
into the modern world.

It would be interesting if we were able to follow the wide
wanderings of this great Heaven-god of the Aryans in all the
lands of the Near East during the second millennium B.C. Un-
fortunately, history has blurred the record. Until the earth
tells its story to the excavator, we must be content with only
tantalizing glimpses of Ahura Mazda-Varuna and his companions as they appear momentarily through the shadows at
widely separated places in their far-flung domain. They have
left the marks of their presence from the shores of the Mediterranean in the west to the Indus Valley in the east. The large
number of religious terms based on the root *var* point to the
importance of Varuna at some time in the remote past over
all the territory touched by the Indo-Iranians.[11] Some of their
gods found places among the deities of the Cassite dynasty in
Babylon (1743–1171 B.C.). A record of 1380 B.C. rescued by
research from oblivion, shows Varuna and Mithra leading the

gods of the Mitanni in the west. From the Mesopotamian Valley to eastern Iran, beginning before 1000 B.C., there are personal names into which the sacred word *arta* was woven. *Arta* was *rita* or *asha,* the natural and moral order, the distinctive sign of the highest Indo-Iranian deity. According to Assurbanipal's records, the mixed population of Medea, in western Iran, ranked Ahura Mazda and Mithra as the greatest gods in the seventh century B.C. These scattered fragments of evidence, like footprints of his passing, tell us little, but they do reveal that the Wise Lord of the Aryans was known and revered in many areas of the Near East during ancient times.

The story of his adventures in those lands, later held by other gods, we do not know, nor even why he lost his people and his scepter there. Iran he claimed as peculiarly his own. It is certain that he was addressed by many names, for the peoples of Iran were not a unity. Over all the area, the Aryans had overrun and absorbed other ethnic stocks of older cultures. They were divided into a large number of petty states, often in conflict with each other. All knew the celestial firmament with its rhythm of day and night and its regular order as their highest god. The early names, Dyaus, "the Sky," and Varuna, "the Coverer," passed out of fashion. "Wise Lord" was a descriptive title, not a proper name, a designation suitable to the heaven powers of all the groups whether they were called Varuna, Mithra, Zervan, Thwasha or Vayu, and sufficiently universal to facilitate the blending of their cults. The company of the Aryan gods and their ruler, manifest in double form—the sunlit heaven and the starry firmament—were well known over all the land; but it was in the old homeland of the Indo-Aryans, between the Jaxartes River and the Himalayas that Ahura Mazda began to build the career that has made him one of the great living gods of the world.[12]

It was the desperate need of an embattled priest-prophet which gave Ahura Mazda his historic character. Zarathustra was struggling in eastern Iran to preserve what he thought was the right way of life against powerful forces which threatened to destroy the old, good ways. The established order of community life with its ruler, nobles, priests and people, its happy homes, wealth in cattle and rich pasture was in danger. A new teaching was undermining the ancient lore. Zarathustra denounced his adversaries as liars, their gods as demons, and was especially bitter against their ecstatic joy in the sacrificial slaughter of cattle and the drinking of the sacred Haoma, which he called a "filthy intoxicant." [13] His voice was lifted in monotonous lament because of the violence and cruelty suffered by the cattle, the desolation of the pastures and the destruction of the prosperity, happiness and peace of the right-living husbandman and cattle-tender. His own livelihood as a priest was at stake. The whole community was infected. He hoped that he might be able to save his people from disobedience and bad thought toward Ahura Mazda; to ward off heresy from the nobles, the teaching of the "liars" from the community, slanderers from the priestly brotherhood and the bad herdsmen from the cattle.[14]

The ideal as portrayed in his poetic Gathas,[15] was a wealthy and happy society secure on its well-watered, lush-growing pasture lands, loyally obedient to the right order, rejoicing in good dwellings and peace, careful of the cattle and their herdsmen and providing protection for the poor. In spite of the passion of his preaching, Zarathustra found no sympathy for his message. The ruler was hostile, the nobles and his priestly peers kept aloof from him, even the people were not pleased with him. He stood defeated and almost alone, a man of few cattle and few friends. Opposed, betrayed and deserted, Zarathustra at last turned away from his own people to find a generous welcome and success for his cause among the Turanians in the north.[16] Through these years of suffering and strain, in hope and despair, Ahura Mazda was the ever-present com-

panion and confidant of the prophet. Zarathustra needed a
helper strong and wise enough to defend good against evil,
order against strife, justice against oppression, truth against
the lie. His burning desire and hope, refusing to accept defeat,
molded Ahura Mazda into an effective and lovable god.

The Lord of Heaven was certainly no stranger to the tribesmen of Iran at the close of the second millennium B.C. They
saw in him the omniscient ruler, all-seeing, master of time, of
space, of light and law. But a host of other gods were nearer
the people, more useful and therefore dearer to them than
the exalted Ahura Mazda. It was Zarathustra's achievement to
bring him down to man as a powerful, personal, good god,
at grips with evil on earth, working through the right order
of nature and human society, and effective in men of good
thought, good words, good deeds. The fighting prophet saw
his god in conflict with evil, the forces of light arrayed against
the powers of darkness. The lines of separation were sharply
drawn. Two spirits, "the better and the worst in thought and
word and deed," [17] demanded that choice be made between
them. According to an original decree, the one offered life and
a good reward, the other death and the worst things. When
they stood face to face with each other, before the world began, the most effective spirit said to the bad: "Neither our
minds nor our precepts, nor our wills, nor our choices, nor our
words, nor our consciences, nor our souls agree." [18] That battle
challenge has echoed through the universe since the beginning
of time. On the one side stood the spirit of truth and righteous
order, on the other the spirit of the lie and destruction. Many
of the old gods, the Devas, were confused when faced with
the choice of loyalties, chose wrongly and became demons.
All Aryans knew from of old that the supreme Heaven-god
jealously guarded the natural and moral law. Zarathustra appealed to him as Mazda, the wise Ahura, identified him with
the good spirit, and claimed him for his cause.

In this alliance, Ahura Mazda became the source and guarantor of all good things, material and social. The prophet saw the active presence of his god in everything that contributed to the good life of a settled, cattle-raising people. The community was accustomed to treat some phases of its life-activity as dynamic, divine powers. The social unity of cattle, pasture land and people, bound together and to the earth, they called Armaiti. Closely related to Armaiti were Haurvatat and Ameretat, the life-giving waters and the growing vegetation, which together embodied the supernatural potency of health, well-being and long life or immortality. Khshathra was a mysterious, wonder-working force manifested in supernatural beings, in warriors and good men fighting for the right, in the powerful word or ritual which distinguished the good from the evil. The mental-spiritual part of gods and men, living and dead was Manah. It was an active force and, as Vohu Manah, could be a cosmic power. More important than all was Asha. This term included the universal order of nature, the way of harmony in human relations, correct patterns of behavior, the order of right and justice. In the highest heaven, in the life of nature, in the social life of men it was an active agent for health, healing and happiness. Asha worked everywhere and always for goodness. The furtherance of Asha was the supreme duty of Ahura Mazda and faithful men. These divine forces were not clear-cut personalities, nor were they abstractions; they were real, effective potencies related to significant modes of the life of the people. They all contributed to the realization of the good and happy society. Zarathustra made them the active agents of his god. Ahura Mazda was the father of Asha, Vohu Manah, Armaiti, and these three were of one will with him. Of all the dynamic powers which found a place in the later theology, these six were always closest to Ahura Mazda, his inner celestial council. They shared with him the changing fortunes of the centuries.

Through Zarathustra's fiery faith, Mazda attained a status of unrivaled splendor. He ruled from the highest heaven of light, a beneficent spirit, omniscient, changeless and mighty. Memories of his youth as a Sky-god clung to him. He wore the heavens as a garment and was called the brilliant one, the brightest of creation. By his might he laid the foundations of the earth and established the vault of the sky. He gave wings to the winds and the clouds, created the rivers and forests and molded the body of man. By his will the stars followed their radiant paths through the heavens; through him the moon waxed and waned and the seasons swung in regular rhythm. Light and darkness, sleep and waking, and the marching hours of the day were ordered by him. He was a spiritual being, blissful, holy, perfect, righteous, wise and good. As the Lord of the armies of light, he gave well-being, long life, protection, felicity and joy to men who chose the good. Those who loved justice and piety could count on him to give happiness and prosperity. The careful tending of cattle, social order, happy homes and smiling countrysides were pleasing to him. His hand dealt distress and adversity to the makers of enmity, hatred and discord. He was the first and the last, the all-seeing one, whom none could deceive. As the sovereign judge he measured out rewards and punishments. To these attributes which he had had as Varuna, was added a new rôle in the world drama. Like his prophet, Ahura Mazda was at war with the spirit of evil at work in the world, and Zarathustra knew that, at the end, the Wise Lord would lead his faithful warriors to victory.

There can be no doubt that Ahura Mazda was the highest and greatest of the gods in the thought of Zarathustra. Possibly he was the only one, but expressions like, "O Mazda and ye other Ahuras," or "one of you Ahuras" [19] suggest that while Mazda was his supreme heavenly friend, there still lingered on the horizon of his mind the other Ahuras, members of the old Indo-Iranian company of the gods of light. These ancient deities were still active in eastern Iran during Zarathustra's life-time but their names never appear in his Gathas. "Mazda and ye other Ahuras" may refer to the Wise Lord and his divine agents, Asha, Vohu Manah and the rest, through whom his work was done.

If the god of the prophet held the throne of the universe alone, it was not long until other gods crowded into the celestial court and found a welcome and work in the cause of Mazda. Earliest of these were Mithra and his companions. At first the Mithraic religion seems to have been a rival of Zarathustra's faith but time and the development of mutual interests led to reconciliation. Then Ahura Mazda graciously acknowledged that Mithra was as worthy of worship as himself.

Mithra was an old god. Long ago, as Mitra, in association with the Indian Varuna, he had been arrayed in all the attributes of a heavenly god of light. In eastern Iran he drew close to the folk life and became immensely popular as the "Lord of wide pastures," guardian of truth, avenger of broken faith, friend and protector of the poor and oppressed. He was a worthy companion for Ahura Mazda. With him came his closest associates, Rashnu, "Truth," the deity of the ordeal, Sraosha, "Obedience," and Ashi, the goddess of fertility. In the ebb and flow of people and influences, Anahita, the most highly favored fertility goddess, associated with the Jaxartes River,[20] took Ashi's place at Mithra's side. Ahura Mazda offered sacrifices to her and won her promise of help in his program for saving mankind. These gods preserved their personalities and some of them lived dramatic lives of their own during later centuries, but they always remained loyal members of Ahura Mazda's court. Inseparable from the gods were the traditional forms of their cults. Sacrifice, the presentation of sacred twigs (baresma), and even the object of Zarathustra's scorn, Haoma—probably in an altered and less intoxicating form—were woven into the religion and lent their services to the cause of goodness and light.

The local religions of eastern Iran were blended with the Mazdayasnian religion of Zarathustra before the rise of the Achaemenian dynasty.[21] There was little reason for conflict among the gods of the various groups because most of the important figures belonged to the old Indo-Iranian family, and were similar in function if not always in name. The goddesses were not so easily reconciled. There must have been a struggle before the Turanian Anahita supplanted the Mithraic goddess, Ashi. The earth goddess, Armaiti, of Zarathustra's group was above the battle since she held a secure place of long standing in the inner divine circle. When the theology was crystallized and each of the gods found his proper rank, at the top of the hierarchy was Ahura Mazda with his six companions, the sacred seven. The seven were now called the Amesha Spentas, the "Immortal Powerful Ones." There was some hesitation before the personnel of the little group was fixed for all future time. There were many candidates for this company of immortals, but the apparent necessity of selecting seven for the highest rank resulted in the classical list. Ahura Mazda was always central and supreme. Next to him stood the two, who had been called from the beginning "sons of Ahura Mazda," Vohu Manah, the Good Mind, and Asha, Righteousness. These two were really phases of the cosmic activity of their chief. They divided between them the care of cattle and fire. Khshathra Vairya represented power and had control of metal, a memory of the use of molten metal in the primitive ordeals for testing truth and a recognition of the rôle of weapons in maintaining dominion. The goddess Armaiti, Haurvatat and Ameretat, who complete the list, were the old trio embodying the values of the good earth, its waters and plants. Later singers chanted the mystical unity of this group, the most exalted of the gods——

Who are all seven of one thought, who are all seven of one speech, who are all seven of one deed; whose thought is the same, whose speech is the same, whose deed is the same, whose father and commander is the same, namely, the Maker, Ahura Mazda.[22]

Around the celestial seven gathered the other gods. Most important among them were Mithra, Rashnu and Sraosha, the inseparable trio of the Mithraic religion, Vayu, the wind or the celestial atmosphere, and Atar, "Fire." Atar, in his many forms, was especially dear to devotees of a religion of light. He was the sacred, memory-suffused fire of the hearth, the light of high heaven, of the sun by day, of the watching stars at night. He was the essence of Ahura Mazda, symbol of Spenta Mainyu, the Holy Spirit of the Lord. He was the altar fire associated with the ecstatic experience of devotion to the god of light.[23]

During the sovereignty of the Achaemenian monarchs, Zoroastrianism reached out for the missionary conquest of western Iran. By the sixth century B.C., Ragha had become its religious center and the Magi of the Medean kingdom its devoted priests. In the west, the Ahura Mazda of Zarathustra met himself in a different form. From ancient times, Herodotus tells us, the Persians had been accustomed to worship the whole circle of heaven under the name of Zeus, together with Sun, Moon, Fire, Water and Winds.[24] These gods are easily recognized as the old Indo-Iranian group of divinities. This "Zeus" was what Ahura Mazda had been before he was transformed by the experience of his prophet. The Persian kings, independently of Zarathustra, had made him the great god of their empire under the name of Auramazda. He did not stand alone, but in relation to him the lesser deities were not important enough to be mentioned except by the phrase, "and the other gods."

From Ariyaramna in the seventh century until Alexander the Great destroyed the dynasty, the Achaemenian rulers, in set phrases constantly repeated, glorified him as the greatest of the gods, by whose grace they received the kingdom, by whose help they won their triumphs. They boasted in stone of their grandeur and gave credit for it to their god. Typical of many is an inscription of Darius——

A great god is Auramazda, who created this earth, who created yonder firmament, who created man, who created welfare for man, who made Darius king. . . . Says Darius the King: Auramazda, the greatest of the gods; he created me; he made me king; he to me this kingdom granted, the great (kingdom) with good horses, with good men. . . . Auramazda granted me aid, Auramazda I revered, Auramazda, the greatest of the gods. . . .[25]

The blending of the Auramazda of royalty with the god of the Mazdayasnian religion was perfected when the Magi became the official priests of Persia.

As Zoroastrianism spread westward the deities of the new territories joined the company of Ahura Mazda. The unification of all Iran under the Persian kings broke down the isolation of districts and the hostile exclusiveness of local chiefs. Conditions were favorable for the flowing together of influences from many areas and an assembly of the gods. A roll-call of divine names in the fifth century B.C., shows gods gathered from east and west, some hoary with antiquity, others radiant new embodiments of old ideals, some dynamic powers of the social life, some lovely, luminous abstractions minted in the mind, and many who never outgrew their nature origin in Sun, Moon, Stars, Sky, Earth and Waters. Within the framework of the official lists were more than two score of gods "worthy of worship," the Yazatas. Ahura Mazda and the other Amesha Spentas were enthroned above them all. Supreme and glorious, all-wise and beneficent, Ahura Mazda, as the Lord of hosts, directed the campaign of the celestial gods in the cosmic struggle against the demon forces of darkness and evil. Although he was the greatest of the gods, their lord and king, he was not a self-sufficient deity ruling them as an autocrat. He prayed to them for help, offered sacrifices to some of them and acknowledged that things would have gone badly if they had refused their aid.[26]

Ahura Mazda could not be a quiescent being, eternally thinking the thoughts of perfection, in a state of timeless bliss. His creative task was unfinished. As the supreme spirit of goodness he was striving to establish his perfect kingdom on earth. Over against him was the evil spirit, Angra Mainyu, and his threatening array. There could be no peace, no lull in the battle either for gods or men until evil was utterly destroyed. The whole universe was the arena and all living things warriors in the strife. The hosts of light included the gods with their various powers, the Fravashis, celestial spiritual counterparts of all creatures, good men, useful animals and plants. The wisdom of Ahura Mazda directed the strategy of the war. His followers praised him as——

The Creator, Ahura Mazda, resplendent and glorious, the greatest, best, most beautiful of beings, the most constant, wisest, most perfect of form, supreme in righteousness, knowing to do good, giving joy at his good pleasure; who created us, formed us, and sustains us; who is the most beneficent spirit.[27]

As creator of the material world and of all good things, he was the keeper, nourisher, sustainer and protector of those who were loyal to his cause. His all-seeing eye swept the universe. He was the giver of health, lands and prosperity, the source of all happiness to men of good thought, good words and good deeds. Just and merciful, radiant and glorious, his might and omniscience gave assurance to men that some day the sun would smile upon a world in which pain and suffering, sorrow and death would be no more.

Quite apart from the beauty of his character and his ability to give rewards here and hereafter, Ahura Mazda could make a compelling appeal to the fighting spirit of Iran because he appeared as a limited being of perfect goodness, hampered in his plan to create a good world by the work of the mighty, malignant spirit of darkness, as eternal as himself. No hint of responsibility for the pain and sorrow of human existence touched his character. He was altogether good and the maker only of the good. Evil was the creation of the wicked Angra Mainyu. An absolute god, sole creator of all things, must apologize for the evil which mars his work. Ahura Mazda had no need of apology. He was fighting on a battle-field, wide as the universe, to make his vision of the perfect world come true. Gods and men were called to help in winning the final victory for the good.

As Lord of the moral order, Ahura Mazda was best served by ethical conduct in the realm of men. The increased power and prestige of his priesthood, however, gradually added to the potency and dignity of the properly instituted ritual. Zarathustra had taken for granted the fact that sacrifice, prayer, ceremonials, gifts and the singing of praise songs were pleasing to the gods. The accretions of centuries elaborated the order of later service. Good thoughts might remain the concern of the individual conscience but good words tended to be defined in terms of sacred formulae. Repetitions of the Gathas of Zarathustra carried tangible merit since they were the most holy of the traditional literature. Several prayers or spells of almost equal antiquity were even more efficacious in furthering the kingdom of light. One correct recitation of the Ahuna Vairya was worth the chanting of a hundred Gathas, and sufficient in virtue to enable the devout to reach paradise.[28] Speaking the names and titles of Ahura Mazda and the other Amesha Spentas was the most fiend-smiting, best healing, strongest and most effective means of bringing the material world to the fulfillment of man's wishes.[29] Whatever increased the productivity of the earth, improved the health, prosperity and happiness of the family and the welfare of the community always came under the category of good deeds but other actions, too, were necessary to thwart the ever present malignancy of the demon world. Rites of purification with *gomez* [30] and water, proper performance of the *baresma* [31] ceremony, libations of milk and the sacred Haoma, sacrifices of meat, played an important rôle in promoting the cause of Ahura Mazda. An especially virtuous deed was the care of the divine fire, the "Son of Ahura Mazda." All manner of evil might be destroyed by preparing its favorite fuel, feeding it incense, and preserving its flames through the dark watches of the night.[32]

The god of Iran faced a severe test when Alexander the Great crushed the Persian empire in 330 B.C. The rock inscriptions of the Achaemenian kings, proudly acclaiming Ahura Mazda's help in their imperial conquests, endured to mock a conquered people. The royal glory rested briefly upon the futile successors of Alexander, passed to the Arsacidae for four uncertain centuries and, at last, found a favorable sovereignty and renewed splendor in the Sassanians. During these centuries the Magi were chiefly responsible for keeping the fires of the holy religion alight.

The national disaster with its resultant disorder brought distress and suffering to the people. They had been so well taught that life is a long, bitter battle with the implacable hosts of evil that, even in this dark time of discouragement, they did not turn to other-worldliness or despair of life on earth. They kept their vision of the perfect world to be shared by Ahura Mazda's loyal warriors beyond the horizon of some far-off tomorrow. But it was easy to believe that Alexander had been an emissary of the Evil Spirit, and that the destructive fury of the captain of the demons of darkness could be a terrifying threat to the purposes of Ahura Mazda. There must have been many who wondered anxiously whether the power of their god was adequate to support his wisdom and goodness. In the earlier and less troubled days they had been content to leave him less than all-powerful, to place beside him an independent, co-existent spirit of evil, because no faithful follower of Zara-thustra could doubt that good would win the final victory. In the days of defeat, however, when good men were tormented by rampant wrong on earth, there was a need for security, a desire for certainty that the age of future blessedness would not fail. In response, the character of Ahura Mazda was drawn with firmer lines to mark his might and invincible will.

As the religion was being molded into its classical form in the hands of the priests, Zarathustra's vision of the twin spirits, at war since the beginning of time, was elaborated into a phi-losophy of history. The ages of human experience were visual-ized as a spectacular, stormy interlude between two eternities. In the age before creation the two self-existent spirits, good and evil, dwelt in their separate realms of light and darkness. In the age to follow the brief span of man's earthly adventure, the Good Spirit would rule the universe alone. The faithful saw their god as the adorable hero of a cosmic drama in four acts of three thousand years each. In the first act he created, in in-visible form, all good beings to dwell in the harmony and hap-piness of a perfect world. Angra Mainyu, lurking in the abyss of darkness because of his lack of omniscience had no knowl-edge of Ahura Mazda's creative activity. Toward the end of this period, however, he became aware of the excess of light, discovered Ahura Mazda's plan, rushed furiously to an attack but was driven back in confusion. In the second three thousand years, Ahura Mazda brought his good world into actuality, while the Prince of Darkness was busy creating all manner of evil things to oppose the good creations of God. At the be-ginning of the third period, Angra Mainyu came leading his motley hosts of evil and "plunged like a snake through the sky," so that from the highest heaven to the remotest regions of earth, all existence was contaminated by the noxious creations of the demon. This was the darkest age of the world. The Evil Spirit seemed to have the advantage in the struggle. With the coming of the prophet Zarathustra, at the opening of the last act, the tide began to turn. Yet the warfare man knows so well against physical and moral evil must go on until the twelve-thousand year cycle is complete. The militant forces of goodness will be heartened in each millennium of the period of last things by splendid leaders of the lineage of Zarathustra. When their work is finished and the final curtain falls, the whole universe will be purged of pollution in a bath of molten metal, Angra Mainyu will be destroyed or chained forever in the abysmal prison of eternal darkness and the good world of Ahura Mazda's vision will become a reality.[33]

The five centuries between the Achaemenian and the Sassanian dynasties were a time of discouragement but not of surrender for the people of Ahura Mazda. Magi toiled faithfully to spread the gospel at home and abroad. The lost scriptures were being reclaimed and interpreted in the new Pahlavi dress. The names of Ahura Mazda and his great adversary, Angra Mainyu, were given their final form as Ormazd and Ahriman. The lowly folk found comfort in the lesser deities of the heavenly hierarchy who seemed to be closer to the earth and the affairs of men than the high Heaven-god. Thinkers, in quest of certainty or troubled by the untidiness of a split spiritual world, sought a principle of unity behind the warring hosts of the divine and demonic armies. Ormazd was honored still as a great, wise and good god, but rivals appeared to challenge his supremacy or to compete with him for popular favor.

Some intellectuals in the west discovered behind the conflict of the Good and Evil Spirits an older, abstract god, Zervan Akarana, "Boundless Time," from whom both were born. In his earliest form Zervan was simply the firmament with its alternations of the dark and luminous heaven, night and day.[34] Night and darkness meant evil and danger; day and light brought safety and gladness. This contrast of darkness and light was a natural symbol of the cosmic conflict between the twin spirits of evil and goodness. Beyond them, and father of both, was the boundless Zervan. The two warring spirits were easily identified with Ormazd and Ahriman of Zoroastrian theology. Their rivalry was explained in the legend of their birth.[35] In his timeless solitude, Zervan desired a son of beauteous form to rule the universe. When he found that two spirits were in his eternal womb he decreed that the first born should hold sovereignty over creation. By a tricky maneuver, the Evil Spirit appeared first and Zervan could not repudiate his word. He did, however, limit the lordship of evil to a period of nine thousand years and decreed that at the end of that time the Spirit of Goodness would rule the perfected earth for "ever and everlasting." The eternal Zervan thus solved the problem of dualism and gave an absolute guarantee that a time limit had been fixed before the beginning to the destructive power of the forces of evil.

Other thinkers, influenced by the Babylonian star-lore, found comfort for the ills of life and a unity behind the warfare of good and evil by enthroning Fate above all the gods.[36] They gladly admitted that Ormazd might intervene to save a man from the steel grip of destiny, but he rarely did. Fate offered escape from the fear of failure and a bitter consolation in defeat, but Ormazd was a more alluring god for a people accustomed to face life as a battle and trained to accept responsibility for earning the right to happiness. Zervan was too colorless and vague; Fate was too impersonal. Neither of these deities could offer any real challenge to Ormazd who embodied all goodness and wisdom and fought for man's ideals.

The supreme god had a worthier rival in Mithra. He was one of the elder gods, as old as Ahura Mazda himself. Long ago the Mazdayasnians had established a treaty of friendship between the two gods, and Mithra never lost the love and loyalty of the princes and the common people. He was the light of heaven, all-seeing, sleepless, vigilant, touching the lives of men more intimately than Ormazd on his celestial throne. He rode across the heavens in a star-jewelled chariot, with the sun as its single wheel, attended by a retinue of lesser gods. In his dwelling place of pure light, sickness, impurity, darkness and death were unknown. He was the infallible sentinel of the sky, with a thousand ears and ten thousand eyes, hearing everything and seeing all the deeds of men. Guardian of truth, he witnessed oaths and bargains, and brought swift punishment upon the liar. When the poor were injured or wronged, Mithra hurried to champion their cause. No man could deceive him. He was the friend of the farmer and the warrior. He gave warmth and light to the growing plants, fertility to the earth, swiftness to horses and strength to the bodies of men. Lord of hosts, Lord of wide pastures, Mithra was the strongest, swiftest, most beneficent, most intelligent, most glorious of all the gods associated with Ahura Mazda. To those who were loyally devoted to him he gave strong sons, riches, prosperity, flocks, cattle, well-being, victory, and crowned these material gifts with happiness, wisdom, piety and fame.[37] He was the best beloved of gods.

His dominion extended from India, in the east, to Rome in the west. In his later rôle as a savior god, giver of immortality, he followed the far-flung Roman armies over Europe and Africa. He was honored in lands where Ahura Mazda was never known. In his homeland, he and Ormazd were ranked together as the two imperishable, exalted, omniscient, holy ones. Ahura Mazda confessed that he created Mithra as worthy of sacrifice and prayer as himself. The glorious god of light, truth and courage might be nearer and dearer to the people than Ormazd, but he never seriously threatened to usurp the throne. Mithra was always the loyal friend and assistant of his creator. When the priests returned to power under the Sassanians, the time of open competition among the old popular gods was at an end.

The Sassanian rulers of Iran were tireless in their efforts to revive the religion of Zarathustra and to give Ormazd a place of supreme glory among the gods of the world. During the four hundred years of their rule his most powerful rival was the Christian God, but missionaries, martyrs and the armies of Rome on the horizon were not enough to endanger the status of Ormazd in his own domain. For Iran, he was the one and only Lord of heaven and earth, the embodiment of light and truth, eternal, omniscient, the mighty guardian of the good creation. There were subtle changes in his character because of the near presence of his great rival. He had always been supreme in goodness and the implacable enemy of evil. In this period his beneficence was extended to good and evil men alike. As the divine law-giver and sovereign judge he was all-just; now he was willing to be called forgiving and all-merciful.[38] This was as far as he could go to match the bounteous grace of the God of Christianity. Ormazd was a warrior in a grim cosmic battle with evil, in which every act of sin and wickedness done by man was a betrayal of the cause. He remained true to himself. No one could presume upon his mercy. If he was forgiving, it was only on condition that the sinner should resolve to overcome his past evil deeds with future good deeds.

During this period, the supreme grandeur of Ormazd began to dim the early splendor of the six other Amesha Spentas, the holy, immortal companions of the throne. From the beginning they had collaborated with him as beneficent supervisors of earthly well-being. Their practical usefulness continued since they remained celestial guardians of animals, fire, metals, earth, water and plants, but the human values they embodied in ancient times—good mind, righteousness, might, devotion, perfection and immortality—were now absorbed in the character of the god they served. They were archangels rather than companion gods. Ormazd gathered all the qualities of power and perfection into his own glorious being. The archangels were fading into little more than personalized symbols of the divine providential care.

The changing times had a devastating effect upon the old nature gods who had lived on as assistants of Ormazd. Only the sun, the star Tishtar (Sirius) herald of the rains, and Mithra continued to be important. Mithra, the most popular of the celestial company in former times, was greatly changed. Although he was still called the Lord of wide pastures, he no longer watched with sleepless eyes all the dwellings of the Aryans as the friend of the farmer and the poor. No longer, as Lord of hosts, did he drive his victorious chariot to the field of conflict. He surrendered his earthly duties to join the heavenly council as lord of truth and justice, the judge of all mankind. With him on the seat of judgement were Sraosha and Rashnu. These two gods had long been active on earth in the company of Mithra. Originally guardian of the religious community, Sraosha had become a demon-slayer, who patrolled the earth three times during the hours of darkness and sleep to protect men from the dangers of the night. As a member of the heavenly tribunal, he acted as the guide and guardian of the souls of the dead during that anxious interim of three days and nights between death and the morning of judgement at the Chinvat Bridge. Rashnu, as the former judge of ordeals on earth, was promoted from the earthly to the supreme court. There he held the golden balance in which the deeds of men were weighed to determine their fitness for paradise or hell. The large and colorful company of divine figures who surrounded Ormazd before the second century A.D., was reduced to a little company of specialized, executive angels. The sun and rain were still real, too practically useful to be forgotten, but most of the earlier, older deities followed the easy, descending path to oblivion—from gods to angels, to vague symbols, to haunting names in old rituals, to ghostly memories of long-lost friends.

The same process of dissolution overtook the Fravashis. In olden times they had formed an innumerable heavenly army constantly alert to forestall the forces of evil. They were the original spiritual creation of Ahura Mazda, counterparts of all beings who were later given life. Even Ahura Mazda and his archangels had their Fravashis. They were practically forgotten, and the so-frequent prayers for help to this heavenly company dwindled to nothing in the later centuries. The Fravashis of men lost their independent status as spiritual guardians and were identified with human souls. The new intellectual climate caused a serious depopulation of the unseen world.

Before the middle of the seventh century the armies of Allah presented a menace to the domain of Ormazd. In the famous battle of Nehavand (641) they scored a decisive victory, and a short time later the Califs of Islam were in control of the whole of Iran. How soon the majority of Ormazd's followers turned their allegiance to the new god is not known. As people having scriptures, they were exempt from persecution, but the head-tax imposed on non-Muslims, the less onerous duties required by the invading faith, and the fact that all political glories belonged to the elect of Allah were probably powerful incentives to conversion. Extensive literary activity of the Zoroastrian priests in Iran through the ninth century indicates, however, that Ormazd was not immediately deserted in his home land.

The most significant change in Ormazd in this period of humiliation was his drift toward omnipotence. In the early days he had been limited in power. He was the creator of all good things and only of the good, but he was not the only creator. The evils of the world were neither willed nor sanctioned by him. Consequently, his wisdom and goodness were not tainted by responsibility for the sorrows and sufferings of man's earthly existence. He was tempted to accept the scepter of omnipotence by the pressure of other almighty gods. Yahweh of Israel and the God of aggressive Christianity had long ago extended their influence to Iran. Now the youngest of the great gods, Allah of Islam, was becoming the dominant deity in the home land of Ormazd. He could not seem to be less than almighty in this company, but the new dignity brought with it the embarrassment all other omnipotent gods have known—the necessity of explaining the presence and continuance of evil. He still had an advantage over the other gods in that he did not have to apologize for the origin of evil. Ahriman, the author of cosmic disorder, was not a divine creation like Satan or Iblis, but an eternal, pre-existent, spiritual being of godlike power. The real problem for the Zoroastrian was why a god of adequate power allowed evil to continue. The earlier defenders of Ormazd explained that when the two rival spirits met before the creation of the natural world, Ormazd tried to win Ahriman over to the side of goodness, but met only defiant threats of eternal warfare——

And the Evil Spirit shouted thus: "I will not depart,
I will not provide assistance for thy creatures,
I will not offer praise among thy creatures, and
I am not of the same opinion with thee as to good things.
I will destroy thy creatures for ever and everlasting; moreover
I will force all thy creatures into disaffection to thee and affection
for myself." [39]

Ormazd therefore accepted battle for nine thousand years. At the end of that time evil will be destroyed, and the world made perfect as he intended in the beginning.

Thought played many variations on this fascinating theme. Although Ahriman now began to be an embarrassment for the theologians, the long tradition of orthodoxy supported his sinister personality. As he had been from all eternity he remained, a personal embodiment of pure evil, the implacable enemy of the good, malicious, deceitful, luring man to moral disaster, disease and death. Any claim of omnipotence for Ormazd was limited by logical and historical difficulties. He could not destroy Ahriman, who was as eternal as himself, nor could he change his nature, and he had failed to persuade him not to make war upon the good creation. Since the power of Ormazd was supported by omniscience, which his enemy lacked, it would have been possible for him to throw a wall of protection around his creatures and, through eternity, be their constant guardian against the attacks of the demons. But he thought of a better plan. He called a council of the Fravashis, the pre-existent heavenly spirits of all living forms, and asked them whether they would prefer to be eternally protected or to fight out the battle with evil on earth until the devil and his demons were completely destroyed. The Fravashis decided to fight, and so the warfare with evil torments our world period.[40] In the end the power of Ahriman will be destroyed and the warriors of goodness and light will enjoy a life of eternal happiness in a world made new.

In this age of defeat and frustration, thought wavered between the need of a god of almighty power and the desire to preserve his absolute goodness. In the ninth century a champion of Zoroastrianism demonstrated the superiority of Ormazd over his rivals because he alone could claim to be a god of perfect goodness.[41] Using the gods of Christianity, Judaism and Islam as examples, he showed how the problem of evil became insoluble if a god claimed absolute omnipotence as well as omniscience and perfect goodness. The fact of evil in the creation of an almighty god cried out against either his wisdom or his goodness, and without perfect goodness and omniscience, he could not be a worthy deity. The superiority of Ormazd rested on the fact that he was all-wise, all-good, and mighty enough to guarantee the final victory of the good while responsibility for the creation of the world's woes rested upon Ahriman. A creative devil kept God's record clear.

Nevertheless, the dangers involved in calling Ormazd omnipotent weighed less than the advantages in the dark days of Muslim supremacy. This quality satisfied the desire to have him the equal in majesty and might of any of the great gods. It was also a consoling guarantee that he could not fail to realize his plan for the salvation of his people. When devoted Zoroastrians bowed in sorrow and desolation amid the ruins of their lost empire, while evil seemed to be triumphantly at large on the earth, complete assurance of the ultimate realization of the good world was more important to them than saving Ormazd from entanglement in the net of an insoluble theological problem.

A seer of the ninth century, learned in the lore of the gods and aware of the afflictions of Ormazd's conquered land and people, might reasonably have predicted the passing of one of the most heroic and lovable of the great gods, the closing of another chapter of divine history. The royal glory of Iran had left the earth forever. The burden of a foreign yoke and an alien god weighed heavily upon the faithful Zoroastrians who would not or could not find a new life in the service of their conquerors. Three gods of a single lineage, Yahweh, Allah and the God of Christianity, each claiming world sovereignty, were disputing dominion of the West and the Near East. The many gods who had held the lands before them were either long forgotten or fast fading into legendary figures. The restless thought of India and China, a thousand years before this time had thrust aside the personal gods in quest of a timeless, impersonal Absolute. In the pre-empted West there was no career for a god who had lost his sword. The philosophic East could never give more than a secondary place to a deity limited by personality and will. Yet Ormazd, like Yahweh of Israel long before, lived down defeat. There was little chance for him to grow under the shadow of Allah in Iran, but when some of the faithful fled the homeland to find refuge as a compact Parsi community in the tolerant atmosphere of India, the future of Ormazd was assured.

As a World-god he had already acquired all the attributes necessary to make him the equal of other great personal deities. As a creator, altogether good, he was superior to them all since no blame could fall on him for the evils of the world. After the tenth century, he was robbed of that distinction. In an age when the unity of God was an obsession, Zoroastrians were accused of having two gods. They yielded to the theological fashion and made Ormazd a single, omnipotent creator, only to prepare for future generations a more difficult problem. Ahriman might be denied independent creative power but he could not be ignored as an ever-present menace.

From that time until the end of the nineteenth century thinkers were worried by the problem of explaining the existence of Ahriman. Their task was made especially difficult because the Spirit of Evil in Zoroastrianism had always had a clear-cut personality. Long ago the Zervanites had found a divine unity in Boundless Time, from which Ormazd and Ahriman were born as twin spirits. Those who still held this position explained that Ahriman was allowed to exist to prove to Ormazd the absolute power of time and to produce variety in creation. Others borrowed from Islam the suggestion that Ormazd permitted evil in order that his goodness might be better appreciated, or that Ahriman was a reprobate angel who revolted from Ormazd. A more subtle thinker offered the unique theory that Ahriman had his origin from a thought of God.[42] In a moment fraught with limitless sorrow for man, the good God visualized what the nature of his rival would be if he existed, and immediately he was.

By the beginning of the twentieth century the combined pressure of the Hindu environment, Christian missionaries, and western thought made the leaders of the Parsis in India shrink from the dualism which, through all the early ages, had been the shield of protection for the goodness of their god. They compromised by denying the existence of Ahriman. Ormazd stood alone, but the scriptures remained to remind them of the earlier picture of the world struggle. What men of ancient times had thought of as a cosmic warfare of two creative spirits was now interpreted as a balance of creative and destructive phases in the being of the one God. In this dual nature of Ormazd there is a reflection of the influence of Vishnu, the preserver, and Śiva, the destroyer, the two modes of the Hindu impersonal Absolute. But the vigorous personality of Ormazd could not be veiled in verbal abstractions and a personal god who united in his own being both good and evil was troublesome to modern thought. Ahriman lost his historic rôle as an independent enemy of the good but the result was a god with a split personality.

Two decades ago a Parsi priest and scholar saved Ormazd from embarrassment.[43] He restored his character of perfect goodness by putting responsibility for evil upon man. There was an ancient scripture of the Pahlavi period which traced the origin of evil to perverse thinking in the immature minds of the first human pair. When it was first suggested the idea fell upon barren soil, for then Ahriman was alive as an active, creative devil, waging an age-long war with God. It was attractive when Ormazd held the field alone. The revived spirit of the old religion and the modern temper combined to stress human responsibility and to find the origin of both physical and moral evil in the thoughts, attitudes and deeds of men. Ormazd must be absolutely good. When the scriptures speak of the rivalry of the Good Spirit with the Evil Spirit, they could only refer to the struggle of good and evil in the life of man.

Through all his history Ahura Mazda has been a useful,

practical, personal god. Like the gods of Israel, Christianity and Islam, he was bathed for several centuries in the light of Greek thought. They were deeply affected; he went his way unchanged. The mysticism of the Persian Sufis touched him with its poetic beauty but had no power to transform him. For eleven hundred years he resisted the influence of Indian philosophy which would have lured him to lay aside his garment of personality to become one of the ineffable, abstract deities lost in eternal quiescence, before whom human thought falters and fails. A modern group of Parsis, however, are troubled by his personality, because personality implies limitation and incompleteness. They would make him Zervan Akarana, Boundless Time; not the Boundless Time of their far-off forefathers, who was a personal being, but an impersonal god, forever beyond the grasp of human language or the understanding of the mind of man. Ahriman would then be merely the shadow of this god. A characterization of deity so foreign to Zoroastrianism can hardly be more than a temporary eddy in the stream of modern thought.

During recent years, the interpenetration of cultures has put an end to the isolation of the gods. The walls which separate religions are falling. No longer do the great gods meet each other as rivals. They tend rather to share each other's qualities and to blend into one. Because of the prestige of western learning and literature and the work of missionaries, the God of Christianity has greatly influenced the Parsis. Some are inclined to refashion Ormazd in his image, to make him a god of love and grace, a heavenly father, tenderly caring for his children in life's troubled ways.[44] The hard, heroic quality of Ormazd is replaced by a velvet gentleness. He is a shepherd of his people rather than, as of old, the captain of human salvation, leading men in the tragic struggle with evil. This compromise probably comes too late.

There are others in high official positions of leadership who make no concessions to the Christian God. Thoroughly aware of the findings of the sciences and versed in the history of cultures, they can appreciate the unique position of Ormazd among the gods. He appears to them in his historic character as a lovable, limited god of infinite wisdom and goodness, who bears no blame for the evils of nature or of human life. Even though the personality of Ahriman is only vaguely restored, evil is recognized frankly as evil, the enemy of God and man. It is not something to be accepted or explained away or interpreted as a hidden good, but a grim, factual phase of existence to be utterly and relentlessly destroyed. The long eons of world evolution and the ages of man's agonized following of the vision of an ideal culture record the progressive advance of Ormazd toward the perfecting of human life in a natural environment made friendly to man. God is the unseen presence everywhere collaborating with good men to reduce the discord, disharmony, and suffering of man's physical and social life. Ormazd claims and deserves the loyalty of man, for only by man's co-operation can the pain-racked world be transformed into paradise. Every deed of dishonor, every act of treachery, every violation of the moral code, every betrayal of the truth strengthens the power of evil to delay the coming of the divine kingdom. "Whoso furthers health, lengthens life, promotes knowledge, spreads truth, advances peace, or assists righteousness cooperates with the godhead in ushering perfection. Whoso fights disease, death, ignorance, bigotry, injustice, corruption, falsehood, war and wickedness, is a comrade of God in his conflict for the destruction of the powers of imperfection." [45] The battle is long and progress painfully slow, but Ormazd will win at last. He and man together will build the good society of justice, order and peace. The brave, fighting spirit of Zarathustra and his Wise Ahura thus return to hearten the faithful amid the tragic scenes of the modern world.

The intellectual and moral difficulties which threaten the existence of the absolute and omnipotent gods do not touch this restored Ormazd. The modern fashion of finiteness, which some gods are assuming so that men may continue to believe in their goodness, he wears gracefully from long habit. When the twilight shadows gather about him, he will be lost to men, not because he has wandered too far into the shadow-land of abstractions but because his work will be finished when men have acquired his qualities of wisdom and goodness, and are able to take from his shoulders the burden of making and preserving the good world.

CHAPTER V

THE GODS OF INDIA

Upon that excellent glory
Of the god Savitar may we meditate;
May he stimulate our thoughts.[1]

HE galaxy of India's gods is as complex and colorful as the endless variety of her geographical and cultural climate. No one great personal god strides in lonely splendor down the centuries, obliterating his predecessors, reducing his rivals to nothingness, until he holds the throne of the universe alone. In ages long ago the gods of India learned the art of tolerance. The arrogant attitude of the high God of the Semitic-Christian tradition does not appear. There was always room for the old gods if they retained their usefulness and for new gods if they carried gifts in their hands.

Three thousand years ago there were rivalries while the gods of the conquering Aryans were making themselves at home in northern India, adjusting themselves to new climatic and cultural conditions and meeting the older gods who held the land before them. As the centuries passed, the boisterous Aryans were subdued and conquered by the higher culture of the Indus Valley. Their intellectual outlook was so altered, their ideal of perfect happiness so changed that neither their own beloved deities nor the gods of the land could help them in the quest for the new goal. For the thinkers of India no divine purpose threaded the events of history with beneficent meaning; no divine will marshalled all things toward a goal of perfection.

Understanding of the ultimate nature of reality was always regarded as beyond the grasp of man's mind, hence thinkers found no basis for intolerance of the multitude of popular gods. The lowliest worshipper of the lowliest god might glimpse some ray of light from the truth which no one, not even the philosopher, could completely know. Thus the long life stories of the gods of India unfold in the mellow atmosphere of universal tolerance.

When the world-shaking Aryans stormed in from the north over the ancient civilization of the Indus Valley, the gods they brought with them traced their origin to the far-off Indo-European homeland of the long ago. The conquered native deities withdrew into obscurity for a time. Through the veil of neglect we catch only fleeting glimpses of them as fertility figures. Although the newcomers ignored them, they lived on in their old haunts, patiently biding their time.

The Aryan gods were all beneficent nature powers, the old familiar friends and companions of the nomads—the lovely maiden dawn, Ushas, full-formed and radiant, who dispelled the dangers of the dark, touched the sleeping earth with her rosy fingers, threw back the curtains of night and called men to the joy and labor of each new day; the sun, specialized in many forms as the fiery, heavenly charioteer, Surya, the way-finder, Pushan, the vivifier and stimulator, Savitar, the swift strider of the celestial heights, Vishnu; Mitra, light of heaven, companion of the sun; the gentle rain, Parjanya, softly caressing all living things to new growth; the fire, Agni, "thrice-born," as the friendly companion on the hearth, the lightning of the storm clouds and the burning strength of the heaven-ruling sun; the soothing, cooling winds, Vayu and Vata; the destructive lightning, Rudra, with his band of mischief-making storm winds, the Maruts. Over them all was the vast encircling heaven, the Sky-Father (Dyaus Pitar), known to the Indo-

Aryans as Varuna. Associated with the Sky-Father was Prithivi Mata, the Earth-Mother.

These and many more of the lesser phases of the natural world were the trusted divine companions of the Aryans. Their characters and exploits are portrayed in the Vedas, India's most sacred scriptures. They were simply the helpful forces of nature, but emotion, flowing into language, had long ago endowed them with human qualities. They had earned their place in the people's interest and gratitude because of what they could do for man. They were treated as good friends, with perfect confidence in their willingness to help and without undue deference. The Indo-Aryan held his head erect and laughed, even in the presence of his gods.

Two of the early Aryan gods owed their prominence to the peculiar development of the sacrificial technique as a way of guaranteeing the values of life. Soma, the intoxicating liquor, and Agni, the altar fire, were indispensable for the ceremony. When the sacrifice grew in importance as an instrument for commanding the gods and molding cosmic events, these two gods of the earth, mediators between man and the heavenly gods, increased in stature as bountiful bestowers of goods.

By the middle of the second millennium B.C., the Aryans were firmly rooted in the Punjab and were spreading their settlements eastward along the north bank of the Ganges. The environmental conditions of their new homeland had an effect upon the gods. In the intense heat of northern India there was no great need of sun gods. It is not strange that they should fade into obscurity. At the same time, the storm rain, the mighty Indra, who came with his thundering voice and lightning sword to destroy the demon of drought and release the rain over the dying crops and pasture-lands, won a place of special favor.

One god stood out above all others in the early Vedic age.

High heaven, Varuna, the mighty Asura, foremost among all the beloved Aryan deities embodied the idea of cosmic order, *rita*. He supervised the rhythmic flow of seasons, and ordered the path of the sun. Clothed in light as in a garment, he watched from on high the flight of the birds in the air and the movements of men upon the earth. He was the wise, mighty, all-seeing god. The ideals of justice and moral right were associated with him. To him the Aryan turned when he felt the pangs of conscience or the whip of retribution. As the sky-power, Ahura Mazda, had become the high, ethical god of Iran, so Varuna gave promise of becoming the one, supreme master of the Indian gods, sanction of the moral law, guide of human destiny and guarantor of ultimate fulfillment.

> Whoever moves or stands, who glides in secret,
> Who seeks a hiding place, or hastens from it,
> What thing two men may plan in secret council,
> A third, King Varuna, perceives it also.
>
> And all this earth King Varuna possesses,
> His the remotest ends of yon broad heaven;
> And both the seas in Varuna lie hidden,
> But yet the smallest waterdrop contains him.
>
> Although I climbed the furthest heaven, fleeing,
> I should not there escape the monarch's power;
> From heaven his spies descending hasten hither,
> With all their thousand eyes the world surveying.
>
> Whate'er exists between the earth and heaven,
> Or both beyond, to Varuna lies open.
> The winkings of each mortal eye he numbers,
> He wields the universe, as dice a player.[2]

Varuna's people had not been long in their new home before Indra became a rival for his throne. The Indo-Aryans were lovers of life, intensely interested in physical and material satisfactions. As the gracious giver of food and prosperity, Indra claimed an ever larger place in their affection and loyalty. Desire and need enlarged his functions. From him came fertility for their fields; they made him the giver of increase in flocks and herds, strong sons in the family and abundant wealth. As the god of the flaming sword, conqueror of the demons that warred against man's well-being, he became a war god leading their fighting men to victory, a giver of plunder and rich stores of gold.

> Indra bestow on us the best of riches,
> Discernment of the practical good fortune;
> Increase of substance, welfare of our bodies,
> Sweetness of speech and pleasantness of weather.[3]

> Hurrah, let us invoke large-hearted Indra,
> Most manly in the fight for gain of booty;
> Mighty, a very present help in battle,
> Slayer of Vritras, winner he of riches.[4]

Though Indra was boastful and self-assured, he himself acknowledged the majesty of the older deity:

> These Asuras have lost their powers of magic.
> But thou, O Varuna, if thou dost love me,
> O King, discerning truth and right from falsehood,
> Come and be Lord and Ruler of my kingdom.[5]

The contention for supreme place between these two gods was still undecided when other factors in the cultural development made their rivalry meaningless and undermined the importance of all the older gods.

Before thought turned critical eyes upon the Vedic deities, the naïve early appreciation of them as helpful nature powers was already lost. They never outgrew the marks of their nature origin but they were thoroughly humanized. Even their bodily appearance was similar to that of the Aryans. Like their wor-shippers they delighted to drink, feast, fight and dance. The poets sang their praises as personal beings with glorified human qualities. The priests organized them into classes, as guardians of the order of the world. Each god was specialized in his par-ticular task but was often called upon for service in other realms. There were gods of the earth, the air and the sky; there were divine warriors, priests and artisans. They rose and fell in rank; old gods withdrew into oblivion and new ones were created following the altered interests of the folk life. Always they were many—a brilliant company serving the needs of men.

There was an early drift toward unification of the many gods in the Vedic custom of applying the same attributes to any member of the divine circle. While each one retained his own peculiar function, they all possessed the common qualities of power, beneficence, wisdom, generosity and beauty. The idea began to emerge of a godhead behind the gods, a single divine nature of which the individual deities were merely special mani-festations. One singer saw in several important gods related to fire, light and lightning, only the changing forms of a single celestial friend——

> At evening he is Varuna and Agni,
> Ascending in the morning he is Mitra.
> As Savitar he moves through air's mid region,
> As Indra warms the heavens from the center.[6]

Another took in a larger group:

> They call him Indra, Mitra, Varuna, Agni,
> And he is heavenly nobly-winged Garutman.
> To what is One, sages give many a title:
> They call it Agni, Yama, Matariśvan.[7]

Carried to its logical conclusion this movement of thought alone might have made of the many gods only manifold phases of one.

Search for an answer to the problem of cosmic origins began early. Varuna, Agni, Indra, Soma and Surya were for a long time the favorite candidates for the title of creator but later sophistication snubbed all the familiar gods. Perhaps the universe was older than the gods. Perhaps it had its origin in fire, or water, or breath, or desire, or the magic word. There were many answers. In the vast chaos of primeval waters was a germ, or a cosmic egg from which the creator emerged to make the world; or Prajapati, "Lord of creatures," produced the universe from his own being; or Purusha was sacrificed and from his various parts came the gods, nature and man. The simplest solution of all was to create a god, Viśvekarman whose name meant the "All-maker." All attempts to solve the riddle ended in doubt.

> Who verily knows and who can here declare it,
> Whence it was born and whence comes this creation?
> The Gods are later than this world's production.
> Who knows then whence it first came into being?
>
> He, the first origin of this creation,
> Whether he formed it all or did not form it,
> Whose eye controls this world in highest heaven,
> He verily knows it, or perhaps he knows not.[8]

During this quest for ultimate origins the old gods received warning that thought was pushing beyond them to find a deeper and more universal cosmic power.

A more serious threat to the status of the Vedic gods came from the growing importance of the sacrificial technique. The power of the ritual was so magnified that it tended to reduce the gods to puppets pulled by priestly strings. The mighty, world-shaking Indra lost much of his dignity and splendor when the sage, Vamadeva, could walk the village ways crying:

Who for ten milch-kine will buy from me my Indra?
When he has slain the Vritras, let the buyer give him back to me.[9]

The masters of the sacrifice were masters of the gods——

> Verily there are two kinds of gods,
> For indeed the gods are the gods;
> And the Brāhmans, who have studied and teach the sacred lore,
> Are the human gods.[10]

In the properly performed ritual was an energy, an effective work, *karma,* which controlled the order of the world. The ritual word of power was *Brahman.* This force which controlled the gods and spanned time and space was like an immanent cosmic energy, a fundamental reality, the soul of all existence. In the presence of this super-personal power, Brahman, the colorful, personal gods were little more important than men.

Centuries in India had left their impress upon the Aryan invaders. The rude, rough life of their past was mellowed and changed by the intellectual and social influences flowing in from more intimate contact with the pre-Aryan people and by a steady advance in culture. To the Kshatriyas, the intellectual and ruling class, the years brought ease, security and an ever-increasing abundance of physical well-being. With luxuriant leisure came sophistication. The pressure of a stimulating alien culture with its novel ideas and strange gods opened the door to further speculation and doubt. Aristocratic thinkers had begun to question their theological heritage, to pioneer along new paths of religious thought. The Brāhman priests were not innovators. They were content to walk in the old ways but when the intellectuals of the ruling class yielded to the lure of change the priests followed. They were dependent upon these aristocrats for their livelihood; since they had no power to eradicate new ideas, they adopted them, stamped them with the hallmark of orthodoxy and reconciled their traditional theology with the philosophic novelties. This process of growth by tolerant synthesis of old and new dominates the development of Indian religious thought. Whenever a group emerged, powerful and important enough to challenge the traditional position, the priests found a way to welcome it into the fold and spread over it the mantle of orthodoxy. This practice is the key to the philosophic unity and the practical multiplicity of the Hindu family of gods.

In the first millennium B.C., intellectuals formulated an ideal of salvation that demanded no service from any of the ancient deities. Vedic religion with its promise of earthly happiness and a happier heaven was ruined by the emergence of the twin concepts of karma and rebirth. Karma meant that every deed had an exact and just reward; rebirth meant that every man must return repeatedly to life on earth in the form dictated by his karma merit or demerit. The result of the new world-view was that the old spontaneous joy of living, the lusty Aryan manner of fulfilling all desires was sicklied o'er with cautious asceticism. If karma weighted every act it was necessary to curb desire. Human life was infected with transiency and every death was a threat. Beyond the portals of each new birth the menace of karma lay in wait for the soul. It might be possible to control karma, and build the merit that would bring the individual back to a satisfying life. Even then the eternal round of existence on the wheel of rebirth became an intolerable burden since every life, even the noblest and best was marred by pain, suffering, sickness, the absence of loved ones, lamentation, grief, old age, despair and death.

Indian thinkers turned their faces away from the transient joys of earth toward an ideal of perfect bliss, eternally free from the wheel of rebirth. On the road to that goal every soul walked alone. The old gods were useless. They could still offer happiness here and in heaven, but heaven could no more be a permanent home. The driven soul was forced to find its way back to a new embodiment on earth when its karma-merit was exhausted. The gods shared man's fate. They too were souls caught on the wheel, seeking, like man, the bliss of eternal emancipation. They too were helpless before the ultimate question—how to escape the eternal transiency of earth and heaven, the endless immortality of birth and rebirth in lives threaded with sorrow. Karma spread its net over all existence. Not only the life of man but the whole universe moved in vast recurring cycles under its sway. Both gods and men were caught in its universal net.

From the eighth to the sixth century B.C., a multitude of intellectuals sent thought out on the wings of speculation in all directions, seeking for the path that led to the realm of bliss eternal. In relation to the total population, however, those tortured by this problem of salvation were at first decidedly a minority. A considerable proportion of the Kshatriya class retained for centuries the traditional Aryan zest for the joys of life in this world. The intellectual ferment of the age touched them only to produce greater sophistication. They denied the gods, were skeptical of the after life and refused to have anything to do with karma and rebirth. The lowly folk and their priests were little troubled by the new ideas. Immersed in the cares and joys of daily life they asked no more than a comfortable earthly existence crowned with heaven. For them the gods of their fathers were entirely sufficient. Many restless thinkers, however, could no longer find peace in the householders' estate. They assumed the ascetic rôle and wandered in quest of an answer to life's riddle. They did not deny the gods, rather they regarded them with compassion as fellow pilgrims through the mazes of existence, but they expected no help from them.

While Aryan and pre-Aryan cultures blended during this

era of transition the most striking result was the change in the intellectual climate. The men seeking a new synthesis were worried not about the fate of the gods, but because the values of life and the validity of the Vedic way of salvation were undermined. They could not rest until they had found a substitute for the lost security and certainty of final bliss. The common problem was to escape the tyrant karma which bound the suffering soul on the wheel of rebirth with the strong cords of desire. The common goal was realization of perfection and bliss. The methods varied and set the style for the salvation quest of India through all later centuries.

During this same period emerged the idea of God as the one, all-enfolding, immanent, spiritual reality. It was not the result of any theological synthesis of the Vedic gods, nor the final term of a long historic development of any one of them, but a new creation. Streams of thought, old and new, flowed together—the old idea of rita, a universal cosmic order, underlying the world of change; the new concept of karma as an ultimate law threading the events of time and holding in its vast web the total universe; the early, neglected insight that the many-named gods might be only manifold manifestations of one; the more recent interpretation of the energy of the sacrifice as an effective cosmic force controlling nature and the gods, binding time and space, active in earth and heaven. These various threads of thought indicate a drift toward some idea of a fundamental unity underlying the universe. Still, even in combination, these various elements could yield only a purely intellectual concept heavily weighted toward the idea of an impersonal, cold, mechanical force.

The thinkers of India, however, were seekers after salvation and not merely intellectuals. In their long periods of lonely brooding on the problems of life, they acquired the art of drifting into the mystic trance in which they were lifted beyond bodily feeling, beyond consciousness, beyond mental activity, to an experience which afterwards they described as joy, peace, freshness and bliss. In such moments, the individual self, Atman, seemed to be blended with a vaster self beyond the limitations and bondage of the earthly embodiment. It may have been this experience which gave vitality and meaning to the idea of a divine reality beyond the actual world. The impersonal, sacrificial Brahman was interpreted as the spiritual soul of the universe, and the soul of man was one with it. This thrilling discovery transformed the world. Souls who knew that "Atman is Brahman" no longer plodded, sorrow-laden and alone through the painful cycles of rebirth. They were eternally safe in the enfolding being of God.

> Self is below, above, behind, before, right and left— Self is all this. He who sees, perceives, and understands this, loves the Self, delights in the Self, revels in the Self, rejoices in the Self—he becomes a self-ruler; he is lord and master in all the worlds.[11]

> All this is Brahman [neuter]. Let a man meditate on that (visible world) as beginning, ending, and breathing in it. . . . He [Brahman] is myself within the heart, smaller than a corn of rice, smaller than a corn of barley, smaller than a mustard seed, smaller than a canary seed or the kernel of a canary seed. He also is myself within the heart, greater than the earth, greater than the sky, greater than heaven, greater than all these worlds. . . .
> He who has this faith has no doubt.[12]

Brahman was one, the self of all selves, immanent in the world yet free from the flux of karma-driven events, closer to man than his own heart-beat, yet beyond the grasp of knowledge, desireless, timeless, changeless, impersonal, the infinite ocean of being. No attributes were adequate to describe it. The enraptured seer knew only that it was *sat-chit-ananda*, ineffable perfection, complete existence, super-consciousness and absolute bliss. In its ultimate nature this Brahman could have no purpose, no interest in threading a plan through cosmic

history, no will to dominate the drift of time. Other lands
might trust the purposive will of a powerful, personal god
who could shepherd all things toward a far-off perfect goal;
the mystic saints of India saw only sorrow, weariness and utter
futility in the cyclic movement of temporal events. In their
desire to escape they dared the ultimate optimism, the supreme
egotism, and identified the soul of man with the eternally
blissful Brahman.

This super-personal Absolute differed in origin and nature
from the older Vedic deities. They began as real forces of nature and as gods were always separate from man. Brahman had
its origin as an interpretation of the ecstatic experience of salvation and, as god, was one with the soul of man. In that age,
when the all-absorbing quest of the world-denying seer was
the discovery of a way of release from the karma-driven wheel,
the joy and peace of the ecstatic trance was immensely important. It was a foretaste of the eternal bliss. Other seekers
after salvation made different interpretations. The Jains and
the Sankhya intellectuals, who denied Brahman, knew the experience and interpreted it as a realization of the true self, the
Atman, eternally perfect and free. The early Buddhists found
in the same mystic flight, assurance of the Nirvana state of
emancipation but no sign of either Brahman or Atman. Yet
all groups agreed in describing it as blissful and perfect existence—*sat-chit-ananda*. Since the Jain and Sankhya philosophers stopped with the human soul as ultimate, the divine could
mean no more than the perfect qualities belonging eternally
to all souls, obscured now by the veils of time and sense. For
them the story of the gods came to an end. Those who read in
the soul's experience a cosmic depth and meaning, and glimpsed
through windows of insight the ineffable Brahman, found a
god able to shelter within its omnipresence all lesser and
limited deities.

The gods who served the Aryans before the emergence of

Brahman lived on for centuries undisturbed, and non-Aryan deities joined the celestial company. Brahman excluded no useful god. An Absolute that could never be defined, which gathered all souls, divine and human, into the enfolding unity of its own being, made theological controversy meaningless. The personal gods who came to man's help in times of need, were nearer and dearer to the common folk than Brahman, yet Brahman could not be jealous of them, for all were merely manifestations of its own meaning. Rivalries between lesser gods could always be overcome by remembering that devotion to one was really devotion to the other, since all were one in Brahman. Shafts of criticism aimed at the limitations of the personal, popular gods fell harmless to the ground, for none of these deities could ever be expected to embody the final and absolute truth. All pointed beyond themselves to the eternal, unknown ONE.

During the period from the sixth to the first century B.C., the way of salvation by sacrificial technique steadily lost ground before the intellectuals' way of salvation by knowledge and the way of salvation by faith emerging in popular religions. The divine figures presented a colorful confusion. The Aryan deities rubbed shoulders with the older gods of the land. New divine names appeared among the familiar company. Tribal gods, deified heroes, village deities, somber, spiritual beings haunting the woods and waters, were side by side with the ineffable ONE of the philosophers and the gracious personal gods. As the Aryan culture was tamed and transmuted by the Indus culture into Hinduism, the deities of both groups changed, rose or fell in status or vanished. Many of the older Vedic gods withdrew into obscurity; others were reduced in rank. The greatest of the early gods, Varuna, lingered on as an insignificant deity of pools and waters. As the sacrifice became less important, Soma was shorn of his power as the giver of immortality and came to be associated with the moon. The mighty Indra became only a shadow of his former self but never lost his sovereignty as chief of the Aryan deities, the famous thirty-three. Out of the forests, hills and jungles beyond the borders of the Aryan settlements spiritual beings of many kinds crowded in. The old method of reducing the divine population by blending deities of different names into one was often useful when tribes and their gods were united under a single ruler or when it was necessary to find a place in the established hierarchy for a rising, popular god. Always behind the stage on which the gods moved and changed loomed the cosmic concept of karma, holding the thought of the intellectuals in thrall. Under its sway they lost all confidence in the usefulness of the deities of their ancestral faith.

While conservatives were trying to bring order into the growing family of celestial beings, and the more radical thinkers were treating them all with indifference, pushing beyond them to an anchorage of eternal bliss in Brahman, or in the untroubled deeps of the true self, two great gods of the people, Vishnu and Śiva, strode with their retinues to the center of the stage. They were just at the dawn of their careers when Brahman was enthroned as the ultimate divine reality. Yet within the framework of tolerance they were able to achieve such importance as savior gods as to overshadow all their peers and to share together for more than two thousand years the devotion of India's millions. Their gradual rise to supremacy covered centuries of religious transition in which rivalries of regional rulers, competing ideals and methods of salvation, restless speculation regarding origins and the growing importance of tribal religions beyond the pale of Brāhmanical practice and Vedic lore constantly changed the status of the personal gods. Only the ineffable, impersonal Brahman remained undisturbed.

The exaltation of Vishnu and Śiva did not doom the lesser gods to death. So long as the threads of memory held them in the cultural web, they lived on, but they could be no more than minor figures. For a time the two great ones had a companion of equal rank, the creator, Brahmā, the personalized form of the impersonal Brahman. The three together were the Trimurti, the Hindu trinity, considered as three forms of the same God. "Brahmā, the creator, Krishna (Vishnu) the protector, and Śiva, the destroyer, are three appearances of the Father God." [13] The ultimate ONE could say, "I am Vishnu, I am Brahmā, I am Śiva." [14] The rôle of creator, however, became an empty honor when thought viewed the universe as an eternal recurrence of vast cycles of change, under the control of karma. Priests might praise Brahmā as "the Supreme One, the Mighty, the All-seeing, the Ruler, the Lord of all, the Maker, the Creator, the Chief of all, appointing to each his place, the Ancient of days, the father of all that are and are to be;" [15] others, whose eyes were open to the sorrows of life expressed doubt and distrust of his worthfulness as a god——

> Why does not Brahmā set his creatures right?
> If his wise power no limits can restrain,
> Why is his hand so rarely spread to bless?
> Why are his creatures all condemned to pain?
> Why does he not to all give happiness?
> Why do fraud, lies and ignorance prevail?
> Why triumphs falsehood,—truth and justice fail? [16]

Intellectuals denied that any god created or controlled the world. Brahmā fell back into a place of relative unimportance, while Vishnu and Śiva rose to take their places among the few gods who have been able to weather the storms of history until modern times. They knew how to kindle the fires of devotion in the hearts of men. The sickness of karma could not touch them. Through their boundless grace the drab insufficiency

of life was lighted by assurance of freedom from earthly bondage and the guarantee of endless heavenly joy.

The Vishnu of popular Hinduism was not a direct development of the Vedic Sun-god under whose name he was admitted
to the later pantheon.[17] In the beginning he was the divine
leader of a clan, the Satvata section of the Yadava people,
dwelling on the fringe of the Aryan settlements in the north-
west. His people knew him as Vāsudeva. Whether the name belonged to a beneficent celestial figure, giver of wealth, or to
a tribal hero identified with the god of the clan is uncertain.
The essential traits of his character were established before he
swung into the orbit of Aryan priestly influence. His followers found favor in his sight not by sacrifice but by simple devotion. He was Bhagavata, "the Adorable One." The quality
of *ahimsha* (non-injury) was pleasing to him. His protecting
care and gracious helpfulness won for him an enduring place
in popular favor. Other clans of the same people were drawn
into the fold of the religion of Vāsudeva; when the tribes were
united, the blending of their gods followed. By this process
Krishna was joined to Vāsudeva. Originally a Rajput clan hero,
Krishna had been deified by his people and associated with the
activities of an original fertility figure—a cowherd god. In
the background were other similar deities—Balarāma, a harvest
god, Baladeva, a god of the plow and husbandry who won only
a minor place in the hierarchy. Through union with Vāsudeva,
the human hero rose above the limitations and trammellings
of local nature deities while retaining the memory of his exploits which endeared him to the folk.

As the supreme god of a powerful combination of clans,
Krishna-Vāsudeva was important enough to challenge the attention of the Brāhman priesthood. By various identifications
the new god was given a welcome into the Aryan fold. An
ancient sage of the Vedic tradition, another Krishna, spread

the mantle of his orthodoxy over Krishna the Rajput hero. Narayana, god of primeval waters in the Aryan heritage and associated with creative power, was identified with Vāsudeva. This was a transient and ineffective union. The Aryan god best qualified to give his name to the new and powerful deity of the popular religion was the former Sun-god, Vishnu.

In the olden days, when the Vedic gods were at the height of their glory, Vishnu had a relatively unimportant place. During the centuries he had grown in stature, not through any new devotion to the sun, but because popular legends credited him with significant services to man. It was he who had out-witted the evil Asuras and saved the world for gods and men. Because of that exploit he had gradually displaced Indra as the demon slayer. He had drawn closer to the common people than the other heavenly gods because of his connection with the household cult. From the earliest times he was known as the god of the "three strides," traversing earth, air and heaven. His third step carried him into the realm of eternal light, "the third heaven of heavens," a glamorous place where the gods feasted together from a lake of honey. It was linked in the minds of the people with hope of immortal bliss in a celestial home. Even when sophistication was clouding the earlier faith, the hope lived on—"He who has understanding for his chari-oteer and who holds the reins of the mind, he reaches the end of his journey and that is the highest place of Vishnu." [18] As a god rising in popular favor while the other Vedic deities were sinking below the horizon, Vishnu could be gracefully identi-fied with Krishna-Vāsudeva.

The resulting union gathered into one divine figure a heav-enly god of light, enriched by the Aryan heritage, a popular god of grace and beneficence, and a deified human hero, revered for efficient service in time of need. The lowly folk-god had become a supreme, cosmic deity worthy of complete loyalty and devotion. High above the bondage of karma which held all

other souls, human, sub-human, and super-human in its re-
lentless coils, he extended his saving grace to all who trusted
him with devoted faith. In times of dire earthly need he came
to earth in bodily form——

When virtue and morality decline and sin and wickedness increase,
I create myself and take my birth in the families of good men. And
assuming human form I restore peace by destroying all evils.[19]

While he was thus a gracious savior god he was at the same
time, in the minds of philosophers, only one form of the personal manifestation of the ultimate Brahman.

Of all India's gods, Śiva alone is Vishnu's peer. He had his
birth in the ancient, native culture long before the coming of
the Aryans. Excavations at Mohenjo-daro, dated in the third
millennium B.C., have brought to light representations of fertility goddesses, phallic symbols, and figures in the posture of
yoga.[20] These signs of an austere god, associated with fertility,
point to the Śiva of later history. When the Aryans and their
shining gods first met the native people, they called them
phallic-worshippers. This term was used to describe the defenders of a great city conquered by the war-god, Indra. On
one occasion the Vedic singers asked him to prevent those
"whose god is the phallus" [21] from disturbing their rites. If the
thread of Śiva's life story runs back beyond the Mohenjo-daro
evidence, he is the oldest living god of the world. Unfortu-
nately the record of twelve centuries of that history is still
hidden from view.

In the second millennium B.C., the invading Aryans had to
reckon with the ancient gods as dangerous enemies. They
despised their phallic rites but held them in awed respect as
dealers in death and destruction. As the centuries passed, the
spread of the Aryan settlements eastward brought them into
more friendly relationship with the native folk. The Atharva
Veda reflects the cultural interaction through which some of

the divine figures of their former foes were taken into the company of the Aryan gods under the name, Rudra-Śiva.

It was natural that the religious leaders should see in their own destructive Storm-god, Rudra, a being akin to the native gods. The dangerous elements of nature were associated with him. He was the destructive lightning of the storm who came howling over their homes with his retinue of violent winds, the evil, mischievous Maruts. Cows and men were killed by his thunderbolts. From the storm clouds, lit up by lightning, he was described as blue-necked and red of countenance. He dwelt in remote places, the lord of mountains and forests. Women going for water often saw him, lying along the mountain clouds, watching them. He was not a gentle god but he might be made beneficent by the proper technique. The correct offerings warded off his destructive power and won from him protection against the evils under his control. Anxiously they appealed to him——

Oh Rudra, do not in thine anger injure our children, our descendents, our people, our cattle, our homes and do not kill our men. We invoke thee always with offerings.[22]

Like Rudra, the gods of their former enemies were associated in the minds of the Aryans with hostility and danger. They dwelt far from centers of civilization, haunted the wilderness, waste places, rivers and mountains. Menacing elements of the natural and human environment—poisons, diseases, serpents, storms, thunderbolts, thieves, highway robbers, violent and lawless men lurking on the forest paths—were associated with them. They were the patrons of workmen, potters, cart-makers, carpenters and other artisans skilled in the crafts of the older civilization. The outcasts beyond the Aryan pale in all directions were under the protection of some one of these gods. They were known by many names, Śarva, the swiftest of archers, launcher of the thunderbolt, Bhava, the king, lord of land

and air and sky, overseeing everything on earth, the fierce Ugra, ruler of the four quarters of the lower world, Mahadeva, the great god. Some of them were called Bhutapati, lord of spirits, and Pasupati, lord of beasts, a title reminiscent of the deity pictured in the Mohenjo-daro material. In the Atharva Veda, Rudra is merged with these gods.[23] Their names, titles and functions were applied to him. In the approved Indian manner, out of the many deities arose one divine figure with many names, but best known as Śiva, the auspicious.

Some centuries later, in the great epic, Rudra-Śiva appears adorned with the highest attributes, perfectly at home among the Aryan gods. In him the age-old religion of India, with its roots deep in the soil, asserted its rights to equal sovereignty with the Aryan Brahmā and the Aryanized Vishnu. The memory of his past still clung to him. He was a powerful, wrathful, impetuous god, always associated with death, disease and destruction but at the same time generous and bountiful, a beneficent protector, giver of food, able to fulfill all desires. His terrible might and ruthless strength were a shield against all evils to those who knew how to trust him. Lord of death, poison and dangerous things, he was also the great healer, the master physician bringing health, wealth and happiness to his devotees. He retained his old reputation for love of waste places and austere practices. He was the divine Yogin, surpassing all others in rigid asceticism. Aryan scorn no longer kept the ancient mother goddesses in obscurity. They emerged as the wives of Śiva, gathered from many regions, Uma, Parvati, Durga, Kali, Karali and others. Only shadowy names of their former consorts remained as they joined the retinue of the single, powerful god. For the first time the lingam appears in the literature as the symbol of his creative power and the skull as the sign of his activity as the destroyer. In Śiva were combined in stark realism two phases of nature's way with man, the one bringing all living things into existence in the passionate fires of creative reproduction and the other driving all life inexorably toward the dark halls of death. Master of life and lord of death, he was a god of grace and blissful salvation to those who would trust him with perfect faith and love.

Meanwhile, thinkers lifted this personal god with his vivid qualities into the realm of philosophic abstractions. The unborn, the unchangeable, the creator of the universe, he was "the one God concealed in all beings, all-pervading, the internal soul of all beings, presiding over all actions, the support of all beings, the witness of all, the life-giver, absolute and without qualities." [24] Like Vishnu, Śiva was thus blended by thought in the obliterating unity of the impersonal Brahman. Yet both of these great gods eluded the invitation to philosophic devitalization. While rigorous Indian thinkers allowed them no more than an exalted status among the other beings in the shadow-play of time, they continued to serve as real, personal gods for the common man in quest of help and salvation.

During the last twenty-five centuries the gods of India have wavered between two attractions. On the one hand, was the intellectual interest which would sink their personal distinctiveness and reality in the eternal Absolute without qualities, on the other, the hunger of the human heart clinging to them as real and helpful heavenly friends. Philosophy tended to lose the world, man, and man's divine companions in an all-inclusive ONE which even thought could not grasp. The people wanted gods who were personal and accessible to the call of human need. A characteristic reconciliation was offered in the fifth century A.D.——

There are two states of this Brahman; one with, and one without shape; one perishable, and one imperishable; which are inherent in all beings. The imperishable is the supreme Brahman; the perishable is all the world. The blaze of fire burning on one spot diffuses light and heat around. So the world is nothing more than the (manifested) energy of the supreme Brahman. . . . Brahmā, Vishnu, and Śiva

are the most powerful energies of god. Next to them are the inferior
deities; then, the attendant spirits; then, men; then, animals, birds,
insects, vegetables.[25]

The struggle of popular religion to save the personal gods from
being swallowed in the formless unknown or reduced to dancing puppets in a maya world of illusion became acute in later
centuries.

Both Vishnu and Śiva were remarkably efficient as popular
gods. They demanded no difficult intellectual attainment, no
austere and painful discipline. A pure heart and loving faith
directed to either of them could lift the soul above the bondage
of karma and give assurance of eternal bliss. Different in
origin, development and character, the two gods had been
shaped by cultural influences to serve a single end. They were
co-workers in the cause of man's salvation. There were times
when they seemed to be rivals, each claiming to be older and
superior to the other. Two streams of Indian culture met in
them and flared up momentarily into antagonism. Vishnu bit-
terly declared that Śiva was a god created for the deliberate
purpose of leading men to hell. Old tales record this rivalry
of the gods. Once when Brahmā and Vishnu were disputing in
regard to seniority, Śiva thrust himself between them and
asked whether either of them could reach to his head and feet.
Brahmā tried and failed but covered his chagrin by lying.
Vishnu tried and admitted failure. Then Śiva graciously pro-
claimed Vishnu the first of all the gods. The final formula of
harmony was found when Vishnu said, "He who worships
thee, worships me. There is no difference between us two." [26]

While the gods served a common purpose as saviors, they
were always different in character. Śiva, in his many moods, is
a picturesque figure. As the dancing god he spans the ages to
salute his counterpart recovered from the Indus Valley culture
of five thousand years ago. With his lingam and skull, the

twining serpents, the Ganges River in his hair, the poison mark-
ings on his neck, his drum and trident and his company of
wives, he is a vivid symbol of India's ancient faith that nature
even in her most dangerous moods is not an implacable enemy
of human hopes.

The wives of Śiva are as colorful as he and probably much
older. The lovely Uma and Parvati of the Himalayas are
beneficent goddesses, embodying the beauty and joy of life.
Durga and Kali are dark and forbidding figures. Before she
was drawn into the company of Śiva, Durga was a virgin goddess of the Vindhya mountains, famous for her chastity, but
delighting in wine, flesh, and animal sacrifices. Later she became a destroying fury, a many-armed champion of the gods
in the war against a giant who was threatening the divine order.
Kali is the most formidable of all Siva's retinue. With her
necklace of skulls, girdle of severed human hands, her many
arms and dripping sword, she is a nightmare vision. She dances
on the bodies of the slain and devours the dead. Sometimes she
is shown with one foot on her prostrate husband, gleefully
holding aloft a human head. Pestilence and destruction attend her. She is the lust of life culminating in death.

These goddesses are very ancient figures. Before the coming
of the Aryans they were the earth-mothers of fertility. Still,
the wives of Śiva are the givers of protection, wealth, fertility
and blessings, and are nearer to the earth than the gods. Philosophic thought has often lifted Śiva into an ethereal divine
state of eternal quiescence, but the goddesses have never left
the earth. They remain as the *Śakti* of the god, the driving,
creative, female energy as the active principle in all life. During
the last thousand years his wives have claimed as many devotees
as Śiva himself.

Associated with Śiva are other popular gods. One of them,
Ganeśa, had been his companion since the far-off days when
he roared over the Aryan settlements as Rudra, the destroying

storm. Then, as Ganapati, he was the leader of the wild rout of Maruts. He was a mischievous, dangerous and tricky being who had to be placated by offerings. Centuries of culture mellowed his character and transformed him into a kind and helpful god, a giver of prosperity and abundance. Through some strange chance of history he was confused with Brihaspati, the Lord of Prayer, patron of sages and wise men. With the double reputation for wisdom and wealth, Ganeśa, the elephant-headed god, became one of the most popular folk deities, invoked at the beginning of work and worship, patron alike of the scholar and the man interested in worldly goods.

The holy river, Ganges, elder daughter of the Himalayas, belonged naturally to Śiva and his mountain wife, Parvati. Ganga appears, in her river form, entangled in the gleaming masses of Śiva's hair. The dark and dangerous elements in the nature of the great god and his wives probably drew the War-god, Skanda (Kartikeya), into his train. The origin of Ayenar, another of Śiva's divine friends, is shrouded in mystery. Legend says that he was born through the union of Śiva and Vishnu. He is known as the hard-riding master of the demon hosts, but he has been tamed to service as the night watchman of south Indian villages. The bull, Nandi, Śiva's favorite mount, shares the divinity of his master.

The personality of Vishnu has none of the vivid high-lights and contrasting shadows characteristic of Śiva. He resembles the familiar, high gods of all the world. From the beginning he was a lovable, gracious and beneficent friend of man. When he was still a young god, his devotees came to him, not with gifts of blood, nor bearing the marks of austerities, but with simple faith in his power to help and save. They learned to trust him for all desired goods. Later, as their supreme god, he gave the best of all boons, blissful emancipation. He was the protector of mankind, the preserver of the world. Ever watchful as the savior of men, in times of tragic need he left his high heaven and came to earth in bodily form to stem the tide of evil.

India knew many incarnations of this benevolent god. When in primeval ages, the demons were overpowering the gods, the divine company assembled to churn the ocean for the elixir of life and immortality which would give them victory. Vishnu then assumed the form of a tortoise on whose broad back they could pivot the mountain with which they were doing the work. When the earth was submerged in a flood, he came as a great fish, piloting the boat of Manu safely through the waters. Whenever convulsions of nature, the arrogance of demons or the pride and greed of men threatened human welfare he appeared in the appropriate form. Thus he took the form of a boar, a man-lion, a dwarf and Rama with the axe. Most important of all were his incarnations in human form as Krishna and Rama. In these beloved figures the high god of grace came fully within the reach of love and understanding. They were men, adorned and glorified with legends which endeared them to the hearts and minds of the millions. They were God, firing the heart with devotion and giving confident assurance of salvation. Another human teacher, Gotama, the Buddha, was also recognized as an avatar of Vishnu. At the end of the age, when good declines and evil grows, he will come again as Kalki, to make the great restoration and usher in a new cycle of cosmic history.

The wife of Vishnu, Lakshmi, is a beautiful goddess of prosperity and good fortune. Her devotion to her husband brought her down to earth with him in his human incarnations. She appeared as Krishna's favorite, and the ideal of perfect womanly virtue as Sita, the wife of Rama. The faithful companion and helper of Rama in his great battle with the prince of demons for the rescue of Sita was Hanuman, chief of the monkeys. This association has given him divine rank. As the conqueror of demons and hostile spirits, a god of strength and wisdom, unselfish, and faithful, he has been a valuable friend of the village peoples.

Vishnu and Śiva, with their wives and companions, play the important rôles in the cosmic drama. The creator, Brahmā, appears occasionally but has only a minor part. As the great theme unrolls through the centuries hundreds of other gods and innumerable hosts of spiritual beings, good and evil, cross the stage. From the vast, ultimate and unknown Brahman behind the scenes to the local village goddesses, they come in endlessly varied form and character, are lit up by some pathetic or thrilling episode and then vanish. The central theme is man's salvation. Entangled in the snares of desire, struggling to free himself from the sorrow and pain of the wheel of rebirth, man seems to have only a lowly place in the play. Yet all the gods serve him. They draw their splendor and glory from their usefulness in rescuing him from the tragedy of time, their ability to guarantee a happy ending to life's drama.

The primary importance of the salvation quest in dictating the character of the gods is shown in the struggle between philosophy and faith after the ninth century A.D. From the age of the Upanishads, India had been accustomed to think of ultimate reality, the supreme Brahman, as utterly beyond description and beyond the grasp of the mind of man. This agnosticism regarding the true nature of God created no difficulty, since all the familiar gods who guaranteed human values were taken as manifold manifestations of the unknowable. It did not matter that intellect failed to overleap the gulf between man and the unknown ONE when all knowledge needful for salvation was assured by the revealed truth of the Vedas and Upanishads, by tradition, by divine incarnation and by mystic experience.

When Śankara used the sacred scriptures themselves to make the unknowable, super-personal Brahman the only reality and the universe of man's experience an illusion with no more real-

ity than a troubled dream, many religious thinkers came to the
rescue of the personal gods. If Brahman alone were real, then
the world, man's individuality, his hope of personal enjoyment of eternal bliss and his beloved gods all drifted into the
realm of relative reality. It was no comfort to the common
man, who hoped for the happiness of heaven through faith
in a divine savior, to be assured that by true insight he would
realize union with the impersonal Brahman and sink into the
eternal perfection and peace of the divine being "as a raindrop
sinks into the silent sea." For the souls still confused by the
maya world, Śankara did offer for worship a shadowy, personal form of god, Iśvara, but this concession was not enough.
Intellectuals and mystics, poets and devotees, during the following centuries insisted upon a real, personal god who could
kindle in the heart of man the fires of devotion and guarantee
the bliss of personal salvation. In deference to scriptural authority they were all willing to make an intellectual bow to
an ineffable spiritual reality beyond the personal gods. Almost
without exception they believed that the individual soul in its
true being was one in essence or in qualities with Brahman.
The real burden of their protest against Śankara's indefinable
Absolute lay in the desire for assurance that beyond this life of
sorrow and frustration they might enjoy an eternity of personal happiness.

The champions of the values of popular religion drew the
picture of god in various ways. Ramanuja took his stand, like
Śankara, on the sacred scriptures and tradition. On their authority he defined Brahman as a person—the only uncondi-
tioned personality. All suffering souls and the material world
were the body of Brahman. He was the soul of all souls. Because of his grace, kindness, love and generosity, he has assumed
many forms and has been incarnated in visible shape to bring
to men wealth, earthly love, truth and salvation. He descended

not only to lift the burdens of earth but that he might be accessible to men as they are. The saved soul abides in Brahman, forever free from desire, forever released from the wheel of rebirth, to enjoy eternally as a conscious person the divine bliss.

Following Ramanuja, from the twelfth to the seventeenth century, a long line of thinkers and poets combined the intellectual appreciation of the supreme god of the philosophers with the emotional attitude of the devotee to a human incarnation. Nimbarka recognized God in three forms—Brahman, the impersonal Absolute, Vishnu, God in highest personal form and his incarnation in Krishna and his spouse Radha, as the savior of infinite grace.

Madhva retained the same emphasis but changed the rôles of the divine actors. Vishnu was given the highest rank, exalted above the universe which he creates, maintains and dissolves in cyclic rhythm. He is known as Narayana, Parabhagavan or the Brahman of the Upanishads. His sons are Brahmā and Vayu, who is the savior of mankind. As the savior, mediating between the high god and man, Vayu was incarnated many times. He was best known as Krishna and Rama through whose grace man is assured of salvation.

The influence of Moslem monotheism made itself felt in Indian popular religion in the fifteenth century. Kabir is an example of the resulting synthesis. He disclaimed polytheism and the limitations of sects and creeds to sing the glory and grace of the one God, the same in all religions, an immanent presence in all existence. He might be called Ali, Hara, Karim, Rama or any of the divine names, but for Kabir the best name was Rama. This unseen God of grace and truth and love transcends the universe and pervades all nature. The life of man in sorrow and gladness swings to and fro in the ocean of divine joy.

From the beginning until the ending of time there is love between
  Thee and me; and how shall such love be extinguished?
Kabir says: "As the river enters into the ocean, so my heart touches
  thee." [27]

In the sixteenth century, Tulsi Das won immortality by his
poetic preaching of god in human form. He recognized that
the ultimate, divine reality must be beyond personality, void
of all change, indivisible and beyond definition, but since the
only god man can adore must be personal, the supreme Lord
incarnated himself and came close to man in Rama.

Let those preach in their wisdom, who contemplate thee as the
Supreme Spirit, the Uncreate, the inseparable from the universe, rec-
ognizable only by inference and beyond understanding: but we, O
Lord, will ever hymn the glories of thy incarnation.[28]

This god, who came to earth in human form, waits now in
heaven as a personal savior to welcome all who trust him with
loving devotion.

Tukaram, the poet teacher of the Maratha people, in the
seventeenth century, molded God to the needs of the folk in
much the same way. As a philosophic thinker he accepted the
traditional idea of a god unlimited by qualities and beyond
understanding. As a religious man he sang songs of devotion
to the personal god, Vishnu, in his human incarnation as
Krishna and made manifest to the eyes of love in the idol Vitoba.

> Thy nature is beyond the grasp
>   Of human speech or thought
> So love I've made the measure-rod,
>   By which I can be taught.
>
> Thus with the measure-rod of love
>   I mete the Infinite.
> In sooth, to measure him there is
>   No other means so fit.

Not Yoga's power, nor sacrifice,
  Nor fierce austerity,
Nor yet the strength of thought profound
  Hath ever found out thee.

And so, says Tuka, graciously
  Oh Krishna, take, we pray
Love's service that with simple hearts
  Before thy feet we lay.[29]

As a god within reach of the common man, Vishnu had an advantage over Śiva. Devotion to Vishnu did not need to span the chasm between god and man for he was incarnated in several human forms. Śiva had no incarnations. Śaivite groups felt the same compulsion as all others in India to define the ultimate god as eternal, infinite, all-transcending, formless, timeless and perfect. The final word in the interpretation of god as the Absolute had been said by Śankara. Later Śaivite teachers brought the god nearer to men either through loving faith in Śiva as a personal figure, or through the immanent presence of god in the world as Śakti, his creative energy symbolized in mother form, or by the tangible symbol of the lingam in which Śiva was immediately present to the devotee. As a personal god, Śiva was all truth, all bliss, all love, offering the soul an eternal, conscious existence of bliss in heaven.

The ignorant say that Love and God are different;
  None knows that Love and God are the same.
When they know that Love and God are the same,
  They rest in God's Love.[30]

In the atmosphere of intellectual tolerance, characteristic of India, the presence of no single god dominates the centuries. From the primitive experience that nature in some of her phases did give help for man's immediate needs, there developed through the later ages of sophistication, the faith that behind the visible universe of change and futility were beneficent spiritual beings, able and willing to guarantee the realization of man's deepest and noblest desires. All the modes of human dependence upon nature in her superhuman moods of mastery, all the hopes which thrust through frustration in quest of fulfillment, all the mystic and intellectual efforts to find spiritual kinship for the soul in its lonely wanderings through the wilderness of rebirth were free to crystallize around some form of god. There was no dogmatic insistence upon any narrowly defined interpretation of the divine nature. From the capricious gods of the villager to the All-soul of the philosopher there was a limitless range. Within the boundaries of sacred scripture and tradition, thought, colored by desire, could find god personal or impersonal, one or many, or at the same time impersonal, personal, one and many. For the intellectual, god could be the Absolute, without qualities, formless, all-pervading, all-enfolding, in the ocean of whose boundless being the restless waves of human generations, sunlit by gladness and darkened by sorrow, will find at last the bliss of eternal peace. For those who felt more comfortable in the presence of a personal god, there were the two high deities, Vishnu and Śiva. Around them, ranging in rank from heaven to earth, a host of other personal gods served the needs of men. India could know god not only as lord but as mother too, in Lakshmi, Lila, Uma, Parvati, Durga, or Kali. When Vishnu and Śiva seemed far-removed in the quiescence of desireless bliss, the divine mother, immanent in the desire-driven world as the creative energy of god, filled the earth with the divine presence.

Still nearer to man than any of the exalted figures dwelling in eternal glory in their gorgeous gem-set heavens were the human incarnations of Vishnu. Untold millions of India's people found the end of their quest for God in one of these saviors in human form. Through loving self-surrender to Krishna or Rama, they attained surcease from sorrow and confident assurance of eternal joy. For those who could not lift their eyes beyond the tangible present, God might be found in his image or symbol or through the guru as religious guide and mediator. In all these manifold ways India read the relation of the inscrutable universe to the needs and hopes of man. Thought interpreted these many forms of God as merely varied modes of visualizing the unknown ONE. Historically and practically they were diverse gods to whom philosopher, priest and peasant lifted pleading hands for help in a world still untamed to the service of man.

During the last two centuries the gods of India have been enveloped by transforming influences flowing in from the outside world. Christianity, backed by the power and prestige of the West, confronted the native deities with a supreme personal god claiming to be the one and only ruler of heaven and earth and brooking no rivals. Neither the limited, local divine friends of the folk nor the impersonal Absolute of the philosophers could evade criticism in the presence of this challenging foreign deity. A more compelling factor of change was the economic penetration of the land which unsettled the balance of India's ancient social security in family, village, caste and guild. The complacency with which the intellectuals had viewed the age-old problem of evil and suffering in a world ruled by karma was rudely shattered when the net of social maladjustment spread to include all classes. They were compelled to come down from their towers of detachment to struggle with the real evils, old and new, menacing the traditional way of life. The need of social reformation forced a new interpretation of Brahman through whom, in the past, had come anæsthesia from earthly suffering and sorrow by meditation or devotion. This trend was strengthened by knowledge of the cultural values and ideals glorified in western literature. Another pervasive influence, impossible to ignore, entered the thought of India through the science of the West. Thus an interaction on Indian soil of religions, civilizations and cultures began a new phase in the life-story of the ancient gods.

In the first half of the nineteenth century, when the prestige of Christian Europe was high in the Orient, a group of intellectuals in the Brahma Samaj reshaped the supreme being of Hinduism to meet the ethical god of the West. They were anxious to clear away the underbrush of popular polytheism, the thick jungle growth of spiritual beings thronging the lower levels of the Indian scene and at the same time to meet the urgent call to social reform. At first they defined God as a personal being with sublime moral attributes, later as the Father of men, rewarding virtue and punishing sin and at last as a trinity in unity, Father, Son and Spirit. The later divisions of the original Samaj drew still nearer to the Christian viewpoint. In the assertion that God is mother as well as father, there is a glimpse of the old India. This blend of Brahman with the Christian God became widely known because many of the most influential leaders of modern Hinduism were associated with some division of the Samaj, but the theology was too feebly rooted in Indian soil to become popular.

Toward the close of the nineteenth century, another effort to modernize India's god was made by the Arya Samaj. Its founder, Dayanand Sarasvati, boldly met the charge of polytheism leveled against Hinduism by asserting that the sacred Vedic scriptures taught monotheism. In the Vedas he found one supreme being, Brahman, the most high, the almighty lord, the soul of the universe. His chief attributes were truth, intelligence and happiness. He was absolutely holy and wise, omnipresent, incorporeal, unborn, immense, omniscient, omnipotent, merciful and just, the maker, protector and destroyer of worlds. He judged the actions of men according to his immutable laws of justice and equity.[31] A deity arrayed in so many divine qualities could meet the Christian God as an equal. Sarasvati felt that Brahman made morality more secure be-

cause he did not forgive sin. Eternal souls move through the
cycles of rebirth earning their rank according to the inflexible
justice of karma. Although at times he was described as all-
pervading, this god was as detached as the deity of the western
Deists, a cosmic witness of the working of the universal law
of karma.

More attuned to the cultural soul of India is the modern development of the ancient Brahman of the Vedantic tradition.
Conscious of the values of Christianity and Islam, yet loyal to
Hinduism, Ramakrishna was convinced that all religions were
reaching toward the same god, the nameless deity with many
names. He is known as Śiva, Vishnu, Allah, Jesus and Brahman
but best of all as Kali, the great Mother. This was a synthesis
true to the classical Indian manner. Ramakrishna's brilliant
pupil, Swami Vivekananda, made the adjustment of the unknowable, impersonal, quiescent Brahman of philosophy to the
pathetic need of the people for alleviation of their social ills.
Like all his predecessors, he knew that the unknown god was
one, eternal, absolute, perfect, the only true reality, concealed
in the superficial world of change, but because of that he is the
soul of all souls and all men are divine. He is not the quiescent
eternal but the true humanity of man. Consequently true
worship of god means service of man. This was a practical
corollary preached by the Tamil saints centuries before, but it
seemed to be a vital, new interpretation of Brahman in the
modern age when intellectuals could no longer take flight from
the world's woe in mystic union with the passionless god beyond the dream-drama of time.

A poetic interpretation of this god, who had his origin in
the age of the Upanishads, is offered to India and the world in
the writings of Rabindranath Tagore. In his thought, science
and naturalism are blended with idealism. He defines God as
the concrete universal, an immanent spirit, manifested in the
whole growing universe. Brahman is the world-conscious be-

ing, who is in his essence the light and life of all. While he is impersonal, man can commune with him only as a personal being. He is infinite love and light and joy. "Love is the ultimate meaning of everything around us . . . it is truth; it is the joy that is at the root of all creation. It is the white light of pure consciousness that emanates from Brahma." [32] God "is there where the tiller is tilling the hard ground and where the pathmaker is breaking stones. He is with them in sun and in shower, and his garment is covered with dust." [33] Creation is the self-limitation of his love, yet in his own nature he is eternally perfect and complete. He is the immanent presence in nature, the true humanity of man. "The same stream of life that runs through my veins night and day runs through the world and dances in rhythmic measure." [34] Through the magic of a poet's words a god who was a purposeless Absolute becomes the immanent presence of love and joy in a naturalistic, growing universe.

All of the many modern modes of India's vision of the meaning of the universe for man go beyond the colorful galaxy of gods who served the earlier generations and who still linger about their ancient shrines. Most of the new gods are varied ways in which the unknown ONE who stood above the many lesser figures has been changed under the molding influence of new knowledge and growing desires. Sometimes, in the interest of social values, the gods are denied. In this cause the Deva Samaj, "the science-grounded religion," directs a vigorous polemic against the supreme deities of all religions. The Jains still find divinity, but only in the perfected soul of man. Almost without exception, Indian thinkers still seek for a spiritual anchorage beyond the naturalistic world—either as an Absolute, or a supreme, personal god or as eternal souls. The quest for god as the path to eternal bliss has been a passion. Modern science has weakened the tone of assurance but the faith remains.

J. C. Ghose illustrates this mood.[35] He is able to view the ideas of god in all religions as merely blundering guesses, and philosophies as nothing more than rationalizations of those inadequate ideas. He knows that the existence of god cannot be proved and believes it is better so. Any faith in god must be built on the firm foundation of the sciences and science allows us to believe, if we can, that in the universe there is a power which is forever moving things from the good to the better. This is a god very different from the "ONE only, without a second" of the ancient days, but faith can clothe him with all the essential qualities to give comfort and security in a world that still frustrates the noblest hopes of man.

CHAPTER VI

BUDDHAS AND BODHISATTVAS

I take my refuge in the Buddha,
I take my refuge in the Teaching
I take my refuge in the Order.[1]

HE gospel of the good life, preached by Gotama to the people of north India in the sixth century B.C., depended not at all on any god. The cultural spirit of the age was troubled by a philosophical problem which theology could not solve. The beautiful simplicity of the earlier religion in which the gods could give wealth and well-being here and a happy heaven hereafter had been destroyed by an intellectual and social climate embodying transmigration and karma. The hope of a good life on earth, continued in a permanent after life of bliss, had been replaced by the dread prospect of an endless wayfaring, through successive lives on many levels of existence, under the control of karma, the inexorable law by which the deed done dictated the future. The ancient Aryan deities were still within call and new gods were appearing from beyond the horizon of Aryan culture, but thoughtful men found them inadequate. The conviction grew that they too were caught in karma's net and were wending their ways, lonely like men, through the painful paths of the worlds. The prospect of this endless round of lives forever weighted with sorrow, wearied the minds of thinkers. One problem held them enthralled—how to escape from the pitiless wheel of rebirth. In the sixth century no supernatural being had been endowed with the power to meet this problem nor the wisdom and grace to show the way to release. The task was man's alone.

A philosophic drift in the development of the old religion had brought the universe to a focus in the soul of man. In the Vedic age the gods were all-powerful but in the period of the Brahmanas the priests, by sacrifice, ritual and spell had become masters of the gods, commanding and controlling them. The karma energy of the sacrifice became an all-effective cosmic force. Man, as priest, wielded divine power. The final step in human aggrandizement was taken when the anxious questers after salvation interpreted the experience of mystic ecstasy as a realization beyond bodily senses, consciousness and intellect, of a reality characterized as perfect bliss. Some called it the ineffable spiritual Absolute (Brahman), pervading all existence and identified the human soul (Atman) with it. Some were content to know that they had found the true nature of the human soul and needed nothing more ultimate. For the Upanishad intellectuals, the Sankhya philosophers and the Jains this was the end of the quest. Man needed only to realize his own eternally perfect being. He, himself, was the divine reality. Salvation was a homing of the soul from its wanderings in the realm of sense and illusion. The goal was the same for all; each group found the way to it by its own special path.

In the region of Magadha, Gotama, a youthful aristocrat of the northern clan of the Sakyas, was wrestling with the same problem that distressed his contemporaries.[2] He was troubled by the transiency of happiness, and the burden of the restless, purposeless pilgrimage of souls from life to life, from world to world. He had lost confidence in the technique of the priests, in the wisdom of the old scriptures and in the efficacy of those higher souls whom men called gods. The heaven of the older faith had no lure for him because it was infected with karma and therefore with transiency. He could appreciate the prac-

tice of yoga, the mystical method of meditation, as a valuable
instrument of insight but through it he caught no vision of
the divine all-soul, Brahman, nor of the eternal, static perfection of the individual soul. Through disciplined meditation the
seer might penetrate far vistas of the soul's journeying, but not
the end of the quest. The philosophers seemed to him to be
weaving ropes of sand, lifting ladders into the unseen which
led they knew not whither. The Jain asceticism attracted him,
both because he was conditioned by his Hindu environment and
because it appeared to be a logical way of wearing thin the
threads of the clinging bonds of karma, but experience taught
him that it resulted only in a weakening of the body and a
dulling of the mind and gave no clear view of the practical
path to follow.

Gotama weighed the world views and salvation techniques of
his day and found them all inadequate. He was in search of a
way of living, under the control of the will, available to all,
by which the individual could work out his own salvation
through stages of progressive attainment until all entanglements in sorrow and world-ill were outgrown and final emancipation realized. All metaphysical speculations he brushed aside
as irrelevant. He asked no help of the gods, and firmly refused
to follow the fashion of philosophic flight into the vague unknown. His was a practical problem.

Through analysis of the nature of existence, Gotama discovered that the individual was enslaved to the immortality
of rebirth by the clinging of desire which established habits—

the karma-bearing element in the changing flux of personality.
By knowledge, right attitudes, and right behavior these bonds
might be broken. Then one might live detached from the al-
lurements of the world, become master of self, enjoy life without the pain of possessiveness, happy in the assurance that at
death there would be no more rebirth, that the foretaste of joy

experienced in mystic meditation would be completed in the eternal bliss of Nirvana.

By his solution, Gotama became a successful "Teacher of the Way." Much later the Buddhist books formulated his gospel of salvation into a system. The foundation stones of the structure were the four noble truths regarding sorrow, its nature, cause and cure, and the eight-fold path, a practical program of discipline to attain self-mastery, freedom from the bonds of desire and, at last, release.

Gotama proved his program by his life. He became a Buddha, an "Enlightened One." Disciples who learned how to walk in his way tasted the joys of Nirvana. The great teacher always refused to speculate about the future existence of the individual in whom the fires of rebirth had been quenched forever. It was enough that a foretaste of Nirvana experienced in this life had shown it to be——

the harbor of refuge, the cool cave, the island among the floods, the place of bliss, emancipation, liberation, safety, the supreme, the transcendental, the uncreated, the tranquil, the home of ease, the calm, the end of suffering, the medicine for all evil, the unshaken, the ambrosia, the immaterial, the imperishable, the abiding, the further shore, the unending, the bliss of effort, the supreme joy, the ineffable, the detachment, the holy city.[3]

He who through moral living and meditation had won to wisdom and enlightenment was described as "profound, unmeasurable, hard to fathom like the great ocean." [4] It was no easy path to follow and every man walked alone. Even the "Way-master" could do no more than spur the traveller on by the assurance that at the end of the trail were the joy and bliss of Nirvana and freedom from the weariness of rebirth.

> Let all-embracing thoughts
> For all that lives be thine,

An all-embracing love
For all the universe
In all its heights and depths
And breadth, unstinted love,
Unmarred by hate within,
Not rousing enmity.

So, as you stand or walk,
Or sit, or lie, reflect
With all your might on this:
—'Tis deemed 'a state divine.'

Ignoring sophist's views,
The good—with insight filled,
And purged of appetite
For sensuous delights——
Shall never see rebirth.[5]

This gospel pointed the way to self-salvation through knowledge, moral living and mastery of desire. The followers of Gotama had not forgotten their fathers' gods. They often spoke of them, but none of the celestial company whose generous bounty the ancient seers had sung could give the gift they sought. What the gods could not do their teacher had accomplished. To men wandering, deluded by desire, on paths leading to destruction, he showed the good way.

During his lifetime Gotama was accorded all the reverence and honor India has always given to her saintly men of wisdom, the great teachers of the truth that saves. He was called the "Way-shower," the "Good Physician," "Savior," the "Enlightened One." After his death, the prestige of the truth he embodied, the molding pressure of influences filtering in from the cultural environment, the philosophic activity of monks and the adjustment of the Buddhist gospel to the needs of laymen combined to transform the human Gotama into a divine being and to surround him with a vast array of glorious, godlike figures, his terrestrial and celestial companions in Buddhahood. The rival gospels of Gotama's day, the Sankhya philosophy and Jainism, offer a striking contrast to the Buddhist story. They have come down through more than two thousand years in the same culture, lived on after Buddhism declined in India, without finding anything more divine in the universe than the soul of man. The Buddhists, who denied the existence of a soul, gradually built out of the person of Gotama and the truth which he embodied a profusion of spiritual beings.

The process of Gotama's exaltation was complex and cumulative.[6] From the beginning he towered above ordinary men, even though he was thoroughly human. The beloved Ananda, who attended him like a faithful shadow, knew well his many moods. As all men, he felt hunger, thirst and the weariness of long journeying. His feet were wounded by stones and his heart by calumny and the faithlessness of those near to him. Often in the loneliness of the far ways he remembered with longing the beautiful natural scenery of his early home. There was a human touch in his eagerness to win his kinsmen of the Sakya clan to the cause. Yet with all his humanity, neither monk nor layman was content to leave him on the human level. He was a teacher of the way, but much more than a teacher. Not only did he teach the truth, he channeled it and actualized it in his own life. He was the Way, the Truth and the Life. His wisdom and powers far exceeded those of common men. He was the Arhat, fully enlightened, perfect in knowledge and conduct.

Because his truth was the guarantee of their salvation, his early disciples magnified his wisdom. He, himself, claimed to know only the truth that saved. When his followers, disputing with the Jains, asserted that he knew everything, saw everything and had a limitless power of vision and knowledge, he corrected them. Yet no one could doubt that he had all the knowledge of the perfect seer. He knew the possible as possible

and the impossible as impossible; he could visualize the ripen-
ing of karma, past, present and future; he knew where all
paths of conduct led and all the factors of existence; he could
read at a distance the thoughts of both friends and enemies;
he knew at once the capacities of every one he met; he could
recall numberless former existences; with his universal eye he
could see beings passing away and being reborn according to
their karma; his mind and knowledge were completely released from all bonds and limitations.[7] The later church made
him omniscient.

In ancient India truth drew its authority from the teacher,
and the teacher had authority not in his own right but because
he was one of a long succession of seers who had transmitted
that truth from the remote past. Gotama received in fullest
measure the reverence and honor accorded the bearers of this
heritage. The message he brought to the world was not his
alone but the one truth, the same always and everywhere,
taught by a long succession of Buddhas through measureless
ages. Thus the prestige of the law and lore he embodied, exalted Gotama above humanity as a teacher of gods and men.

Reverence for the great Master soon led his followers to
overlay his real, historic person with marvellous qualities. They
pictured him as remarkably beautiful, tall, winsome and of
incomparable grace. His body bore the thirty-two marks of a
perfect being. Men were entranced by his voice and none could
resist the charm of his smile. None of the physical feebleness
of ordinary men was allowed to touch him. He could make
his body serve his will and, if he had wished, could have prolonged his life for millions of years. A halo of light always surrounded him but at the time of his realization of the truth and
at his death his body shone with the radiance of the sun. The
highest names of honor of both gods and men were claimed for
him. He was called the Victorious One, the Great Being, Maha-
paruna, and the favorite religious title of the gods, Bhagavat,

the Adorable One. The austerities of his early career clothed him with the esteemed virtues of the Yogin. Some titles no man nor god could share with him in this age of the world. He alone was Tathagata, one who has arrived at the truth, who has followed by will and wisdom the difficult path to perfection.

Gotama was a peculiar being, not a man, not a god, but a Buddha. Since he had passed beyond the limitations of time, space and the conditioned generation which ruled earth and all the heavens, he was the highest and most perfect being. The human teacher men could know. The real nature of a Buddha was beyond human understanding. Thus the historic Gotama became merely a temporal manifestation of a transcendent Buddhahood, an earthly embodiment of the eternal law, the truth made alive to be the teacher and savior of men.

Legends gathered about him to glorify his previous lives and to give his career on earth a supernatural quality. It was accepted without question that every individual had been driven through a numberless succession of existences under the deathless urge of karma, but Gotama was not like the others. His journey through the worlds had been a steady progress leading up to his final rebirth as the great teacher of the truth. Imagination, working with old folk tales, embroidered the successive stages of his advance from life to life with heroic episodes to glorify his generosity, courage, self-mastery, wisdom, his love of animals and men.

In one of his existences in the long ago, when as the ascetic Sumedha, he was taught by Dipankara, he made his vow to become a Buddha. Many other Buddhas of the celestial realms predicted that his vow would be fulfilled. Through 100,000 ages of the world he labored toward his goal in life after life until finally he was born in the Tusita heaven. There he waited until the old creator god, Brahmā, visited him to urge his descent to earth for the salvation of men. A survey of the world revealed to him that the time had come. Then he chose the continent, the district, the family and the mother for his last rebirth. His mother conceived him while she was dreaming that a white elephant entered her side. Marvels attended his birth. The thirty-three gods in Indra's heaven rejoiced. Celestial music filled the air. Gods and heavenly rulers did homage. The young child stood saluting each of the six directions of space; he took seven steps to the west and shouted, "I am the chief of the world." [8] Brāhman wise men examined him for the auspicious signs and prophesied that he would become either a universal monarch or a Buddha. By such legendary lore Gotama was transformed into a supernatural being and might easily have become a god in the Indian manner.

The Buddhists of the early church, however, could have found no advantage to themselves nor honor for their teacher in making him equal to the gods, even the highest gods. These celestial beings enjoyed privileges beyond the human, were good friends of man, but the monks did not envy them. Some of them dwelt in the world of sense, some in the realm of pure, spiritual joys, some in the formless world of thought, but wherever they were, karma and eternal change ruled them. Not even Brahmā, Vishnu and Siva were exempt. So little was existence as a god esteemed that the Buddhist books represent it as an easy step from the human level (even animals who ate the body of a perfect saint were reborn among the gods), but it was also a calamity, for the path was infinitely long that led from the divine realms to final salvation. Gotama was much superior to the gods. His grandeur consisted in his wisdom as the teacher of the way, not as a giver of gifts. His followers were devoted to him, cherished every relic and revered every place made holy by his presence but they did not pray to him. Salvation was a personal achievement. Gotama was as helpless as the gods to donate it. He showed his dis-

ciples a path leading to Nirvana, a way to be walked alone
without help either heavenly or human.

> By self alone is evil done,
> By self is one disgraced:
> By self is evil left undone.
> By self alone is one purified:
> Purity and impurity belong to self.
> No one can purify another.[9]

Knowledge of the truth led, through strictly controlled
conduct and concentrated meditation to the realization of wisdom. Only through long and difficult discipline could the candidate for salvation become a seer and a saint. Although the gospel was preached to laymen, the distractions of daily living
dimmed any hope that they might attain Nirvana as householders. For their more modest needs the Hindu gods, in spite
of their limitations, were still useful. They could do what they
had always done—give earthly goods, long life, health, wealth,
wisdom, power and glory, even happiness in heaven. Only the
gift of final release was beyond their power. Gotama, himself,
had urged the layman to respect the gods and make use of
them——

> Revered and honored by him, the gods honor and revere him in
> turn. They surround him with their care as a mother the child of her
> body. The man who enjoys the favor of the gods sees only happiness
> around him.[10]

King Aśoka, a good Buddhist layman, called himself a "favorite of the gods." For centuries after Gotama, Buddhist
teachers maintained consistently this early attitude toward the
Hindu gods. They did not deny them, but they argued vigor-
ously against the idea that any personal, divine will could control or check the rolling wheel of rebirth. It pleased them to

picture Indra and Brahmā leading vast multitudes of gods to listen to the preaching of Buddha in celestial assemblies. Supernatural beings of all kinds in hundreds of millions served as background for the resplendent figure of the Buddha.

Buddhas were teachers of wisdom and the way, not yet heavenly helpers for the householder. In the early scriptures are the names of seven of these celestial beings who attained Buddhahood in the long past ages. They completed their earthly pilgrimages as men many millions of years ago and no one could hope that these far-off, glorious figures might be enlisted to serve the needs of common men. Even as Buddhists, men were dependent upon the Hindu deities for help in daily living.

After the time of Aśoka a change came over Buddhism. As the religion drew closer to the people, it developed gracious and powerful divine helpers of its own who could offer the greatest of all boons—an easy way to Buddhahood. This development was fostered by the influence of the Indian environment. The Buddhist laity lived as members of the Hindu community, in friendly relations with the priests and gods of Hinduism. The rise of Buddhist deities patterned on the Hindu models might have resulted simply from this free, tolerant interaction of the two religions. Actually the germ from which they grew was latent in the interpretation of the career of Gotama as a savior.

The early church had taught that he had labored through many lives to attain the wisdom that made him a Buddha. Through pity for human suffering, to provide a cure for earthly sorrow, he had endured ages of toil. The period of the preparation of a Buddha was modestly stated in the early texts but the later records made it incalculably long—in one case more than 540,000,000,000,000,000 ages of the world. At last Gotama attained the wisdom, glory and power that gave him lordship over the Tusita heaven. Yet for man's sake he left his blissful realm, humbling himself to human rebirth, to bring the saving truth to the world. The marvellous compassion of the Buddha for the sufferers on the wheel of earthly sorrow made the idea of saving oneself for the bliss of Nirvana appear selfish. It seemed nobler to follow the example of the great Master, to take the vow of love to all creatures, to enter upon the path that led to Buddhahood. Those who dedicated themselves to this career were called Bodhisattvas. The term was first used to describe Gotama when he left his home in quest of enlightenment. Later the time of his entering on the Buddha-path was pushed back to that day, millions of years ago when, in the presence of the ancient Buddha, Dipankara, he took the vow to attain omniscience. During all the intervening ages he was a Bodhisattva, filled with love and compassion for suffering humanity.

When this idea was established it was easy to believe that in the deeps of the limitless universes and in the far spaces of the unseen worlds and heavens there were innumerable other Bodhisattvas on their way to Buddhahood. These transcendent beings, powerful, wise and beneficent, still kept their contact with the earth. Because of their vows of love and service they were ever ready to bring men providential care, rescue from danger, help in trouble, guidance on the way to heavenly happiness. The Bodhisattva vow committed them to transfer their merit and the fruit of their age-long labor to others that they might be saved——

For the sake of all sentient beings on earth,
I aspire for the abode of enlightenment which is most high;
In all-embracing love awakened, and with heart steadily firm,
Even my life I will sacrifice, dear as it is.

In enlightenment no sorrows are found, no burning desires;
'Tis enjoyed by all men who are wise.
All sentient creatures from the turbulent waters of the triple world
I'll release, and to eternal peace them I'll lead.[11]

For the ordinary householder the way of salvation as an Arhat, a saint self-saved, was too difficult; the stupendous task of becoming a Buddha was far beyond his powers. It was much simpler to claim, by loving devotion, the services of these celestial saviors and to fashion from the vague multitude distinct individuals endowed with the qualities necessary to satisfy the deepest desires and meet the many earthly needs of men. Since such divine beings had no roots in history there was no reason to limit their number or their powers. In this way the Buddhism of the layman acquired a galaxy of Buddhas and Bodhisattvas to outshine in splendor and surpass in usefulness the gods of other Hindu religions. The Buddhism of India which in its early Hinayana form had felt no need of divine helpers in the quest for salvation, in its later, Mahayana development gave to Asia some of the most gracious deities the world has known.

While popular devotion was transforming the Bodhisattvas into celestial, personal deities, Buddhist philosophers developed the idea of Buddhahood, the essence of all Buddhas, into a cosmic Absolute. Underlying the transiency and ceaseless change of all existence they found an eternal reality, the ultimate impersonal divine being, the ground of all that is. As the water of the vast ocean remains the same, although the waves rise and fall endlessly, so in all temporal and finite things, the Absolute abides as their essential being, the same in all creatures, changeless while they change. No words can describe it and no knowledge fathom it. It is eternal, immutable, ineffable, unthinkable, Tathatā (suchness), Bhūtatathātā (permanent being), Pāramarthā (absolute truth), Dharmadhātu (the essence of truth). As the basic reality of Buddhahood, it is the body of truth, the Dharmakaya.

The varying ideas of the Buddha in philosophy, in theology, and in history were reconciled by the doctrine of the Trikaya, the three-bodies. The Dharmakaya is the true nature of all the

Buddhas viewed as the impersonal Absolute. The mind of mortal man, unable to escape the shadow-play of relativity and change can never grasp this reality. It is ineffable, the Void. The Sambhogakaya is Buddhahood personalized, as an object of devotion. Thus the glorious divinities, as the embodiments of the supreme perfection of love, life, light, compassion, healing and grace may be visualized. In this form the Buddhas appear in celestial assemblies. The Nirmanakaya is the incarnation of the eternal truth on earth, in human form, for the salvation of men, when they have "become unbelieving, unwise, ignorant, careless, fond of sensual pleasures." [12] Although pity for humanity moved the Buddha to assume a human body, this manifestation could only be a partial and illusory vision of the true reality.

Theologians were tempted by this pattern to arrange the celestial hierarchy into trinities. A great variety of interesting combinations were produced in the countries of the east. A classical arrangement, known over all the Buddhist world, was made in Nepal. It consisted of five trinities, related to the zenith and the four directions of space. The Absolute Being in each group was called Adi-Buddha. The Sambhogakaya forms were the celestial Buddhas, Vairocana, Akshobya, Ratnasambhava, Amitabha and Amoghasiddha. Corresponding to them, as earthly manifestations, were Krakuchandra, Kanakamuni, Kasyapa, Sakyamuni (Gotama) and the future Buddha, Maitreya. Between the celestial and earthly Buddhas were placed five Bodhisattvas, Samantabhadra, Vajrapani, Ratnapani, Avalokiteśvara and Viśvapani. Under the influence of later Hinduism, the celestial Buddhas were given wives. Some of these divinities were apparently never more than names; a few of them made their way into all the lands of the Orient and live today in the hearts of the Buddhist millions.

When the types were established the number of divine beings in the Buddhist heavenly hierarchy could be endlessly increased. The early scriptures were content with nine earthly Buddhas, including Gotama. Tradition in Ceylon modestly increased the number to twenty-four. In contrast, Mahayana Buddhism gave desire and imagination free rein, especially in the creation of compassionate and servicable Bodhisattvas. Moreover, with the new flexible formula for divine beings, many useful members of India's multitude of gods were selected for initiation into the Buddhist fellowship. During the period when the elaborate later pantheon was being built, the northern Buddhists were in immediate contact with Zoroastrian influences. Some of their shining deities bear an Iranian stamp. The Mazdean identification of truth with light is reflected in the names and luminous qualities of the most popular Buddha of all, Amitabha, "Boundless Light." His other name, Amitayus, "Boundless Life" or "Boundless Time" also suggests the influence of Zoroastrian theology.

Not only was there freedom in the creation and adoption of deities, but the system makers rearranged the functions and positions of celestial Buddhas, Bodhisattvas and earthly Buddhas to meet their momentary interests. Gotama Sakyamuni might be presented in any rank which seemed to give him greatest glory. Answering the call of man's desire, divine beings multiplied in the unseen realm, until the number of individuals in each class of the divine hierarchy grew to astronomical proportions.

The way in which the Buddhist imagination could play with vast numbers of superhuman, supernatural beings is well illustrated in one of the earliest Mahayana Sutras, *The Lotus of the Good Law*, which is probably not later than the second century A.D. Gotama, or Sakyamuni, is the chief figure of a congress at which innumerable Buddhas, Bodhisattvas and divinities are assembled to hear him preach. Seated on the Vulture Peak, he becomes the center of a vast panorama in which countless universes in all directions are illuminated before the eyes of his awed listeners. His audience is composed of 1,200 Arhats, 2,000 monks, 6,000 nuns, 80,000 Bodhisattvas; Sakra, the ruler of the celestials with 20,000 gods, the four rulers of the cardinal points with 30,000 gods in their train, Śiva with 60,-000 gods, Brahmā, with 24,000; eight Naga kings, with many times 10,000,000,000,000,000 Nagas, four Kinnara kings, with many times 10,000,000,000,000,000 followers, four Gand-harvakayikas, with many hundreds of thousands of Gandhar-vas, four demon chiefs, with many times 10,000,000,000,000,-000 demons, four Garuda chiefs, with many times 10,000,000,-000,000,000 Garudas.

When they were all assembled a ray from the forehead of Gotama lit up 1,800,000 Buddhafields in the eastern quarter of the heavens and all the beings in each of the six states of existence became visible. In all the other directions of space, Buddhafields were revealed in limitless profusion. This was a worthy theater and an impressive audience, even for the preaching of a Buddha, but it was not yet complete. When Sakyamuni reached a dramatic point in his recital, Buddhas came flocking in from all directions in numbers as countless as the sands of the Ganges. They were followed by Bodhisattvas innumerable.[13]

Other scriptures are equally extravagant. The *Mahavastu* speaks of 8,000 Buddhas who bore the name Dipankara, and 300,000,000 others called Sakyamuni, the name of the great teacher who brought the gospel to the modern world.[14] The text describing the paradise of Amitabha says that 1,296,000,-000,000,000,000,000,000,000 Buddhas are revealed by the light streaming from each of the many lotus flowers there; [15] and at least eighty-one quintillion other such Buddhafields star the deeps of space.

Among all these millions upon millions of divinities, Gotama Sakyamuni is the only one who has a factual basis in history and he taught a way of salvation without dependence upon the help of any god. The other earthly Buddhas described in the texts are merely replicas of him. His career as a savior, visualized by later thought as a long labor, lasting through many ages, served as the pattern for the beneficent Bodhisattvas. His final status as a Buddha, allowed imagination to people the innumerable universes of Buddhist cosmology with similar blissful beings. The Hindu gods of Gotama's day retained, throughout, their old status as candidates for salvation from the wheel of rebirth. They were always helpful friends of man, and a few of them joined the Buddhist ranks as Bodhisattvas.

In spite of the apparent complexity of the teeming multitude of deities, Buddhist theology is simple. In contrast to the gods of Hinduism, who have their separate personal histories, the Buddhist pantheon consists of only earthly Buddhas, Bodhisattvas, and celestial Buddhas, artificial constructions, endlessly repeating the stages in the career of Sakyamuni. Philosophically there is only one divine reality, the changeless, unknowable Being, manifested in personal form in the Buddhas of bliss, accommodated to human frailty in the Bodhisattvas, embodied age after age on earth in the appearance of a human teacher to guide man's blundering steps back into the path of truth and salvation. Radiant through all the splendid deities, latent in all living things is the ultimate ONE—but this Absolute, under whatever name, whether as Adi-Buddha or Dharmakaya, gets little recognition from the humble people struggling with the problems of life and dreaming of bliss eternal. The important deities are the Bodhisattvas who are ever-present helpers in time of need, and a few great Buddhas specialized in the fulfillment of human desires.

Almost all the figures of the Buddhist pantheon were created in India, but many of them won to great importance and popularity only after they left their homeland; and some were profoundly altered by the cultural conditions of the lands through which they travelled.[16] The stamp of India was so clearly upon them before they began the march for the conquest of the world that at any time from the second to the ninth century A.D., a Hindu worshipper could have found under Buddhist names all the typical forms of his own gods. In several cases the attributes, symbols, titles and gestures were identical. The Dharmakaya closely resembled the impersonal Brahman. Vishnu, the personal form of the Absolute, coming to earth in human embodiments whenever man desperately needed a savior, was the Hindu parallel of the Buddha manifested in his several earthly appearances as the physician of souls. The wives of the gods were similar, and sometimes a Buddhist deity could borrow a wife from his Hindu contemporary. A common culture marked the divinities of the two religions with a family resemblance.

The pantheon of Indian Buddhism was resplendent with a large number of divine beings of all ranks, but only a few were practically important. Out of the long list of Buddhas named in the legends as saviors on earth, Sakyamuni alone was deeply revered. The mythical Dipankara received some reflected honor because Sakyamuni took the bodhi vow before him millions of years ago. Associated with them was Maitreya, the Buddha to come. He is now ruling the Tusita heaven as a glorious Bodhisattva of love. Like Kalki, the future avatar of Hinduism, and Saoshyant, the coming savior of Zoroastrianism, Maitreya will some day appear upon the earth. Meanwhile he watches over the teaching of the faith and sometimes makes revelations.

Of the five celestial Buddhas who stand out from the background of the millions ruling the unseen universe, Vairocana and Amitabha have won the world's deepest devotion. Both were Buddhas of light. Vairocana's name was derived from a Sanskrit word for the sun. The common identification of truth and goodness with light may have given these two deities their brilliant quality, but it is more likely that the presence of other great gods of solar origin helped to determine their character—the beneficent Vishnu with his gorgeous gem-set heaven, and the Persian Mithra, captain of the hosts of light. Vairocana was a vague figure and often was no more than another name for the impersonal Dharmakaya.

Amitabha became a vivid personality. In the long ago, when he was a monk, he heard an ancient Buddha describe the glories of innumerable Buddhafields. He made a vow to achieve a paradise eighty-one times more perfect than all the others, and to guarantee that all who call upon his name in faith would be rescued from the wheel of rebirth and born into that heaven of bliss. After ten million years his labors were complete and he now presides over the Western Paradise, waiting to welcome all who accept his gift of grace. India listened to Amitabha's invitation and was not greatly impressed. Śiva and Vishnu offered salvation on the same terms. Moreover, the strenuous way to salvation, as an Arhat, or to Buddhahood, by the path of the Bodhisattva, was still the official teaching of the Buddhist church. Amitabha had to wait for his great triumph in the lands of the farther east.

Among the multitude of Indian Bodhisattvas, the three who embodied wisdom, power and pity were most highly honored. First and chief was Manjuśri, the prince, called also Vagiśvara, "Lord of Speech." He appears on the scene full-formed as the active personal manifestation of wisdom, the highest virtue of a Buddhist saint. When the other Bodhisattvas were given wives he remained single, although sometimes he appropriated the wives of his Hindu friends, Vishnu and Brahmā.

Power was embodied in Vajrapani. India had known him since ancient times as the mighty Indra of the storms, wielder of the thunderbolt, and later as ruler of the heaven of the thirty-three gods who had been companions of his youthful glory. He joined the Buddhist company as a guardian deity. When Buddhism made his lightning weapon, the *Vajra*, a symbol of truth and of creative power his name acquired a deep mystical meaning.

After the second century A.D., the most popular of all the Indian Bodhisattvas was the pitying Avalokiteśvara, called also Mahakaruna, "the Great Compassionate One," or Lokeśvara, "the Lord of the World." He was the spiritual son of the Buddha Amitabha and shared with him the Western Paradise. The Bodhisattva Mahasthamaprapta, who embodied strength and light, was the third member of the trinity in this heaven, but the overwhelming splendor of Avalokiteśvara doomed him to perpetual obscurity. While Amitabha dwelt, quiescent in the blissful realm his grace and love had long ago prepared for man, Avalokiteśvara was an active, universal providence, surveying with infinite pity the wretched plight of men who were groping in sorrow through the evils of life, blinded by lust, hatred and stupidity. His power was as limitless as his pity. In times of terrifying danger on land or sea, in all the many modes of misfortune, in prison or in danger of death, it was only necessary to call upon Avalokiteśvara to be immediately delivered. He could save from sickness, protect from poisonous snakes, ferocious animals, robbers, demons, and the destructive forces of nature. By his spiritual power he was able to meet every need. Strong, highly gifted sons and beautiful daughters were his precious gift. In order to do his great work and reach every creature he assumed any form necessary for the task. He might appear as a Buddha, any one of the Hindu gods, a monk, a Brāhman priest, a demon, a man, a woman, a little child, or a great multitude of other forms, and so bring all beings everywhere help in trouble and release from sorrow. This omnipresent, merciful being was all-sufficient for the needs of men on earth, and at death he led the way to the celestial paradise.

The later texts magnified his saving power and extended it to incalculably remote past ages of the world and to all realms of existence. Gods and ghosts, demons and the damned in hell, as well as men, were comforted and saved by his boundless compassion. After the sixth century, when the creative energy of the Indian gods was represented in female form, the goddess Tārā joined him as a wife to share his qualities and his labors. She was miraculously born of a tear which fell from his left eye as he was gazing in pity upon the suffering world. Under most of her 108 names she was a gracious and lovely figure, but sometimes she showed the effect of her friendly association with Kali, the terrible wife of Śiva. Then she appeared as a dark goddess, garlanded with skulls, a furious destroyer, a slayer of evil beings.

Associated with these active deities were others of the same rank with little honor in India but famous in the farther east. Kshitigarbha, an old deity of the earth, vaguely related to Akashagarbha of the air, assumed control of the underground realm where the colorful hells of Hindu cosmology were located. As a Bodhisattva, he undertook the special task of rescuing the victims of these places of torment. Suffering on earth through sickness was relieved by Bhaishajyaguru, master of spells and king of healing. Although he became the Buddha of a glorious Eastern Paradise, he was hardly more than a name in his home land. The Bodhisattva Samantabhadra was a purely imaginary creation to give a place in the divine company to the quality of kindness. These three celestial beings could meet genuine needs, but their real careers began only after they left India.

During the early centuries of the Christian era Mahayana Buddhism developed the characteristics which made possible its remarkable success as a missionary religion. It could offer eternal salvation to any individual of any culture or race. The ideal and technique were adjusted to the capacity and desires of each person. While Buddhahood was preached as the final end of the way for everyone, the bliss of paradise was offered as an alluring way-station for those who desired immediate happiness at the close of this life's sorrowful journeying.

The cosmic theatre in which every man played out his part was magnificent in size and splendor. Out from our little earth, in ten directions of space, were millions upon millions of celestial universes radiant with the light of their resident deities. Above the earth was a series of heavens and below an array of hells with exquisite tortures to provide artistic retribution for every form of wrongdoing. Buddhism pictured each person, bearing his burden of karma alone, as he wandered through life after life, on earth, in the heavens and in the dreadful halls of hell. To rescue the individual from this tragic fate it brought its brilliant company of Buddhas and Bodhisattvas as omni-competent saviors. They were specialized to respond to all the worthy desires of man. The philosophers knew that the ultimate divine reality was ineffable, a blazing light in which personality and all other attributes were obliterated, but to lost souls confused by the illusions of time, the divine being came in gracious personal forms.

These shining deities could give health, strength, wisdom, kindness, children, safety from danger and providential care to make existence on earth satisfying. When death came to the man who trusted them, they snapped the chains of karma and ushered him into the glories of the celestial paradise from which the only path led on to Buddhahood. All the lands of the Orient yielded to the lure of the Buddhist gospel. As the religion adjusted itself to the various cultures, the divine figures also made themselves at home. While they retained the essential qualities given to them in India, some of them grew in importance in the new conditions, and some were changed by association with the native gods. In every country the most popular Buddhist deities were Amitabha of the Western Paradise and his spiritual son, the compassionate Avalokiteśvara.

Buddhism won its place in China primarily through the help

its kindly deities could bring to the common folk. The Chinese intellectuals had long abandoned belief in personal gods and in the idea of life after death. They could appreciate the impersonal Absolute of the Buddhists, for the Tao of Chinese philosophy was also an indefinable, all-inclusive reality. The two ideas were, however, poles apart. Buddhism snubbed the world of actuality to honor the ultimate spiritual unity as the only real. Chinese intellectuals found the reality of the Tao in the actual, material world of which man is a part. The Buddhist Dharmakaya could be manifested in any number of superhuman, spiritual beings. The Tao was simply the order of nature.

While the intellectuals were emancipated from the gods, the Chinese villager still looked for help in need to old-time nature deities or familiar divinities of folk tradition, but they had no god who had conquered the dark realm of death. Long before Buddhism came to China many had sought means to avoid the reckoning with man's ultimate enemy. They were looking for an "Elixir of life" or some way of orientation to the cosmic forces that would prolong life indefinitely. The Buddhist celestial company brought the answer to their problem and, to the multitudes immersed in the anxieties and frustrations of daily living, they offered generous aid.

China learned to revere five of the host of heavenly Buddhas. Sakyamuni (Shih-chia-mou-ni) was always given a central place as the Buddha of the present age of the world, but his celestial companions, molded by thought according to the heart's desire, seem to overshadow him in importance and usefulness. A blaze of brilliance suffuses these divine figures. Vairocana (P'i-lu-châ-na), called "The Great Sun," was the very embodiment of light. He was so often identified with the ineffable Absolute that his personality and his paradise failed to capture the hearts of the folk. His double, Locana, was also glorified as the eternal light and truth, the source of all the Buddhas. A thousand lotus petals surround his throne and each petal is a universe. In each universe are a hundred-million worlds. Every universe has its Buddha and each of the thousand-times repeated hundred-million worlds has its Sakyamuni. These divine beings are merely multiple manifestations of Locana who is the source and origin of all.[17]

More useful to the Chinese people was the healing Buddha, Bhaishajyaguru (Yao-shih Fu), enthroned in his Eastern Paradise of light. Associated with him were two Bodhisattvas, the Treasury of Medicine and the Treasury of Healing Herbs. These two were the sun and moon drafted into the Buddhist company of shining ones. By the fulfillment of his vow to save mankind from disease, Yao-shih Fu made his merit available to all who came within the hearing of his name. His grace and redemptive healing were freely given to all who were cripples, ugly, stupid, blind, deaf and dumb, lepers, insane from suffering, the incurables, the friendless and homeless, the poor and sorrowing, women who desired to change their sex because of the misery of their lives, victims of the cruelty of the law, wretches awaiting the executioner's axe, all who were crushed in body and soul under their endless misfortune. Since all this service was provided by the conditions of the vow through which he attained Buddhahood, he continued to be an omnipresent savior even as a quiescent Buddha.

However helpful the other great Buddhas might be, the most popular of them all was Amitabha (O-mi-to Fu) because he brought the boon no Chinese god could give. His name was a magic word to dispel the terrors of death and lead even the lowliest to the Western Paradise of bliss.

The Bodhisattva, Avalokiteśvara, achieved an immediate triumph in China. Through his boundless compassion and love, he could serve the people as an all-sufficient savior. In all realms of existence, among all conditions of men, he was ever present and swift to answer the cry of need. His Chinese devotees not only magnified his attributes as a universal providence but transformed him into a goddess. Both male and female forms appear in the temples, but after the twelfth century he was known primarily as Kuan-yin, the Goddess of Mercy. Many separate elements may have combined to produce the change. His nature as the embodiment of compassion and pity, his special function as the giver of children, and the fact that he could appear at times in the form of a woman may have prepared the way. His feminine sex was probably established through the presence in China of several female deities who were performing on a modest scale the same services he rendered with all the power and splendor of a cosmic savior. The converted demoness, Hariti, who became a tender protector of children, the Chinese Queen of Heaven, who rescued sailors from the dangers of the sea, and the Princess of Motley Clouds who protected women and gave children, duplicated some of Kuan-yin's most important work. Contemporary Nestorian teaching concerning the Christian Queen of Heaven, the Virgin Mary, may have been a further factor. To fix the feminine character of Kuan-yin, an old legend praising the filial piety of Miao-shen, a Chinese maiden of ancient times, was rewritten about the twelfth century as a Buddhist tract. Through suffering, sacrifice and self-mutilation, in devoted service to a harsh father, Miao-shen attained supernatural powers and became a Bodhisattva. The legend identified her with Kuan-yin. Theoretically these Buddhist deities were sexless and able to appear in any form. The Chinese selected the Goddess of Mercy as the most satisfactory manifestation of the love and compassion of the divine nature.

> . . . Trusting in her power
> A fiery furnace becomes a cooling lake of water,
> Waves cannot drown.
> Through her kindliness of heart
> Shivered is sword of executioner.
> Accursed poisonous herbs

May life endanger, but——
Think upon the Lotus Law
And you will then be healed.
Mid thunder-clouds and lightning,
Hailstones and floods of rain,
Look up to Kuan-yin.
These all shall vanish.
Kuan-yin's wondrous knowledge
Can save a world of sorrow.
'Tis mercy upon mercy——
Purest Light! [18]

Power and strength to support the loving labors of Kuan-yin
were supplied by her companion of the Happy Land, Maha-
sthanaprapta (Ta-shih-chih). The Bodhisattvas, Manjuśri
(Wen-shu) and Samantabhadra (P'u-hsien) added their con-
tributions of wisdom and grace.

Maitreya (Mi-lo Fu), who will come as the last teacher and
savior in our world-period, acquired a new and amusing form
in China. He was pictured as a fat, jovial figure, laughing at
the world over the expanse of a mountainous stomach. The
artists confused him with Pu-tai, a famous fat monk of the
ninth century.

Buddhism taught the Chinese to believe in retribution for
evil deeds in a series of eighteen picturesque and gruesome hells.
Ten of the worst of them were ruled by fearful figures who
knew how to fit the punishment to each man's peculiar taste in
sinning. Overlord of all the hells was Veda (Wei-to) who came
with Buddhism from India. Chief of the terrible ten was fierce
Yen-lo, the Chinese form of Yama, the first ancestor and lord
of the dead in Hinduism. Even on their own account, the
bravest and best of men might quail before the prospect of fac-
ing the dread judge, but the central importance of filial piety
and reverence for ancestors made the Chinese masses especially
susceptible to the terror of this novel institution brought to

them by the Buddhists. A busy career was thus made in China for Kshitigarbha (Ti-tsang) whose vow as a Bodhisattva committed him to the task of emptying all the hells. In China he dwells among the damned, preaching the gospel to them and offering the gift of Amitabha's boundless grace—a place in the happy Western Paradise. Like other Buddhist deities he assumes innumerable forms in his saving work. Surrounded by the ferocious devil torturers, he is a being of infinite tenderness, the beneficent "Master of the Kingdom of Death." Through his efforts the shackles of evil have fallen from countless millions who now enjoy the bliss of Heaven. Until the last soul is saved, Ti-tsang will remain in hell.

This brilliant company of immigrant deities provided help for the Chinese people in all experiences from birth to death and beyond. Since they had become Buddhas and Bodhisattvas through vows of self-effacing service to others, it was of their very nature to give freely. They were not grudging gods, demanding obedience and submission, threatening sinners with the whip of punishment. The tyrant karma which held men on the wheel of suffering was their enemy as well as man's. With limitless love, power and pity they came to rescue humanity from the entangling coils of pain.

Philosophers knew that these celestial beings were only appearances assumed by the Absolute to lure souls out of the bondage and illusion of existence. The earthly teachers, the heavenly saviors and the Buddhas in their shining paradises were all means of leading earth-bound beings to the ultimate goal of Buddhahood, the timeless perfection of Nirvana. For the Chinese folk, the Buddhist deities were living persons. Their images in the temples, bearing their characteristic symbols and signs, made them vividly real. Benign and gracious figures they survey the human scene with far-seeing eyes. There was a tendency to arrange them in trinities—O-mi-to Fu, Ta-shih-chih and Kuan-yin of the Western Paradise, or the three great

Buddhas, O-mi-to Fu, Yao-shih Fu with Sakyamuni between
them. The Buddha, the Truth and the Church were represented
by Sakyamuni, Vairocana and Locana. Often Sakyamuni appears in a triad with the two great sages of China, Lao-tzu and
Confucius.

With these important deities Chinese Buddhism honors a
great company of saints among whom the first ten disciples of
Sakyamuni are the most important. A group of twenty-four
gods are enlisted as guardians of the law and the church. Con-
spicuous among them are the four Kings who, in India, guarded
the dwellings of the gods on Mount Meru from the assaults of
demons. In China they were identified with the heavenly rulers
of the four quarters of space and the four seasons. The guardians are an international group. Some of them are deities of
Confucian and Taoist folk religion, drafted into the service of
Buddhism. From India came Wei-to and Yen-lo, doing double
service as guardians and lords of hell, as well as two of the
greatest Hindu gods—Brahmā (Ta-fan) and Indra (Ti-shih).
In addition to the twenty-four, two ferocious figures often
stand on guard at the entrance to the temples—Hêng and Ha,
"Snorter" and "Puffer"—two forms of Vajrapani, the name
assumed by Indra when he joined the Buddhist ranks in the
early days as the bodyguard of Gotama. If this identification is
correct, the ancient Hindu deity, dwelling with the thirty-
three elder gods on Mount Meru, may be meditating on the
futility of embracing a new religion when he views himself as
Indra among the guardians, while in his Buddhist form he is
reduced to a mere watchman at the gate.

In the seventh century the gracious Buddhas and merciful
Bodhisattvas began the task of taming the rude, primitive customs of Tibet.[19] They seemed strangely out of place in the new
land. The native Bon religion was an adjustment to the harsh
realities of life on the Tibetan highlands where nature rarely
smiled, and earth gave her gifts grudgingly. There man lived

dangerously. He learned to be wary of the menace of the forces which played with his life. The awe-inspiring mountains, crowned with eternal snow, frowned down upon his feebleness. Too often nature turned toward him a face of cruelty in the dangerous gorges and the treacherous mountain ways, the fierce winds, violent storms and bitter cold. He learned to translate the many modes of menace to his security into demons, ghosts, fiends and devils of all colors and shapes. Some of the sky powers were friendly, but the Tibetan found it necessary to devote a large proportion of the technique of his religion to controlling the dangers surrounding him, subduing the demons and undoing the evil work of hostile spirits. The Buddhist deities were compelled to adapt themselves to this task.

Wise teachers and noble saints guided Buddhism through the centuries of struggle as its great array of deities proved their worth in the new land. The Tantric form of Buddhism, with its powerful spells and charms to direct the divine energy against the forces of evil and command good fortune, proved effective. The Vajra, Indra's demon-slaying thunder-bolt, symbol of divine power, of truth, of love, of creative energy, entered the warfare against the demons.

Not only did the entire personnel of the Buddhist celestial company come to the service of Tibet but with them came a large number of the Hindu gods. The ultimate supreme Being was called Vajradhara in Tibet. This was the Adi-Buddha, or Dharmakaya, the one, only reality of which all the multitudinous personal deities were merely manifold phases of manifestation, but he was only a figurehead, and played a minor rôle. The central group was composed of familiar figures—the five celestial Buddhas, with their Bodhisattvas and earthly manifestations. Tibet added another group of five celestial reflexes of the Buddhas and five wives. There was no theological reason for limiting the number. A title, a quality, a mood or a special task was sufficient to create new forms of what was in reality the eternal ONE. The "Thousand Buddhas" which became traditional in Tibet were a modest limitation of the possibilities of the Buddhist galaxy. These celestial figures appear blazing with light, embodying all the qualities man most desires in his gods, but the special tasks of their new home caused them to assume also fierce and demoniacal forms before which no fiend, demon or devil, however terrible, would dare to make a stand. Among these high Buddhas, here as elsewhere, the most important were Amitabha of the Western Paradise and the healing Buddha, Bhaishajyaguru, who was represented in seven forms.

Among the Bodhisattvas, Manjuśri had his Indian rank as the Prince, the first of the company. It seems strange to see this sweet-voiced deity, the embodiment of wisdom, appearing in Tibet not only in his kindly form but also as an angry fury, and in still more terrible guise as the "six-faced dreadful king demon," decorated with skulls, wreathed in flames, trampling on prone, tortured bodies. With him were the other well-known saviors who delay their entrance into Nirvana because men need their help—Samantabhadra, Maitreya, the loving one, who watches from the Tusita heaven to guide and give revelation, Vajrapani, the powerful defender, Kshitigarbha, and the Lord of Mercy, Avalokiteśvara. The combined powers of all these deities seemed entirely adequate for security in this life and joy in the life to come.

Avalokiteśvara was the world's best beloved Bodhisattva, but in Tibet, his wife, Tārā, the Goddess of Mercy became the most popular of all the heavenly host. She took care of the poor, banished grief, fear and distress, gave children, wealth, happiness and prosperity. Devils, plagues and poisons she could utterly destroy. When death came, she led the soul to the Buddha realm and the bliss of Nirvana.

Hail! O verdant Tara!
The Savior of all beings!
Descend we pray thee, from thy heavenly mansion at Potala,
Together with all thy retinue of Gods, Titans and deliverers.
We humbly prostrate ourselves at thy lotus feet!
Deliver us from all distress! O holy Mother! [20]

Loveliest of the heavenly friends of the Indo-Aryans three
thousand years ago was the dawn-maiden, Ushas, goddess of
light and morning. In her Buddhist form she was highly honored in Tibet but time and travel marred her once beautiful
form. The name Marichi, "the Resplendent," is true to her
original nature, but the virgin queen of heaven has been confused with fertility figures and associated with the pig as the
symbol of fecundity. Her lotus throne is supported by a pig.
Seven pigs draw her car and one of her three heads is that of a
pig. In her mild mood she has all the lovely qualities of her
prototype, the goddess of dawn, with the added grace of a
Buddhist Bodhisattva. Like Tārā and the other deities she assumes a fierce form, crowned with skulls and wreathed in flame,
for her warfare with the powers of evil.

The ten chief disciples of Sakyamuni and the great historic
teachers of the faith receive their proper share of divine honors.
The life of Padma Sambhava, founder of Tibetan Buddhism
was so embroidered with myths of his supernatural birth and
his miraculous exploits in the destruction of demons that he
rivaled the celestial deities in popular devotion. Since 1640 the
Grand Lamas have been gods on earth, the Panch'en Lama an
incarnation of Amitabha and the secular ruler at Lhasa, the
Dalai Lama, an incarnation of Avalokiteśvara. When either of
these Grand Lamas dies, the embodied deity is at once reborn
in the child destined to succeed him. By this theory, the lineage
of the Dalai Lama was carried back to primeval times, for
Avalokiteśvara was identified, not only with the succession
of priestly rulers of the land, but also with Padma Sambhava

of the seventh century, who introduced Buddhism into Tibet, and finally with the good spirit of the mountains who first evolved man from the monkey.

The gods who guard the law in Tibet are an awe-inspiring army as becomes a land infested with dangerous demons and destructive fiends. Some of them are native deities, drafted to serve the new religion; many came from India, and some seem to be products of nightmare imagination. They have a furious and menacing form. Śiva and his wife, Kali or Durga, arrayed as the death-dealer and great destroyer, were excellent models for deities enlisted to destroy the armies of fiends and devils. The guardian kings and generals are like Śiva, and the goddess, Lha-mo, Queen of the warring weapons, resembles Durga. There is a great array of these defenders of the faith, terrible in appearance, and the consorts of the guardians are more deadly than their lords.

Among the lesser gods who bow humbly before the greater glory of the Buddhas, are Indra and his once glorious "Thirty-three." Some of them guard the ten directions of space with Brahmā in the central heavens. Indra, Yama, Varuna, Kubera, god of riches, Agni, and Marut have other stations. Name and fame carried them beyond the borders of their homeland, but under the shadow of the new religion their grandeur departed. They became servants and suppliants in a strange land. Yet all this multitude of lesser gods could be useful in acquiring health, wealth, long life, mastery of enemies and protection. In a universe crowded with supernatural beings, the Tibetan lived under the protection of a multitude of spiritual defenders. From his personal protective divinity, who never left him, to the demon kings, guardians and celestial Buddhas and Bodhisattvas, he could select a divine helper for every time of need.

In the seventh century Nepal was a dependency of Tibet. From the Buddhist homeland through Nepal the cultural paths were opened for the Buddhas and their heavenly host to win the northlands. From Tibet in the thirteenth century they went on to Mongolia.

The march toward the Pacific for the mastery of Korea and Japan was mediated through China. All the familiar deities had taken up their work in Korea by the sixth century. The historic Buddha, Sakyamuni, was honored but somewhat obscured by the greater glamour and usefulness of his companions. The healing Buddha, with his attendant medicine kings, the Sun and Moon, the great Bodhisattvas Manjuśri (Moonsoo) of wisdom, Samantabhadra (Pohien) of kindness, and Maitreya (Miryuck) the coming Buddha, performed the same services in Korea as they did in China. Greatest of all were the Buddha Amitabha (Amida) of the Western Paradise and his associate Avalokiteśvara (Kuan-scieum). These two deities deserved their popularity. Avalokiteśvara shepherded, consoled, rescued and benefited men as an omnipotent providence in the troubles of daily living; Amida graciously welcomed the lowliest of earth's wayfarers into his happy homeland when death marked the end of the way. There they would "enjoy unspeakable bliss and happiness through everlasting ages." To complete the divine circle of security here and hereafter, Kshitigarbha (Chijang) came with the Buddhist hells to Korea to rescue all unfortunates who ignored Amida's gospel and wandered into these dismal torture chambers of the underworld. The great divinities were accompanied here as in other lands, by the gods who guard the religion and the church, but in the gentler cultural climate of Korea they had no need of the fierce and frightening forms assumed in Tibet.

Buddhism entered Japan in the late sixth century with a letter of glowing recommendation from the ruler of central Korea.[21] With it came the culture and practical arts of the continent. The primitive Japanese were awed by the elaborate trappings of the new religion, and the miracle-working craftsmen, artisans, builders and physicians who came with it were a great help in making its welcome sure. The value of the culture of the mainland gave it prestige. When Buddhism was established, students went to the continent to search out all its treasures and bring them to Japan. By the eighth century all the much-travelled Buddhist deities had arrived to serve and save the land of the rising sun, many of them to assume new duties and new forms. With their usual tolerance they made no attempt to displace the native gods. Tactfully, it was arranged to have the supreme Japanese deity, the Sun-goddess, Amaterasu-Omikami, announce from her temple at Ise that she herself was one with the great sun Buddha, Vairocana. When the ultimate divine reality of Buddhism was thus identified with the highest Shinto deity, it was an easy step to recognize the many gods of Japan as manifestations of other figures in the Buddhist pantheon. The two celestial families could dwell peaceably together.

Because of the sharp sectarian divisions of Buddhism in Japan the importance of the several deities varies from group to group. Vairocana (Dai Nichi) has an exalted rank not only in his own right as the absolute ONE, but through the central importance of his counterpart, Amaterasu, the divine ancestress of the imperial family. Sakyamuni (Shaka) received little honor until Nichiren became his champion in the thirteenth century and acclaimed him the greatest of all the Buddhas, since he alone had any reality as an historical figure. The Buddha of light and healing, called in Japan Yakushi, with his attendants Gwakko and Nikka, sun and moon, attained great popularity, but had to share his honors with the saint, Binzuru, who was closer to the people. This monk was well known in India and China as a member of the early church who, in his younger days, broke the vow of chastity. As a result his entrance into Nirvana was indefinitely postponed, and he was given the task of protecting the church and helping men in trouble. In Japan he was confused with the healing Buddha, and took over his functions as the king of medicine. The memory of his lapse of long ago still lingers, for his statue always stands outside the temple. His service and popularity are proven by his well-worn figure, sadly defaced by the rubbing hands of the multitudes in quest of a cure.

The great Buddha, Amida, won another triumph in the island kingdom. None could compare with him in popular favor. His gracious gift of eternal happiness, so easily attained by simple faith or by the repetition of his name, endeared him to all classes of the people. His attendants in the Western Paradise, Avalokiteśvara (Kwannon) and Mahasthamaprapta (Sei shi) shared his glory. In Japan, Sei shi added wisdom to his original quality of strength. Kwannon was her usual compassionate self, an ever present help in every hour of trouble.

The two Bodhisattvas, Manjuśri (Monju) and Samantabhadra (Fugen), who embodied wisdom and kindness, were unchanged in Japan, except that Fugen's compassion was extended to include sympathetic understanding of the hearts of men. He could also prolong the span of life. These two benevolent beings often appear in a trinity with Sakyamuni.

The conqueror of hell, Kshitigarbha (Jizo) grew into a remarkably versatile and serviceable deity among the Japanese. Some of his new characteristics he took from native Shinto gods, others from his companions in the Buddhist hierarchy. The work of rescuing souls from the hells, to which he is pledged as long as the wheel of rebirth turns, is his main interest. That he may reach all forms of living things and lead them to Amida's paradise, he takes six forms, one for each of the six realms of life—hell, hungry ghosts, animals, demons, men and gods. Through his great compassion for sufferers, he sometimes substitutes himself for them in hell and on earth does the work of those too heavily burdened. He heals the sick, wards off disease, forewarns against fire, gives children and helps women in childbirth. As Jizo of the victorious army, he helped to quell a rebellion in the eighth century. He has taken the place of an old Shinto god of the highways as the guide and protector of travellers. He is best loved as the friend and guardian of little children. When they die, they go to the bank of an under-world river, Sai-in, where they play with pebbles. As they are busy with their building, a fearful demon comes roaring among them to torment and terrify the helpless little ones. Then Jizo rescues them, and while they cling to him trustfully, he shep-herds them to Amida's heaven. Not only dead children but the living, and not only children but anyone suffering or in trou-ble, may call upon Jizo for help.

The children have another protector in Hariti (Kishimajin), the former demoness who, since her conversion to Buddhism, has been the savior of suffering women and little children over all Asia. Her companion in travel, Marichi, the ancient Indian goddess of the dawn, appears without the pig's head which marred her loveliness in Tibet. In Japan she became the pro-tector of warriors and guardian against the ever-dreaded men-ace of fire.

The Shingon sect has a much more elaborate pantheon than any of the other divisions of Japanese Buddhism. Early in the eighth century the celestial hierarchy of Tantric Buddhism was imported from India to China and from there the founders of Shingon brought them to the Islands. In this way the list of the five great Buddhas of meditation was completed in Japan. The five Myo-o, the fierce forms, which these beneficent beings assumed in their warfare with evil, seem out of place among the deities of Japan. They were terrible in appearance but very useful in overcoming evil desires, folly, ignorance, calamity, illness, poison, insanity and all the ill effects of demons, dark-ness and death. With them came a large number of Hindu gods. The great deities Indra and Brahmā and the goddesses, Hariti and Marichi, followed the Buddhas everywhere. In addition Shingon brought to the service of Japan, Agni, Sarasvati, Var-

una, Vayu, Prithivi, Ganeśa and Kubera. The strange fortunes
of gods is well illustrated by this group of wanderers in a foreign land. Sarasvati, wife of the supreme creator, Brahmā, became a goddess of love and happiness. Varuna, who once ruled
as the highest of the Vedic deities, appears as a god of luck and
a protector of sailors. Ganeśa kept his ancient rôle as the giver
of riches, but is represented locked in a close embrace with a
female counterpart. Kubera, another wealth-giver, becomes
also a god of happiness, a protector of warriors and savior of
sailors in storms. The Japanese hunger for happiness, love, long
life and wealth was met by at least eight of these lesser gods,
two of them native to Japan, three from India and three from
China. One of the emigrants from China, Hotei-osho, a jolly
priestly figure with bald head and an enormous belly, can be
none other than the famous monk, Pu-tai, who in China was
confused with the future Buddha, Maitreya.

The supernatural beings who guard the law and the church,
and the rulers of the infernal regions came with Buddhism to
Japan with little change in character. The most picturesque
of the underworld figures is still Yama (Emma-o), the judge of
hell. Some sardonic imagination wove around him a legend of
poetic justice. In ancient Indo-Aryan times he was simply the
first ancestor who travelled the road of no-return and arrived
in the realm of death. There he became king. When hells were
invented in India, he was made the Judge of the dead. Buddhism spread the story over the Orient that he is compelled to
suffer some of the torture he metes out to others. Three times
a day the lictors of hell seize him, open his mouth with an iron
hook and pour molten metal down his throat. This daily torment makes hell momentarily miserable for Emma-o, but being a god, he lives on through the ages, happy and undamaged.

With its vast company of Buddhas, Bodhisattvas and super-
human saints, its assembly of gods gathered from all the cultures of the Orient, and its innumerable hosts of supernatural

beings of lesser rank, Buddhism has provided divine help for all the various needs of mankind more lavishly than any other religion the world has known. Twenty-five centuries ago the sage, Gotama, taught that no god can give man salvation; that emancipation from the sorrows of bondage to the wheel of rebirth could come only by a way of living, leading to true insight, the realization of supreme wisdom. He made no effort to destroy the popular faith in the gods, but treated them as transient phases of the ever-changing flux of the phenomenal world which had no permanent reality. The long line of intellectuals who developed his doctrine has maintained through the centuries that the true reality is beyond time and change, formless, not to be grasped by the intellect, an eternal existence of perfect bliss. This reality is Buddha, and Buddhahood is the ultimate goal of every earth-bound being. All living things in all the infinite universes, in all the many states of existence are potentially Buddhas. But this supreme Being can never be defined. It is impersonal, indescribable, infinite. It is the only reality. Consequently, the celestial multitude of personal Buddhas and Bodhisattvas are illusory accommodations to man's limitations, helpful in leading souls out of the deceptive mazes of ignorance and desire to wisdom and salvation. "There is no Buddha outside the heart," said Bodhidharma in the sixth century. "Save the reality of the heart all is imaginary. To imagine a Buddha outside the heart, to conceive that he is seen in an external place is but delirium." [22]

All the glorious company of Buddhist deities created by imagination to meet the manifold needs of men dissolve into the ONE, known only by the wordless mystery of mystic insight. Images of Buddhas and Bodhisattvas with their calm and compassionate faces, looking out upon the worshipper with kindness and mercy from the deeps of a great peace, are to the senses what their celestial counterparts are to the mind. Both image and idea are practically useful to pilgrims on the path toward truth, but personal gods with qualities are no more real as spiritual beings than as figures of clay or stone. The real Buddha is beyond form, or words, or ideas.

> There is a reality even prior to heaven and earth;
> Indeed, it has no form, much less a name;
> Eyes fail to see it;
> It has no voice for ears to detect;
> To call it Mind or Buddha violates its nature,
> For it then becomes like a visionary flower in the air;
> It is not Mind, nor Buddha;
> Absolutely quiet, and yet illuminating in a mysterious way,
> It allows itself to be perceived only by the clear-eyed.
> It is Dharma truly beyond form and sound;
> It is Tao having nothing to do with words.[23]

The gods of Buddhism have no need of apologists as they confront the modern world. It would be meaningless to try to prove the existence of these lovely creatures of imagination and desire. As symbols of ideal values and as aids to daily living, they serve, as all gods do, for those who still need them. But Buddhist intellectuals in Ceylon and Siam, in China and Japan are proud that Buddhism can meet the age of scientific thought with an advantage over western religions in that it is not fettered to the idea of a personal god who created and directs the course of world events.

The two great divisions of Buddhism differ now as in past centuries. While neither of them would cling to the "superstition of God," [24] Buddhist teachers of China and Japan posit a Buddhahood, realized in personal experience, deeper than the unstable, flickering flux of physical, social and intellectual activity; the leaders of Ceylon and their western converts return to the teaching of Gotama and, like him, put no faith in gods or absolutes.

The beliefs in soul and God are the mistaken inferences of primitive mentality. . . . The end of religion is always salvation, a larger, freer, more satisfactory and more abundant life. It does not consist in the profession of a belief in God, soul and immortality as recorded in scripture or condensed in a creed. God, soul and immortality are the illusions that have crept into religion and without their suppression religion cannot appear in its true colors.[25]

Buddhism in the modern world tends to be agnostic or indifferent to the gods as it was in the beginning.

A man is his own helper: who else is there to help? [26]

Chapter VII

THE GODS OF CHINA

Man follows the laws of earth;
Earth follows the laws of Heaven;
Heaven follows the laws of Tao;
Tao follows the laws of its intrinsic nature.[1]

HE lost past is now speaking to us from the earth in China, lifting a little the veil that hides the earliest records of the ancient gods. For five hundred thousand years or more, this historic land has been the home of man. It will probably be forever impossible to do more than conjecture what friends those primitive earth-dwellers found in nature to help them in their fight for life, but light may be expected to break from the buried cities to reveal more clearly the prehistoric stories of the gods who greet us in the earliest written sources.

Scholars of a generation ago could speak with great assurance regarding the primeval gods of China. More knowledge makes the modern student cautious. The written sources are rich in records which describe in detail the misty times of the long-lost, legendary past. While these texts were accepted as trustworthy for the early ages, it was fashionable to find at the very beginning of Chinese history a supreme figure, called Shang-ti or T'ien, ruling from heaven in solitary splendor. This high god embodied the moral order, presided over human destiny, established and removed rulers by his decree. Missionary scholars found resemblances between him and Yahweh of

Israel. Of course the sources mentioned many lesser divine beings, but the great Heaven loomed so large that it was easy to ignore them and to speak of a virtual monotheism in the dawn age of China.

Higher criticism of the texts ruined this picture by demonstrating that none of the literature in its present form can be dated earlier than the first millennium B.C.[2] The scholars who wrote the Odes and Annals of that era were certainly far removed from the earliest Chinese ideas of deity and their highly sophisticated views of Shang-ti or T'ien a far call from the time of origins. The gods of the various states, welded together by war to make the greater, later China, had a long and separate history before the Chou rulers assumed the mantle of sovereignty in 1121 B.C.

Like all primitive farming folk, the Chinese were bound emotionally to the powers of nature which influenced their well-being. In their desire for the goods of life they were anxious, troubled and grateful, as nature in her many moods withheld or gave her bounty. More than other peoples they seem to have been attuned from ancient to modern times to the natural world, to the year rhythm, in friendly familiarity with the actual forces of heaven and earth. Some phases of nature were especially important as givers of material benefits. By sacrifice and petition the people reached out for help to these friends in heaven above and earth below. They appealed to clouds and the fertilizing rain, sun and moon, winds, mountains, rivers and the grain-producing soil. Very important from the beginning were the ancestral spirits. They kept their interest in the living and were able to give constant guidance and help, or to cause trouble if they were neglected. Whatever may have been the fate of the common dead, the ancestors of the royal house at least dwelt in the heavens. The spirits of great men were so important that from ancient times there was a tendency to associate them with the nature powers. Thus the minister of agri-

culture of the legendary ruler, Shun, was identified with the
Grains, and the ancestors of the royal house shared the cult of
Heaven.

In all the cultures of the early world the emotional attitude
to beneficent phases of the sky gave to Heaven an exalted place,
usually the supreme place among the helpful nature powers.
The all-seeing, all-covering, all-enfolding Heaven was high
above all other deities. The orderly movement of sun, moon
and stars, the flow of seasons, day and night, were under its
direction. From it came light and warmth, rain and snow, the
storm of thunder and lightning to refresh the parched crops and
pasture lands. These lesser manifestations of nature's activity
were gods in their own right, but far above them was the majestic Heaven ordering and controlling all. Out of such simple
beginnings grew some of the greatest gods of the ancient world.
In the early days of the Chou dynasty, high Heaven, under the
names Ti, Shang-ti or T'ien had already attained this supreme
status among the gods.

The difficulty of following the paths of the gods through the
shadowed realm of prehistory has been partially relieved during recent years. From the graves and buried ruins of the capital city of the Shang dynasty, which preceded the Chou, come
inscribed bones that were used to seek guidance and help from
the unseen powers concerned with human welfare.[3] Their evidence indicates that Shang-ti and T'ien, so easily identified as
one in the writings of the Chou period, were in origin and development separate gods before they met and blended three
thousand years ago.

That Shang-ti of the Shang people and T'ien of the Chou
should unite in a single Heaven-god would suggest that their
relation to the sky was common to both from early times. The
story of their lives as independent gods is obscure. On the
oracle bones of Shang, Shang-ti often appears as a god in the

heavens who sends down blessings to men. He is a giver of goods, rainfall, crops, guidance, advice on military and material problems. The royal ancestors, addressed as Ti, were associated with him and, from heaven, continued to direct earthly affairs by their wisdom and power. This picture of a Heaven-god, sharing devotion with the spirits of dead kings, provides the evidence for prehistoric times of the relationship between Shang-ti and the ancestors of the ruling house which continued in the state cult through all later Chinese history. In this earliest glimpse of him through the veils that hide the beginning, Shang-ti appears as the beneficent Heaven, humanized by man's gratitude for his generous gifts.

Lack of prehistoric evidence beclouds the ancient history of the Chou deity, T'ien. In the earliest literary sources this god is Heaven, fully arrayed with attributes as a divine friend and ruler. It would be reasonable to assume that T'ien as he meets us on the horizon of history is the developed form of the primeval Sky-god of the Chou people. The early pictograph for T'ien was the figure of a man with a large, round head. Several Chinese interpreters [4] have seen in the character a natural way of representing Heaven. The lower part of the pictograph is the archaic sign for a man and the round head represents the disk of the sky. The combined symbols would mean the circular expanse above man, that is, heaven. After a penetrating study of the history of the character, however, Professor Creel is convinced that it came to mean heaven only after a long development. Originally it was simply a pictograph of a "great man" and denoted a man of eminence and authority. It was specialized in meaning to refer to the "great ancestors" and especially the ancestral kings as a body. The separate individualities of these spirits faded out in time. As a unified power controlling human destiny they were treated as a single, rather vague, awe-inspiring, over-ruling intelligence acting from heaven. At last the character, T'ien, moved in meaning from "the spirits who dwell in the sky" to "the place where the spirits dwell"—Heaven.[5] If this interpretation is correct, it reveals that the association of royal ancestors with the sky was common to both Shang and Chou tradition. By whatever devious paths, the gods, Shang-ti and T'ien, travelled through the prehistoric ages, they arrived at the same goal.

It was the Chou conquest of the Shang culture that forced the two originally separate gods to pool their powers. They were sufficiently similar to merge gracefully into one Heaven-god who united in his own being the characteristics of both. He was called, sometimes Shang-ti, more often T'ien, and sometimes by the composite title, "Sovereign Heaven, Shang-ti." The name Shang-ti, meaning "The Ruler Above," long retained a personal flavor while T'ien, "Heaven," lent itself more easily to an impersonal interpretation of cosmic control. In the early literature and bronze inscriptions, the term, T'ien, was used four times as frequently as the more personal Shang-ti and Ti, but this may mean only that the ruling Chou preferred their own divine name to the term Shang-ti of the conquered people.

While the Heaven-god held the place of highest honor, he was not alone. A galaxy of nature powers, useful in the practical life of the people, shared with him the offerings of the official cult and the affection of the folk. Most important of these were Sun, Moon and Stars, the three luminaries of heaven, Mountains and Rivers, the Spirits of Heat and Cold, Rain, Storm, Thunder and Lightning, and the Spirits of Soil and Grain. Among the bright gods were men who had earned divine rank—culture heroes and ancestors who had done great deeds or displayed remarkable virtue. Appeals for help to the various classes of gods were made in orderly fashion by the proper person, at a fixed time, with correct decorum. The Emperor represented all the people in the great sacrifices, to Heaven in winter and to Earth in summer:

The feudal lords sacrificed to Heaven and Earth and to the three luminaries, as well as to the mountains and rivers in their territories. The ministers and great officials performed sacrifices to the spirits of the house and to the ancestors. The lesser officials and common people did no more than sacrifice to their ancestors.[6]

These lesser gods, greatly altered by local legendary lore, lived on in the popular religion until modern days. From early Chou times, T'ien towered above them all and for the intellectuals soon became the one, supreme god.

Before the Chou dynasty began to be troubled by social distress, this great deity embodied, under his two names, the characteristics of a personal, heavenly ruler, supreme in moral grandeur, intelligence and power. As the impartial "Parent of men" [7] he fixed the relationships and duties of the people and gave them rulers and teachers. He was compassionate and granted satisfaction to the desires of men. The cry for help in time of trouble always came to his ears, but only the virtuous man received an answer to his prayer. After examining the behavior of men he gave rewards to the good, sorrow and punishment to the wicked. From him the king received the decree of sovereignty, and was charged to labor with compassionate anxiety on behalf of the people. The virtuous ruler received as Heaven's gift, wisdom and honor, dignity and prosperity. T'ien ordained the social order and was especially angry with the king who failed in his duty. Sometimes he seemed very human, enjoying the gifts of his people and pleased when men were helpful and obedient to the moral law. At other times he appeared in awe-inspiring majesty, a god of sovereign power, greatly to be feared. Heaven in angry mood might send down upon the hapless folk disease, misery, famine and destruction, but material blessings, rain, rich harvests, enduring prosperity, joyous days and long, serene life also came abundantly from his generous hand. These two moods of the celestial ruler are reflected in the Odes.

Great is Shang-ti, beholding this lower world in majesty.
He surveyed the four quarters, seeking for some one to give settlement
    to the people——
How vast is Shang-ti, the ruler of the people below!
How arrayed in terrors is Shang-ti, with many things irregular in his
    ordinances.[8]

    Heaven is sending down death and disorder,
    And has put an end to our king.
    It is sending down those devourers of the grain,
    So that husbandry is all in evil case.
    All is in peril and going to ruin;
    I have no strength to do anything,
    And I think of the Azure Vault.[9]

    How beautiful are the wheat and barley!
    What shining produce we shall receive!
    The bright and glorious Shang-ti will give us in them a good year.[10]

    The proud are delighted,
    And the troubled are in sorrow,
    O Azure Heaven, O Azure Heaven!
    Look upon those proud men,
    Pity those troubled ones.[11]

    In the early centuries of the first millennium B.C., T'ien or
Shang-ti was moving toward the heights of celestial majesty as
a solitary, supreme god. At the same time, Yahweh of Israel
and Ahura Mazda of Iran were taking their first steps toward
monotheism. Like them T'ien rose above all other nature powers by acquiring the attributes of sovereignty. He was powerful, wise, beneficent, all-seeing, the guardian of the moral law.
No other Chinese god could compare with him in authority. He
dominated the domain of nature and the destinies of men.
Earthly dynasties rose and fell by his decree. All signs pointed
to a development of T'ien that would give him a place among

that small company of great, personal gods the world has known, each of whom claimed to be the supreme, only ruler of the universe.

As the centuries passed, however, it became clear that the Heavenly Emperor of China was not free to follow the divine path to enthronement as a supreme, personal god, lonely lord of heaven and earth. The traditional seasonal ceremonies of the state cult kept him trammelled by association with the lesser nature gods concerned with the welfare of the people. On the level of the folk religion he was always the highest of the gods but never the only one. The intellectuals, on the other hand, came to acknowledge only one, sovereign, cosmic power, but gradually washed out his personality. On these two levels the divine saga of China moved down the centuries.

After the eighth century B.C., the old order of society began to crumble. Traditional patterns of behavior, established through ages of experience and sanctified by honored, ancient names, were challenged by novelty in social relations. In spite of his mandate from Heaven, the Emperor often was unable to exert effective authority over strong and turbulent states. The relationship of subject and ruler was in practice set aside when the prince of a powerful state acted for the Emperor in maintaining order. Serfs rose to positions of influence, acquired property and power. The merchant class flourished and grew wealthy. Sons were strangely unfilial. A subject was not a subject, nor a prince a prince according to the traditional meaning of these "names." The good old ways were yielding to modernism. In the earlier agricultural life desires were simple; fed by opportunity they multiplied and grew, reaching out for luxury, prestige, wealth, honor, power and pleasure. Restlessness fell upon the states like a disease. Ambition drove powerful rulers into dangerous political and military adventures. War fed the earth with the bodies of men and wasted agricultural wealth. Oppression and injustice crushed the weak. Poverty and hunger made miserable the life of the poor man. Insecurity threatened all classes.

In such times of social suffering the prophets come. It was the age of the philosophers in China. Through dark clouds of discouragement, these wise men looked longingly back to an idealized past when order prevailed. Unlike so many prophets in times of defeat and despair, they did not project their ideal into the far future nor into another world; nor did they lay the burden of frustrated hopes and unfulfilled desires upon T'ien, to make of him an all-wise, all-good, all-powerful guarantor of the perfect life into whose gracious presence men might flee for refuge from a world sick with evil. Rather the sages of China kept their eyes steadily upon the earthly scene and sought to find the way back to peace, order and blessedness through human conduct, attuned to the impartial, righteous rule of Heaven.

During the first five centuries of the Chou dynasty, China's high Heaven-power had been clothed in the warm coloring of personal qualities. Slowly he began to change as a long line of philosophers, during the Ch'un Ch'iu period (772–481 B.C.) and the age of the Warring States (481–256 B.C.) wrestled with the tide of social distress. The direction of change was implicit from ancient times in the practical attitude of the Chinese toward nature. They sacrificed to rain, earth, mountains, rivers, soil and grain for benefits received, with no veil of mystery to obscure the direct dependence of man upon these phases of the environment for his well-being. Early divination technique assumed a close relationship between man and nature. The religious ceremonial of the state followed the seasons and oriented the desires of the folk to the year rhythm. The forces of nature, the fertility of the fields, the good of the state and the happiness of the people were all intertwined. Harmony of the whole was maintained by correct social and ritual behavior, *li*.

The li constitute the warp of Heaven, the principle of earth and the conduct of the people.[12]

Ideally, Heaven, earth and man were united in a great unity of moral orderliness. Blessedness for man flowed from action attuned to the way of T'ien. Scholars agreed that "Heaven does not speak," but the bitter fruit of social disorder was interpreted as an eloquent warning of maladjustment between the way of man and the way of T'ien. As sages labored through five troubled centuries to find the formula for harmony and happiness in human relations, Heaven gradually assumed a new character. Refined by their thought, T'ien became a universal natural order, giving to every existing thing the formative principle of its being, binding into one vast unity the changing process of nature and culture of which man is a part. Obedience to the divine decrees had practical meaning only as socially approved behavior in all the relationships of life.

Such a T'ien could be a source of strength and confidence to scholars who labored to check the erosion of social institutions by the forces of change. Faith in the efficacy of spiritual beings was fading for many members of the ruling class. The will of Heaven touched them only lightly, with none of the awed sense of responsibility of an earlier day. To a generation drifting from its ancient anchorage, Confucius (551–479 B.C.) preached a return to the old, wise ways of the happier past, and claimed high Heaven as authority for his message and mission. When danger threatened him he was confident that T'ien, who had chosen him to serve the "cause of truth," would allow neither him nor the cause to perish at the hands of hostile men. The T'ien of Confucius was a god to be treated with awed respect as a Heavenly Emperor, not to be met on familiar terms nor importuned for favors, but obeyed and revered as the source of personal virtue and the master of human destiny. Heaven could not be deceived. Before the decrees of T'ien wise men learned to bow without complaining. In this sixth century, T'ien had not yet surrendered all the character of a personal sovereign, but the respectful reserve of Confucius allowed so little emotional glow to touch him that the will of Heaven seems to be hardly more than the decree of destiny; and the austere god is saved only by the overtones of language from being simply the order of heaven and earth underlying natural and social law.

As a master of tradition, Confucius was in sympathy with the reverent attitude of the folk toward the ancestral spirits. He commended the legendary Yü for his filial devotion to the spirits, and stood in full dress as a host to receive the villagers who were performing the ceremonies to drive out evil powers. He, himself, sacrificed to the spirits "as if they were present." [13] His apparently skeptical words—"To devote oneself earnestly to one's duty to humanity and, while respecting the spirits, to keep away from them, may be called wisdom" [14]—should perhaps be read as advice to treat the spirits with proper reserve, avoiding importunity and presumptuous familiarity. Confucius showed no interest in the local and lesser gods of the people; Heaven and the ancestors he served with the correct, ancient decorum, refusing to bend before the rising winds of change.

In the next generation, a determined effort to save T'ien from being transformed into a cosmic fate, or an impersonal natural order was made by Mo-tzu (479–381 B.C.) He complained that the men of his day no longer believed in the active will of Heaven and were in doubt as to the existence of ancestral spirits. All the social evils and moral failures of the age flowed from this loss of faith. T'ien rewarded the sage kings of the glorious past because——

> In the highest sphere they revered Heaven,
> in the middle sphere they worshipped the spirits and
> in the lower sphere they loved the people. [15]

The ancients knew well that the Sovereign on High sees everything that is done in the woods, the valleys and the hidden places into which no human eye can pierce; that he desires the good and hates the evil; loves justice and hates injustice. The men of old sought happiness by obedience to the will of T'ien.[16] Modern men have forgotten. If rulers were really anxious to follow the true way and to benefit the people, they would give careful attention to the will of Heaven.

Heaven loves the whole world universally. Everything is prepared for the good of man. Even the tip of a hair is the work of Heaven . . . Heaven ordered the sun, the moon, and the stars to enlighten and guide them. Heaven ordained the four seasons . . . to regulate them. Heaven sent down snow, frost, rain and dew to grow the five grains and flax and silk so that the people could use and enjoy them. Heaven established the hills and rivers, ravines and valleys. . . . He appointed the dukes and lords to reward the virtuous and punish the wicked.[17]

Mo-tzu enlisted T'ien in the cause of social reform. He praised the goodness and love of Heaven or, in darker mood, confronted the war-maker, the exploiter and oppressor with the threat of Heaven's wrath, or quietly pleaded that the will of Heaven desires men to share their energy, wisdom, and wealth with their fellows. Thus the preacher of peace and love tried to revive faith in a personal, heavenly Sovereign, all-seeing, beneficent and powerful who loves and rewards the good, hates and punishes the evil.

The tide of change was too strong for Mo-tzu. Among the intellectuals of the next generation there was scarcely a sign of faith in a Heavenly Sovereign with human qualities. The personal T'ien of the past was fading back into the natural heaven from which he emerged. Mencius (372–289 B.C.) revered Heaven as the bounteous source from which man and all other existing things have their being. As the gift of T'ien, human nature should manifest in action the virtues of benevolence, righteousness, propriety and knowledge. This is the path (tao) of man which accords with the tao of Heaven. To know one's nature is to know T'ien. To be true to one's nature is to serve T'ien. Harmony with the way of Heaven, as history shows, leads to blessedness, while he who wanders from the way walks the road to destruction. Heaven is the master of events, the dictator of destiny, holding sway above and beyond the area of human action and control. Before the inscrutable decrees the good man and wise, bows in quiet resignation. At times the T'ien of Mencius seems to be as impersonal as a cosmic fate working through nature and human nature, but he is also the source, sanction and support of moral values. T'ien is too cold to stir emotion, yet the sage of perfect sincerity, who embodies the virtues of the Tao easily and naturally, may feel the mystic glow of harmonious unity with Heaven, earth and all.

While Mencius remained loyal to the T'ien of his master, Confucius, at least to the extent of preserving his moral qualities and the old familiar name, contemporary scholars were following their thought through the rhythmic processes of the natural universe, beyond earth and heaven, to a cosmic ultimate with no personal traits. There had been a naturalistic flavor to the phrase Heaven-earth, used since early Chou times as an equivalent of T'ien. In accounting for the origin of existing things the primitive idea of the creative relations of heaven and earth had been gradually replaced by a more sophisticated concept of the dynamic interaction of Yang and Yin. The Yang was the male, active, dry, warm, light phase of the material of the universe; Yin the female, quiescent, moist, cold, dark phase. From these two, all the complex forms of the natural world, including man, drew their characteristic qualities. For the mystic, and the tidy mind in quest of unity, it only remained to project behind the dualisms of Yang and Yin, of heaven and earth, a pre-existent ONE, the impersonal Tao, instead of the celestial T'ien. This step was taken by a southern dreamer, Lao-tzu, whose graphic teachings were eventually assembled in the *Tao Te Ching*.

Tao was an old word meaning path or way. From early times it had been adapted in such phrases as the "tao of man," the "tao of Heaven," to refer to correct orderly behavior, the path of duty. Lao-tzu made it the primordial principle of existence.

Before the beginning of heaven and earth the Tao was. No man can know its real nature. Seen from beyond the beginning in its own timeless inaction it might be called non-being. But since it acts to produce the universe it is also being. It is nameless, formless, changeless, unique, impalpable, yet spontaneously effective in releasing the creative forces from which all existences spring.

> There is a thing inherent and natural,
> Which existed before heaven and earth,
> Motionless and fathomless,
> It stands alone and never changes;
> It pervades everything and never becomes exhausted.
> It may be regarded as the Mother of the universe.
> I do not know its name. . . . .
> I call it Tao and I name it as Supreme.[18]

"The Tao produced one, the one produced two, the two produced three, and from the three the myriad forms of nature evolved." [19] The transformation of the eternal, quiescent, unknowable Tao into the Great Oneness, the mother of the universe, was the mystery of mysteries. From the Great One came heaven and earth, then Yin, Yang and their harmonious interaction, and at last the ramification into all the complex multiformity of the natural world. By this process of continuous extension every living thing derives from the Tao its essential nature. The Tao in a being is the power, principle or virtue of its life. Although the world presents a bewildering variety of existences with different natures, all are harmonized in the universal nature of the Tao. The far-flung universe has emerged from it, yet the Tao is not made less. Beings innumerable are born, die and return to their source, the Tao remains ever unchanged. "The Tao never acts, yet through it all things are done." [20] Its motion is spontaneous. It has no purpose in creation and is indifferent to human values. "Heaven and Earth are not kind. They treat men like straw dogs." [21]

Man as part of nature, one with the timeless Tao, needs no more the favor of any external god. He knows the joy of being naturally an embodiment of the Tao, the security of enfoldment in the order of nature, the feeling of vast power in submissive surrender to become a channel for the irresistible drive of the Tao. Yet the nature of this ultimate source of the universe could never be grasped by the mind of man. It became an axiom that he who defines it does not know it; he who knows it does not define it. In the writings of Chuang-tzu (369–286 B.C.) there is a constant emphasis upon the ineffable quality of the Tao and at the same time a radiant assurance of well-being through mystic union with it.

The ultimate end is Tao. It is manifested in the laws of nature. It is the hidden spring. In the beginning it was. This, however, cannot be explained. It is unknowable.[22]

The universe and I came into being together; and I and everything therein are one.[23] We are embraced in the obliterating unity of Tao.

. . . Take no heed of time, nor of right and wrong, but passing into the realm of the infinite, take your final rest therein.[24]

The Tao pervades all existence, gives to every living thing its proper qualities. By being natural, yielding quietly to the myriad molding fingers of the Tao, the individual finds blessedness. "Repose, tranquility, stillness, inaction—these were the levels of the universe, the ultimate perfection of Tao." [25]

A son must go whithersoever his parents bid him. Nature is no other than a man's parents. If she bids me die quickly and I demur, then I am an unfilial son. She can do me no wrong. Tao gives me this form, this toil in manhood, this repose in old age, this rest in death. And surely that which is such a kind arbiter of my life is the best arbiter of my death.[26]

In an age of disorder and insecurity, when moral standards were shifting and wise men sought in vain for the path to peace and justice, Chuang-tzu and his friends took refuge in the enfoldment of the changeless Tao. This infinite source of being from which all life flowed, was impersonal, unknowable, purposeless, yet by identification with it and willing surrender to it, the Taoists transformed an indifferent cosmic order into a dictator of destiny worthy of trust.

By the end of the fourth century B.C., Chinese intellectuals of all schools had learned to feel at home in a natural universe controlled by the orderly movement of an impersonal law, which found expression in human nature, on the social level, in the moral virtues of love, righteousness, reverence, sincerity and wisdom. The personal god of the long ago was remembered by scholars only in the formal words of state ceremonies, in the familiar phrases of old texts or in the lingering overtones of religious language.

In making the supreme reality one with the actual world in which man finds or fails to find his happiness, the thought of China made a unique choice. All other cultures, in their dark days of defeat and frustration turned from the earthly scene to a supernatural, spiritual realm. A personal god or an impersonal, spiritual absolute, perfect, changeless and eternal, was set apart from the transient, imperfect level of human existence. The true goal of man's soul was in this spiritual homeland. In contrast, China kept the center of reality in the natural world, emphasized social values and honored the moral law as the highest divine power in the universe.

During the third century, T'ien was completely identified with the order of nature. Under Heaven's omnipotent law the celestial bodies, the "10,000 things" of earth, the seasons in their rhythmic movement, all life from the lowliest form to man and his social institutions were bound together in a vast unity. "Heaven, Earth and all things are like the body of one man, and this is what is called the great unity (ta t'ung)." [27] While T'ien was the supreme ruler of the universe and the master of human destiny, it was not like the other great gods dwelling in celestial splendor far above the lowly creatures of earth, nor an eternal spiritual being forever changeless beyond the drift and change of man's illusory world. Heaven was near at hand, holding all existence in its eternal order. As the ultimate source of all, T'ien gave to each being its nature and determined the conditions of its individual lot. When the Heaven-given nature was preserved unspoiled, the Tao of Heaven found expression in virtuous conduct, which meant happiness for the individual and well-being for society. [28] Social evil and personal suffering inevitably flowed from corruption of that nature and violation of the Tao. In the early days, when T'ien was a personal god, he watched the deeds of men as the stern guardian of moral values. With steady hand, he measured out rewards and punishments for conduct, good and evil. T'ien of the third century still rewarded virtue and brought calamity upon the evil doer, but in the form of immanent, impersonal law.

Heaven and Earth were the father and mother of men. By a process of evolution, the myriad forms of nature and the human race came into existence out of the original unity. Bound by the bonds of nature and origin to Heaven, man found happiness in harmony with the law of T'ien. The method of achieving that harmony varied with the schools. The Taoists felt that naturalness was enough. "They who follow heaven or the natural order, flow in the current of the Tao." [29] Confucius had taught that man's nature, coming from T'ien, was good and needed only to be preserved in its original purity by education and training to yield the ideal life. Hsün-tzu (d. 238 B.C.) denied the goodness of human nature and stressed the necessity of discipline for the development of the superior man. "The nature of man is evil; his goodness is only acquired training." [30] But when the rules of proper conduct (*li*) are observed, prosperity, safety and well-being follow for state and individual. The sage who embodies the Tao of man has nothing to fear from the Tao of T'ien.

If the right Way of life (Tao) is cultivated and not opposed, then Heaven cannot send misfortune. . . . If a person rebels against the right Way of life and acts unseemly, then Heaven cannot make him fortunate.[31]

Hsün-tzu had no faith in supernatural beings. Belief in ancestral spirits, ghosts and the many gods of popular religion and in the efficacy of prayers to them in times of need he considered "unfortunate." T'ien was the supreme power and T'ien was nature with its "Constant regularity of action." [32] It had no personal qualities to be influenced by prayer, sacrifice or ceremonial rite. Man met Heaven as law, all-ruling and inexorable. His task was to conform, to learn to use nature, to master the art of living within the framework of natural and moral law.

If people pray for rain and get rain, why is that? I answer: "There is no reason for it." If people do not pray for rain, it will nevertheless rain.[33]

How can exalting Heaven and wishing for its gifts be as good as heaping up wealth and using it advantageously? How can obeying Heaven and praising it, be as good as adapting oneself to the appointments of Heaven and using them? . . . If a person neglects what men can do and seeks for what Heaven does, he fails to understand the nature of things.[34]

Prosperity and calamity do not come from Heaven, nor from the Earth, nor from the seasons; man weaves his own web of destiny by his deeds.

Hsün-tzu lived in the later years of a dying era. The long, troubled age of the Warring States was ending on blood-soaked battlefields as the prince of Ts'in welded the weakened kingdoms into an imperial unity by military force. His dynasty passed swiftly. As the third century drew to a close, a period of cultural reconstruction and peace began under the house of Han. Scholars set to work to recover the lost literature of the past or to write it as they thought it should be. The patterns of social life were stabilized and the official religion of the state molded into an instrument to bind the empire to the throne. At the same time the religious thought of Chinese intellectuals settled into a system mature enough to withstand the successive waves of missionary religions and weather the centuries with little change until modern times.

Underlying the differences of the schools there was a generally accepted understanding of the natural world order and of the place of man within it. The supreme cosmic reality was one. It might be called Tao or T'ien or T'ai Chi, "the Supreme Ultimate," or T'ai I, "the Supreme Unity." From it, all things came into being. The original one evolved into heaven and earth, then into the two modes, the Yin and Yang, the endlessly interacting phases of cosmic material. Then followed the five elements, dynamic creative agents, by whose infinite combinations all existences, including man, acquired their characteristic forms. These elements had the qualities of wood, fire, metal, water and earth. From the beginning in the Supreme Ultimate, through the long process of evolution to the bewildering complexity of nature and the social life of man the threads of continuity are unbroken. The universe came into existence, not by an act of creative will but by spontaneous

exfoliation. The ONE became many. Tao was the order underlying all things, the universal law.

Tao is that whereby all things are so, and with which all principles
agree. . . . Tao is that whereby all things become complete.[35]

Tao is the principle of Heaven and of man.[36]

When man obeyed the Tao and was true to the principle of his
own nature he manifested love, righteousness, reverence, wisdom and sincerity in social living. Tao embodied in human behavior was virtue (*te*). The final result of this harmony with
Heaven's law was blessedness in the individual life, prosperity
and peace in the state.

While scholars thought of T'ien as the order of nature or
impersonal law, the language they used in describing the activity of Heaven seemed to imply personal qualities—as when
they spoke of T'ien ruling, giving prosperity, providing food
for the people, rewarding and punishing. The most highly revered books, the Classics and works of the early sages, preserved the memory of the time when Heaven was the Supreme
Ruler acting as a personal god. In the state ceremonies the Emperor and local officials still addressed Shang-ti and the lesser
gods according to the ancient customs, asking for good harvests,
prosperity and peace. The ordinary people of the villages believed in many gods who could help the farmer and householder in home and field. On this level of folk life the divine
population was large and growing. There was a wide gulf between the faith of the intellectuals in T'ien or Tao, as cosmic
law and the naïve faith of the people in the many lesser deities.
In the first century A.D., Wang Ch'ung tried to clear the air,
to free the folk from belief in spirits, ghosts, and gods and to
correct the impression given in the classics and the writings of
the sages that T'ien was a personal being, interested in human
affairs, hearing prayer, rewarding the good and punishing evil.

Wang Ch'ung ridiculed the popular opinion that T'ien lives in heaven like a king in a palace; that he metes out rewards and punishments; that he reprimands sovereigns for misrule; that the thunder is his angry voice and the thunderbolt his weapon. T'ien was not concerned with human affairs. "The literati declare that Heaven and Earth produce man on purpose. This assertion is preposterous." [37] Some people think that "Heaven produces grain for the purpose of feeding mankind and silk and hemp to clothe them. That would be tantamount to making Heaven the farmer of man or his mulberry girl." [38] In reality all Heaven's actions are spontaneous and without purpose. All things are produced by the mingling of the fluids of Heaven and Earth but not intentionally. Heaven does not hear nor speak, nor is it affected by men. Often in the Classics, the sages used the name of T'ien to reinforce their teaching, when they wanted to reform the lawless or frighten the ignorant. In this sense Heaven acts through man. The virtue of the great man is the virtue of Heaven, and when Heaven reprimands, it is through the mouths of the sages.

Wang Ch'ung taught that the life of every one is controlled by fate. The constitution which he happens to receive at birth determines the length of his life, his condition of wealth or poverty, honor or low estate. Intelligence and virtue are no guarantee of happiness. Men of little virtue sometimes attain wealth and honor while those of highest intelligence and virtue remain always poor and wretched. It was no new doctrine that Heaven's fate ruled in human affairs. It was new, however, to teach that moral living had no relation to happiness. The Confucian intellectuals preferred to believe that T'ien ruled as moral law, and that the path of virtue led to the material and social satisfactions of the good life.

While Wang Ch'ung was presenting his reasons for disbelief in all supernatural spiritual beings, the first heralds of the gods of Buddhism arrived in China. These missionaries were so wise and sympathetic in adapting their teaching to the culture and personal needs of the common people that Buddhism became a dominant form of popular religion from the fourth to the ninth century. The radiant Buddhist deities, with their attributes of love and compassion, were very attractive to the Chinese folk. That they might serve the people better, some of the gods changed their forms and took on added responsibilities while new deities were created on the models of their companions to perform special tasks. Thus the celestial Buddhist divinities won a popular triumph in China.

It could hardly be expected that the intellectuals, accustomed to think of the supreme cosmic power as impersonal law, would be attracted by the foreign deities. Buddhist thinkers, however, knew as well as the Chinese that the ultimate reality was not personal, that the personal gods were only a concession to the feeble powers of common men and not the final truth. Behind them was the impersonal Absolute, the Dharmakaya. There was enough similarity between the Tao of China and the Dharmakaya of Buddhism to make a blending of the two possible. Both were impersonal law or truth; both were beyond the grasp of man's intelligence and indefinable; both embodied the perfection which man sought to attain. Yet there was a vast and fateful difference between them. The Dharmakaya was a spiritual reality, eternal and changeless, in whose presence the actual world of man's life was only a troubled drama of shifting shadows. In contrast, the Tao was one with man's real world, the natural and social order, and beyond it the realm of the unknown had no more reality than the stuff of dreams. The gulf between the two divine realities was too difficult to cross. Many Taoist mystics were lured into the Buddhist fold. Occasionally an emperor was converted. The Confucian literati examined the foreign teaching, often approved it as a religion for the common people, but remained true to the classical tradition, to T'ien and naturalism. Yet the presence of the Buddhist spiritual Absolute sometimes colored their thinking during the later centuries.

Although the Confucian school produced no outstanding thinkers during the period of Buddhist popularity, the stream of religious thought continued unbroken and little changed. When philosophy flowered again during the troubled Sung dynasty, Chu Hsi (d. 1200 A.D.) completed the work of his predecessors and gave T'ien the interpretation which has continued unchallenged until modern times. The ultimate source of the universe and the supreme reality, he called T'ai Chi, the Supreme Ultimate. This term he borrowed from Chou-tzu, who took it from the third appendix of the I-Ching, where it had stood neglected for twelve-hundred years. In the beginning was the self-existent, T'ai Chi. It evolved into the two modes, Yang and Yin, then into the five elements and finally into the manifold forms of existence. Through all runs an immanent law which finds expression in human nature in the virtues—love, justice, wisdom, reverence, and sincerity. Heaven is law. T'ien is properly interpreted, sometimes as the sky, sometimes as a ruler, sometimes as a principle. Referring to the inequalities which result from the blind interaction of the cosmic processes Chu Hsi says:

. . . That there is a personal being above us by whose commands these things come to pass, seems to be taught by the Odes and Records —in such passages, for example, as speak of the wrath of the Supreme Ruler. But still, this Ruler is none other than Law. In the whole universe, there is nothing higher than Law and hence the term Ruler.[39]

As the source of all things, T'ien gives to each being, with its nature, the law of its life. When man, as the child of nature, is completely attuned to the law of his being the practice of virtue becomes effortless. In the endless cycles of change and transformation the generations of men rise, have their moment in the sun, and disappear like waves on a limitless ocean. Over all is the ageless ruler T'ien, the universal law.

Three centuries later Wang Yang-ming added a mystical flavor to the relationship between T'ien and man. Either an echo of Taoist teaching or the influence of Buddhism appears in his glowing sense of oneness with T'ien and his stress upon intuition as the source of knowledge of truth and T'ien. He agreed with Chu Hsi that "the highest excellence consists in nothing else than a mind completely dominated by heaven-given principles" [40] but he was more conscious of the all-pervading unity of the universe. Ultimate reality was one, whether known as mind or nature or Heaven.

Benevolence, justice, propriety and wisdom are nature manifesting virtue. There is only one nature and no other. Referring to its substance it is callen T'ien; considered as Ruler or Lord, it is called Shang-ti; viewed as functioning it is called fate; as given to men it is called disposition; as controlling the body, it is called mind. Manifested by mind when one meets parents, it is called filial piety; when one meets the prince, it is called loyalty.[41]

The transition from the personal Heaven of ancient times to the impersonal T'ien came early in China. Confucius marked the beginning of the change. He seems to have retained the traditional faith with a tolerant skepticism toward the popular belief in supernatural beings. By the fourth century B.C. the tide had turned in both Taoist and Confucian thought, away from the idea of a personal god. In all later centuries the intellectuals differed from each other, not on the idea of an impersonal, natural order, but only on the method of realizing the good life by harmonious embodiment of its universal law or Tao. Yet it would be a mistake to think that the intellectuals never treated the impersonal T'ien as though it were personal, or that the terms applied to Heaven in the Classics and surcharged with human qualities were no longer used, or that language was carefully guarded to avoid any suggestion that T'ien might be personal. There was no orthodoxy to combat. Tolerance was the rule and only rarely did a scholar feel called to free the minds of the people from antiquated ideas of gods and ghosts. While the literati had outgrown belief in such beings, they found good reasons for the continuation of the state ceremonies inherited from remote antiquity, which related a farming people to the beneficent powers of nature.

In the official cult the emperor presented the needs of all the people of his empire to the divine nature powers. He alone could perform the great sacrifice to Heaven at the winter solstice and to Earth at the solstice of summer. The memory of far-off times lingered in these ceremonies. Sun, moon, stars, clouds, rain, wind and thunder shared honors with the sovereign Heaven, called by his old name, Shang-ti. With Earth were associated the mountains and rivers. As in ancient times the imperial ancestors received the sacrifice with Heaven and Earth. As the rhythm of the agricultural year swung through the seasons the emperor set the pattern in appeal for the blessings of nature. Governors of provinces followed him but restricted their requests to the divine powers of their territories—especially the mountains, rivers, and the spirits of land and grain. In addition to these nature deities the five gods of the home received official recognition and honor—the outer and inner doors, the well, the hearth and the inner hall. All of these divinities were very old and carried down the centuries the marks of their origin. They lived on because they were real phases of nature helpful to man, or parts of the home charged with memory and emotion.

The intellectuals of the Han dynasty felt it necessary to explain that sacrifices were offered to the nature powers because they were useful and the people looked up to them. They found a practical reason also for the cult of the house gods——

Through the outer and inner doors man walks in and out, the well and the hearth afford him drink and food. And in the inner hall he finds a resting place. These five are equally meritorious, therefore they all partake of a sacrifice.[42]

In addition to the imperial ancestors, the state recognized certain great men, who had starred the centuries of China's history, as worthy of divine honors. They were relatively few before the beginning of the Christian era but increased rapidly in number as the Buddhist influence spread. The great skeptic, Wang Ch'ung, agreed with the *Li Chi* that the cult of great men was reasonable and natural. It was intended to show gratitude for benefits received, just as ancestors were worshipped in memory of their kindness.

An oblation is offered to him who has improved the public administration, who for the public welfare has worked until his death, who has done his best to strengthen his country, who has warded off great disasters, or prevented great misfortunes.[43]

The principle thus stated by the *Li Chi* and Wang Ch'ung, that men may earn the rank of gods by their services, is abundantly illustrated in the long list of popular gods. They are almost all human heroes of historical or legendary fame. Even the divine nature powers were identified with earthly human figures. In ancient times, Chu, son of Shen Nung, was the Spirit of the Grain, and after him, Ch'i of Chou held the same office under the name of Chi. The son of the mythical Kung Kung became the Lord of the Soil. The great rulers, T'ang, the victorious, the peaceful Wen and the warrior Wü were deified. Imperial ancestors, associates of T'ien, could give effective help to the state while the dynasty lasted. Mencius notes that the Gods of Soil and Grain were removed from office and others appointed in their places if they failed to ward off floods or drought.[44] Following this pattern, the appointment of great men to office as divine administrators of various phases of heaven and earth could be endlessly extended. The Buddhist idea of Bodhisattvas, human beings who rose to the rank of great cosmic divinities in fulfillment of their vows to serve mankind, added its weight to the enthronement of human gods and perhaps accounts for the rapid increase in their number after the third century A.D. The Taoist theory of the immortals who prolonged their lives indefinitely fell into the same pattern and provided candidates for positions in the divine government. The heavenly hierarchy was organized on the model of the imperial administration. The offices remained fairly stable; the gods who filled the offices might be changed.

The modern Heaven-god of the popular religion came late to his throne. Only the Emperor, at the proper time, with correct ceremony, was allowed to have any dealings with the old imperial Heaven, Shang-ti. He was far beyond the reach of the people. They were content to depend for help upon the lesser gods. Early in the eleventh century, however, a Sung ruler received a revelation by special messenger from on high and enthroned as the head of the divine government, the Jade Emperor, Yü-huang, under the title "The Great Supreme, Opening Heaven, Holding the Tablet, Regulating the Calendar, Embracing the Truth, Embodying the Tao, the Exalted, Great Heaven Emperor." He became the modern and popular form of the ancient Shang-ti.[45] Common folk ignore his long and awesome title and call him simply, "Mr. Heaven." He dwells in his celestial palace, surrounded by his family and court. In imperial fashion he appoints all the other gods to office. Once every year they report to him and receive promotion or a lower rank according to their efficiency as gods. This modern "Shang-ti of the Azure Vault" rules over a galaxy of gods unborn and unimagined in the days when the original Shang-ti was young. Under his command are not only the old mountain gods and nature powers of earth but also hosts of

Buddhas and Bodhisattvas of the celestial universe and the kings of hell. He is still the master of destiny, as of old, "fixing men's wealth and rank, poverty and low estate," punishing and rewarding with even justice, lord of gods and men.

Before the rise of the Jade Emperor, the most important deity of the popular religion was the god of the great mountain, T'ai Shan, in Shangtung.[46] Since the medieval period (220–618 A.D.) his temples have been erected in all the villages of China. Towering between earth and sky, he served as mediator, to relay petitions to the Sovereign Heaven who could be addressed only on state occasions. T'ai Shan was one of five mountains which have received official honors since the Chou dynasty. The original responsibility of the mountain was to hold the earth steady, to keep the rivers from overflowing, to assemble the clouds, send fertilizing rain and guarantee the harvests. In the spring T'ai Shan was asked to help in the growth of crops; in the fall he received thanks for his protection of the grain. When floods or drought threatened the food supply he was officially reminded of his responsibility. All of his companion mountains served in the same way in their districts. The development of T'ai Shan as a great god of the people came only after the fifth century A.D. Then his position as the "Peak of the East" gave him supreme rank among the mountains, because the east, the birthplace of the sun, was associated with the Yang element of the universe and the origin of life. In 725 he was called "King, Equal to Heaven." Three centuries later a Sung ruler promoted him to the title, "Emperor, Equal to Heaven," and added the attributes "good and holy." In 1370, a Ming ruler stripped most of the gods of their honorary titles and addressed T'ai Shan with simple dignity as "The Eastern Peak." In more recent centuries he has been known as the "Great Emperor of the Eastern Peak."

As Lord of life, T'ai Shan presided over the birth and death of mortals. He dictated the number of years, the wealth, honors and children allotted to each individual. When Buddhism taught the people to believe in an after life of heavens and hells, he became the judge of the dead. A hard-working staff of officials kept a record of deeds, good and evil, done on earth, so that his rewards and punishments were just. His supervision extended not only to the people and their officials, but also to all the lesser gods who had special duties to perform.

Some of the popular gods were very old. The storm-rain has earned the gratitude of man since the dawn of time for its stimulus to growing things and the mastery of drought. Thunder, Lightning, Wind and Rain were divine nature powers in prehistoric China. They have become popular gods in the last thousand years by identification with historic or legendary figures. In the popular pantheon they are known now as the Duke of Thunder, the Master of Lightning, Earl Wind, and the Master of Rain. In modern times, however, the Dragon Kings have largely taken over their old task of providing rain.

In ancient China, the farming unit of twenty-five families expressed the desire for a good crop in a springtime ceremony. Their appeal was made to the Spirit of the Soil from which their food came. In time of drought or flood they turned again to the divine power resident in their farm area. He was primarily a land deity, collaborating with the Spirit of the Five Cereals to produce the crops. This earliest form of the God of the Soil was taken into the official cult. During the Chou dynasty each feudal state had its Gods of the Soil and Grain. Under the Han empire, the land was divided into provinces and smaller administrative units. From the family group at the bottom to the imperial domain at the top, each official district was provided with its own God of the Soil. Working together, the deities of the Soil and Grain cared for harvests but the God of the Soil had heavier duties than his companion. He was identified with the Yin principle of the universe and consequently was responsible for help when there was too much rain or if rain was lacking. Bound to a limited area of land, the god was expected to give protection and bounty to the people in his district. In recent centuries these Gods of Soil and Grain have been able to maintain a feeble existence only by grace of their formal recognition in the official cult. In popular religion their place has been completely usurped by the Gods of Walls and Moats.

As in ancient times honored ancestral figures were appointed as gods of land and grain, so now in the villages and districts, the Gods of Walls and Moats are men who have won the love and admiration of the people during their lives. Like their predecessors, they give protection and good harvests, but the people expect them to provide, in addition, wealth, happiness, security and peace. For greater certainty, the Chinese farmer added deities of his own—the Overseer of the Five Grains, to ward off drought and protect the crops; Hu-shen, to avert hail storms; and Pa-cha, to keep the locusts under control.

Very similar to the Gods of Walls and Moats is the God of the Place (T'u Ti Shen). He might easily be taken for a miniature copy of his greater companions, created to take care of special buildings or limited local areas, but in reality he is the modern form of one of the five house gods of ancient times. In primitive China the soil of the inner court was open to the sky and sacrifices were offered to it. After the feudal era, this deity of the inner court seemed to be lost, but Chu Hsi tells us that the God of the Place of his day (twelfth century) was the same figure the ancients worshipped as the household god.[47] Through the centuries this little local divinity has assumed duties beyond the home. He has become legion. Bridges, public buildings, special tracts of land, as well as houses, have their Place Gods. In all cases he is a protector. In the homes he guards the inmates from danger and sometimes intervenes when the mistake of a heavenly record-keeper would cut off the life of an individual too soon.

Most important of the old household deities is the God of
the Hearth. Popular imagination pictured him as a householder
himself, with a wife and the usual domestic animals. He keeps
an account of the deeds of the family. In ancient times he re-
ported to Heaven once a month but since the twelfth century
his monthly reports have been presented to the God of Walls
and Moats. Once a year, however, he makes the trip to heaven
to present the family record to the Jade Emperor. The two
Door-gods of the early ages have been blended into one, whose
task is to guard the home from evil influences. The ancient
God of the Well is only a memory. His place has been taken
by the God of Riches who gives wealth and happiness.

A military hero of the third century A.D. became the War-
god, Kuan-ti. He was the patron of soldiers, defender of the
empire against disorder. The similarity of his name to that of
the Buddhist Goddess of Mercy, Kuan-yin, who is a universal
providence, has made him immensely popular and extended
his duties as protector against all kinds of evils.

A goddess of mysterious origin, the Princess of Motley
Clouds, spreads her protective care over women. She was given
a place in the celestial hierarchy as the daughter of the God of
the Eastern Peak. The people call her, affectionately, "Madam
Lady," or "The Holy Mother." With her are associated eight
other goddesses specialized to care for the needs of mothers and
little children. Among them they divide the duties of bringing children, supervising the progress of pregnancy, assisting
at birth, caring for the baby's diet, guarding against eye-
trouble and small-pox, and directing the development of early
childhood.

The age-old hunger of man for happiness, security, long life
and wealth, which gave character to the gods in the beginning,
was answered in China by a long list of deities created by Taoist
priests to meet specific needs. Out of the three-fold confession
to Heaven, Earth and Water established by Chang Tao-ling in

the first century came the three agents, San Kuan. The Agent of Heaven gave happiness, the Agent of Earth forgave sins, and the Agent of Water warded off misfortune. Of this type also were the Seven Gods of Happiness and the Three Stars, who gave happiness, honors and long life. All of these popular gods were pictured in human form and most of them were provided with historic, legendary or mythical biographies.

Patron of scholars was the Emperor of Literature, Wen-ti. He was assisted by K'uei-sing, identified with the four stars of the great dipper, and Red Coat. They helped in examinations. Red Coat apparently did not have his heart in pure scholarship for he was the friend of students who were unprepared and helped them through their examinations by luck.

During the Christian era, Confucius has received divine honors from the scholar class. He was given a place among the gods of the state cult because the state used the literati as administrative officials and was interested in the creation of an efficient school system and an educated leadership. According to Confucius' own teaching only a man's descendants could properly offer sacrifices to him, but he was too important in the cultural life to be bound to a single family. An imperial decree of 59 A.D. ordered sacrifices to the sage in the government schools. When the examination system was perfected in the T'ang dynasty (618–907) Confucius became very important for the scholars who were also officials. Temples dedicated to him were built in all the cities of the empire. Honorary titles were showered upon him and the sacrifices flowered with greater brilliance as the centuries passed. The teaching of Chu Hsi became the accepted doctrine after the thirteenth century. As a result the usual skeptical indifference of the intellectuals toward the popular gods was replaced by an active effort to strip them of the extravagant attributes given them by earlier rulers. Only Confucius kept his titles when all the other gods lost theirs by decree of Emperor Hung Wu in 1370.

Some two centuries later his collection of honorary names was dropped and he was addressed in more realistic and dignified manner as "The Master Kung, the Perfectly Holy Teacher of Antiquity." [48] Devotion for Confucius weathered the centuries and respect for him grew. At the dawn of the twentieth century his sacrifices were placed on an equality with those of Heaven and Earth. The beginning of the end came with the revolution of 1911–1912, when the link between government service and the old style of education was broken. The leaders of the new China refused the plea of the literati to continue the cult of Confucius in the schools, even if only as the symbol of a cultural heritage and a bond of national unity.

Since the revolution the gods of the state cult have been neglected. They have begun their pilgrimage into the shadow land of history to join the lost gods of other empires of the long ago. The lowlier divinities of the common people share with their devotees in the convulsive changes which, in pain and anguish, are bringing to birth the new China. They are not likely to survive the ordeal. There remains, however, T'ien of the philosophers, who for twenty-five centuries has ignored or tolerated the growing multitude of popular gods. For two thousand years or more T'ien has been the ultimate, impersonal, cosmic law, dominant in the natural and moral order. The physical and social sciences are now giving to Chinese intellectuals a new understanding of nature, human nature and the social relations of men. The ancient emphasis of the thought of China upon man as a part of nature and the central importance of moral values in cosmic meaning, they find confirmed by science. The T'ien of old will live only as a memory, but the natural and moral values, for which T'ien stood, endure, waiting for the creators of the newer, nobler China to weave them into the tapestry of cultural life.

Chapter VIII

AMATERASU-OMIKAMI

This Reed-plain land of abundant rice harvests is the region my descendents shall rule. Do thou, My August Grandchild, proceed thither and govern it. Go! and prosperity attend thy dynasty, and it, like Heaven and Earth shall endure forever.[1]

MONG the great deities who claim the lordship of the world, Amaterasu of Japan is unique in two respects. She is the only goddess to win a place in that select celestial company of supreme gods, and she alone has a direct lineal descendant living on the earth today. Her relationship to the succession of her descendants has been one of reciprocal advantage. The Japanese imperial line has basked in the prestige of divine ancestry through the centuries, and Amaterasu has been accorded ever more impressive honors to intensify the glory reflected upon the Emperors. The history of religions has known many state gods and many rulers who claimed, through some suspension of the laws governing the birth of ordinary mortals, to be their offspring, but only in Japan has the pattern been carried into the modern world.

Almost two thousand years ago, Amaterasu took the position of leadership among the gods of Japan, but she did not win her high estate without a struggle. History and legend both record the fact that her island kingdom came to her by right of conquest, and history further adds the heresy that she and her people were invaders or immigrants from the continent. During the new stone age, if not from primeval times, the

Ainu dominated the whole territory of Japan. At some period in the first millennium B.C., tribes from the coast of southeast Asia made their way to the southern island of Kyushu.[2] They brought with them a primitive form of agriculture, a matrilinear social structure and probably the Sun-goddess, Amaterasu. Their new home provided a climate similar to that of the coast lands from which they came and furthered their farming and fishing economy. In the course of time they were able to absorb or displace the original inhabitants and to consider themselves hereditary possessors of the area.

To the north of them, on the west coast of the main island, was a powerful rival, Izumo, with a hunting and fishing population differentiated from the surrounding Ainu by their cultural contacts with Korea. These hardy warriors, under the leadership of their Wind-Rain-Storm-god, Susa-no-Wo, must have presented formidable opposition to any programs of expansion entertained by their southern neighbors, for the enmity between Amaterasu and Susa-no-Wo is firmly established in Japanese traditions.

Just before the dawn of the Christian era, the island of Kyushu was touched by a new tide of influences flowing in from the continent. Through immigration or commerce, the clans of the area were introduced to bronze and iron, the horse for riding, the bullock for plowing, and the great advance of irrigated rice culture, all of which enabled them to surpass their neighbors in economic wealth and striking power. Under these circumstances the group that was to become the imperial clan of Japan became strong enough to subjugate and unite the leaders of other tribes, conquer all of Kyushu and push north to establish a capital in Yamato. A long period of conflict followed before the people of Izumo finally surrendered and the Ainu were driven to the mountains and fastnesses of the north. It was during this age of gradual unification of the islands by blood and sword that the accepted theory of the relationships of the gods was worked out, and Susa-no-Wo was relegated to the position of secondary honor as the obstreperous younger brother of the reigning goddess. Through the economic, cultural and political success of the clan group who claimed her as their own and carried her with them to power and glory, Amaterasu-Omikami of the victorious family assumed the throne of high heaven.

Traditions of ancient times, gathered together in the *Kojiki* and *Nihongi* during the eighth century A.D., speak of the eight hundred thousand or eight million gods of early days—a forthright way of expressing their multitude. Only a few hundred of them, however, were important enough to have their names recorded and, of these, a relatively small group achieved distinction. The vast number of deities reflects the early emotional attitude toward the many impressive things in nature. The word *kami*, which came to mean "god," was applied to anything startling, super-usual, awe-inspiring, beautiful, lofty, valuable or worthy of admiration and respect. There were innumerable kami, for mountains, winds, volcanoes, the sea, sun, moon, thunder, lightning, storms, superior men, animals, birds or plants with unusual qualities could stir the necessary emotional response. Out of the general crowd, some rose by virtue of their usefulness to be the real gods of the clans settled in the various islands. The members of this select company were mostly the nature powers which provided the essential needs of physical existence. They were the life-giving, growth-stimulating sun, the fertilizing waters from mountain streams, rivers, rain and storm, and goddesses of the earth, providing food in a variety of forms. Some kami were specialized to ward off disease, to guarantee protection from danger, to promote fertility and to give victory in war. The duplication of gods performing the same services was inevitable, since each separate district developed its own deities and named each of them in its own way, and even divine industry must have experienced difficulty in absorbing 8,000,000 employable deities. When the people were united under a single rule the gods of the dominant clans crowded the lesser figures into the background. Some of them lingered on in their old haunts and some were important enough to be invited to join the company of the great, but always the Sun-goddess of the imperial clan held the center of the stage. The old myths remember, however, that many gods ruled the islands before her, and that only after long and turbulent years of struggle did the divine descendants of the Storm-god of Izumo surrender their sovereignty and yield to her and her divine grandson the lordship of the "Eight-Island Empire."

The old legends tell of the time when, after eight mysterious generations of gods had come and gone from the celestial scene, Izanagi-no-Mikoto, the Male Who Invites, and his sister-wife, Izanami-no-Mikoto, the Female Who Invites, stood upon the floating bridge of the sky, high above the vast expanse of waters and prepared to begin their cosmic reproduction. From their union the islands of Japan were first born and then a vast host of deities. The story of the marriage of a Sky-Father and Earth-Mother appears as a theory of beginnings among many peoples but nowhere is the tale told with such vivid naïveté as in the Japanese myths. Many of the newly born gods bore high-sounding, long-drawn-out names, difficult to make meaningful, but among them also were familiar figures—the nature deities nearly all early cultures have known. Sometimes, through the language of the legends, windows are opened to reveal the primitive struggle for life when the environing world was unkind. The breaking of a drought which threatened the food supply shows through one phase of the divine drama. In the midst of the creative propagation, Izanami, the Earth-Mother was so badly burned at the birth of the Fire-god, that she was forced to withdraw into the underworld realm of the dead. All vegetation died, scorched by the summer heat. Then the Sky-Father, Izanagi, killed the Fire-god with the lightning sword of the thunder storm. As he used the sword, nine gods were born who together represent all phases of the storm—the dark rain cloud, the rain, lightning, thunder, and the striking bolt. Their names, from the hilt in high heaven to the point of the sword on earth, were, the Dark-Mountain-Body Deity, the Dark-Rain-Chief Deity, the Dark-Water-Swift Deity, the Terrible-Swift-Fire Deity, the Swift-Fire-of-Fire Deity, the Fierce-Thunder-Male Deity, the Rock-Splitting Deity, the Root-Splitting Deity and the Rock-Possessing-Male Deity. This struggle of nature forces in which the demon of drought is slain to preserve the crops and pasture lands has left its marks upon the myths of many lands. The extravagant multiplication of the gods involved is peculiar to the Japanese story.

The return of vegetation was made possible as the fatally burned Izanami defied the power of death long enough to give birth to the deities of Water, River-Leaves, Gourd, and Clay Mountain Lady. The latter goddess then married the once slain Fire-god, and produced the Young Growth Deity, source of the mulberry, the silk worm and the five kinds of grain. Granddaughter of their union was the great Food-goddess, Toyo-Uke-Hime-no-Kami, whom the Sun-goddess later found worthy of a place at her side in the temple at Ise.

The vast assembly of deities who crowded the early world of Japan presented an unwieldy mass of material to their biographers. Consistency is not an outstanding virtue in the myths. The gods married and multiplied in profusion. Some of them died and later reappeared in full vigor. They were jealous, quarreled, practiced deceit and fought each other in the best human manner. When one of their number strayed altogether too far from the path of divine decency the eight hundred myriad of his peers met in council on the plain of high heaven to determine his punishment, as a group of earthly chief-

tains might meet to discipline an unruly clansman. From the
High August Producing God, who was sufficiently refined to be
a friend of philosophers, to gods with tails, they were endlessly
varied in form and function. They dwelt in the sky, in the
air, on the mountains, at river sources, on the plains, in the
valleys, in the ocean deeps and in the underworld.

Above this divine multitude, two deities were from the hour
of their birth singled out for special prominence—the Sun,
Amaterasu-Omikami, the Heaven-Shining-Great-August-
Goddess, and the Storm, Susa-no-Wo-no-Mikoto, the Brave-
Swift-Impetuous-Male-Deity. In one version of the legends
they were born, like the other original deities, from the marriage of Izanagi and Izanami who spoke thus——

We have now produced the Great-Eight-Island country, with the
mountains, rivers, herbs, and trees. Why should we not produce
someone who shall be lord of the universe? They then produced the
Sun-goddess. . . .

The resplendent lustre of this child shone throughout all the six
quarters. Therefore the two deities rejoiced, saying:—"We have had
many children but none of them has been equal to this wondrous
infant. She ought not to be kept long in this land, but we ought
of our own accord to send her at once to Heaven, and entrust to her
the affairs of Heaven."

At this time Heaven and Earth were still not far separated and
therefore they sent her up to Heaven by the ladder of Heaven.

They next produced the Moon-god. His radiance was next to that
of the Sun in splendor. This God was to be the consort of the Sun-
goddess and to share in her government. They therefore sent him also
to Heaven. . . . .

Their next child was Susa-no-Wo. This god had a fierce temper
and was given to cruel acts.[3]

According to another account, they were produced by Izanagi
himself as he purified his body after his descent into the underworld in quest of his dead wife. From the left eye of the

Sky-Father came the Sun-goddess, from his right eye, the Moon-god, and from the cleansing of his nose the tempestuous Storm-god, Susa-no-Wo.

At this time His Augustness, the Male-Who-Invites, greatly rejoiced, saying: "I, begetting child after child, have at my final begetting gotten three illustrious children." At once jinglingly taking off and shaking the jewel-string forming his august necklace, he bestowed it on the Heaven-Shining-Great-August-Deity, saying: "Do Thine Augustness rule the Plain of High Heaven." With this charge he bestowed it on her.[4]

At the same time the Moon was given sovereignty over the ocean and the Storm-god dominion on earth. The Moon-god has left no record of interest, but the Sun-goddess and her brother were in constant conflict. He was "always weeping and wailing," as a Storm-god should, and making himself a perpetual nuisance to his illustrious elder sister. A double significance may be read behind these stories of divine family friction. The destructive action of the storm in injuring the rice crops and of the wind in drying up the fields of the farmers is clearly pictured, but the antagonism between the two deities also reflects the long and violent political struggle between the imperial clan with its Sun-goddess and the lords of Izumo with their boisterous Storm-god.

In the earliest accounts the great goddess presided as a queen with human qualities over a heavenly realm where the interests and activities were like those on earth. The gods found their respective places in the celestial court. Some excelled as warriors, others were renowned for wisdom. They had their own residences, sometimes so inaccessible that special messengers had to be sent to call them to conferences. Amaterasu, whose radiance lighted the world, was the most beautiful of all and the most cherished. When Susa-no-Wo, in the course of his tactless pranks, offended her beyond endurance, she withdrew, closed the door of the Heavenly Rock-Dwelling and made it fast.

Then the whole Plain of High Heaven was obscured and all the Central Land of Reed-Plains darkened. Owing to this, eternal night prevailed. Hereupon the voices of the myriad Deities were like unto flies in the fifth moon as they swarmed, and a myriad portents of woe all arose.[5]

The gods hastened to devise a plan for inducing her to return to them. After clever artisans had fashioned a gleaming mirror they gathered together close to Amaterasu's dwelling. The Heavenly-Alarming-Female performed a strip-tease dance which was so ribald that

The plain of High Heaven shook, and the eight hundred myriad Deities laughed together. Hereupon the Heaven-Shining-Great-August-Deity was amazed, and, slightly opening the door of the Heavenly-Rock-Dwelling, spoke thus from the inside; "Methought that owing to my retirement the Plain of Heaven would be dark, and likewise the Central Land of Reed-Plains would be all dark: how then is it that the Heavenly-Alarming-Female makes merry, and that likewise the Eight Hundred Myriad Deities all laugh?"

Then the Heavenly-Alarming-Female spoke, saying: "We rejoice and are glad because there is a Deity more illustrious than Thine Augustness."[6]

When curiosity and jealousy impelled the Sun-goddess to peer out upon her rival, she was relieved to behold only her own glory reflected in the mirror, and the gods were able to draw her forth from her retreat. Thereafter the blessing of sunlight was secure for heaven and earth. Susa-no-Wo was banished from celestial society and Amaterasu reigned in tranquility. She wore the jewels presented to her by her father, Izanagi, when he made her Queen of Heaven. These jewels, the mirror which reflected her resplendent beauty, and the sword given her by her brother,

Susa-no-Wo, were her special insignia, as they were of her imperial descendants.

When any problem confronted the gods, she presided over the council in the Rocky Bed of the Tranquil River of Heaven. In womanly fashion, she busied herself in weaving the garments of the gods and as a priestess she was the central figure in the festivals. She had her celestial rice fields which could be destroyed by storms as those of her earthly subjects so often were. As the supreme goddess, she assumed credit for the cultural values which originally were the work of other local deities. The mulberry tree and the silk-worm, the millet, wheat and beans grown on dry fields, the rice as the seed for wet fields, came from her. Agriculture was her gift to man. From heaven she directed the campaign to subdue the wild deities of earth and establish order among the clans of the Eight-Island-Empire. Peace came at last to the earth as it had to heaven, when the descendants of Susa-no-Wo surrendered their sovereignty to the War-god emissaries of the Sun-goddess. Then followed the act of benevolence which has endeared her to the hearts of her people. She sent down her own grandson, Ninigi-no-Mikoto, to establish an imperial dominion on the "Luxuriant Reed-Plain Land of Fresh Rice Ears," destined to rule over human affairs through eternal ages. His great grandson, Jimmu Tenno, who, 1,792,470 years later, became the first emperor of Japan was fully conscious of the dignity of his commission:

I think that this land will undoubtedly be suitable for the extension of the Heavenly task, so that its glory should fill the universe. It is, doubtless, the center of the world.[7]

The story of the origin and history of the gods, shaped and colored by the editors who recorded the ancient traditions in the eighth century A.D., has given to Japan a peculiar status among the nations of the earth. On the basis of the records of its early religion it lays claim to be a divine land. The islands themselves were born of the original divine pair. All the people of Japan are children of the gods in some way, and many of the great families are able to trace their descent directly from divine ancestors active in the Age of the Gods. The divinity of the Emperor has a surer foundation, a greater splendor than that of his subjects, for no loyal Japanese can doubt that the lineage of the imperial family runs back in unbroken succession to the greatest goddess, Amaterasu-Omikami. The Sun-goddess was worthy of the devotion of the ruling house. In the early days she fostered the agricultural development, the economic wealth and fighting strength which gave lordship to the Yamato clans. Having led them to victory and supremacy on earth, she in turn assumed the highest place among the gods. Izanagi, Izanami and the early gods who had made and ordered the world, graciously presented it to Amaterasu and her divine descendants to hold through eternal ages. It was natural that descent from her should be made the basis of imperial authority. The Emperor's right to rule was based, not on the will of men, nor on moral worth so variable from generation to generation, nor on power which may be overthrown by power, but on the authority of direct, divine relationship to the supreme deity.

After the stormy years of conquest and consolidation of the Yamato culture were over, the life story of Amaterasu became simple and uneventful. Responsibility for serving the people in their many specialized needs rested upon the lesser deities. Susa-no-Wo was still remembered at Izumo. The old nature gods of mountains, rivers, ocean, wind and rain continued their ancient rôles. The gods of thunder and lightning became specialized in the art of war. The "evil-hearted child" of the primeval Earth-Mother, the Fire-god continued to command an awed respect with his moody changes from beneficence to destruction. O-Kuni-Nushi, a son of the ancient Storm-god, won a wide reputation as the master of medicine, of effective

spells and of the spirit world. He sometimes served also as a
god of war. Healing and purification were important enough
to command the attention of several deities. The fundamental
need from the beginning was food and fertility. Male and female phallic figures and an imposing array of food deities
were enlisted in this service. Toyo-Uke-Hime-no-Kami, the
ancient Earth-goddess-of-Abundant-Food, had the special
honor of being called by the great Sun-goddess to her sacred
shrine at Ise. (This may be a polite way of saying that the
shrine originally belonged to her). From the throne and palace
of the Emperor, to the home, family and fields of the peasant,
every call of need could be answered by some deity or group
of deities whom desire and custom had endowed with the
needful powers.

Amaterasu and her colorful company of assistant deities
were still very close to their nature origins, struggling upward
from a primitive level of civilization, when the tides of high
culture from the continent overwhelmed them. Confucian influences had been seeping in for more than a hundred years
when, in the middle of the sixth century A.D., Buddhism came
in a flood to take possession of Japan. The foreign religion
brought a developed philosophy and a glorious array of splendid
deities, who had made a victorious pilgrimage from India across
all the lands of Asia, and came recommended by a Korean
ruler as the gods of all the great cultured peoples of the continent. Their images, scriptures, elaborate ceremonials and
learned priests aroused wonder and admiration in the hearts
of the Japanese, but much more impressive and appealing were
the arts and crafts, practical techniques, medicine and instru-
ments of advanced civilization they brought with them. When
the Prince Regent, Shotoku Taishi, "the Constantine of Japan,"
gave the new religion the effective support of the court, Buddhism was launched upon its long and creative career as the
dominant faith of Japan. Under these strange new conditions,

the native gods were forced to find a working arrangement with the Buddhist deities in order to survive.

Many times, in the shifting scenes of history, gods with a longer experience of culture have overrun and suppressed the simple, homely divinities of preliterate folk. Amaterasu and her friends were saved from that fate by three factors. The Buddhist deities came to Japan on the crest of a cultural invasion, not as the gods of a foreign conqueror; as the legendary ancestress of the imperial family, the great Sun-goddess could not be challenged without undermining the divine authority of the throne; and the tolerant, philosophic attitude of Buddhist leaders in Japan, as elsewhere, led them to welcome the Shinto gods into the fellowship of their own shining celestials, and to give the primitive native figures a dignity and depth of meaning they had not known before. Thus the two families of gods lived together through the centuries in perfect harmony.

The Buddhist deities were equipped to do practically everything that needy humanity wanted to have done. During their wanderings in many lands through many centuries, they had learned to serve all classes, the intellectual and the peasant, wearied men and worried women, souls in torment and saints in rapture. Their many-handed providence extended help in this life; their love and grace guaranteed a blissful after-life in paradise. The Japanese gods could not compare in glamour with these naturalized immigrants, but they were too firmly rooted in the countryside and in native tradition to be neglected. Some of them improved their standing by taking on Buddhist color. The phallic deities toned down their natural exuberance in the presence of the decorous, divine strangers who were superior to sex. Sometimes a Shinto god was absorbed in a Buddhist divinity who did the same work but with more distinction.

The friendly co-operation between the two groups of gods was justified by philosophy at the close of the eighth century,

when Kobo Daishi discovered that the Shinto kami and the
deities of Buddhism were the same divine beings under different forms and names. All were only manifestations of the one
Spiritual Reality, impersonal, incomprehensible, changeless and
eternal, the real essential Buddhahood, the soul of all existence.
This theory won general acceptance and made possible the
identification of any Japanese god with some figure in the
limitless Buddhist pantheon.

Amaterasu was recognized as Vairocana, the Buddha of
Light, called Dai Nichi, the Great Sun. The intention was to
give the supreme goddess of Japan an exalted rank, but in
reality she was being merged in a crowd of Buddhist deities and
robbed of her own original status among the gods. Later
thought tried to make amends, and laid at her feet the highest
tribute Buddhist philosophy could give——

Amaterasu-Omikami is the true body of the Primordial Buddha, all-
pervading, ever-present, having neither beginning nor end.[8]

Beneath fair-sounding words philosophy concealed the kiss
of death for the personal gods, the real friends of the folk,
molded and given character by their needs and desires through
the centuries. Japanese thinkers, taught by Buddhist and Confucian philosophy, became interested primarily in the Absolute, the indefinable divine ground of all existence. For them,
the folk-gods could never be more than temporal manifestations of the original ONE. The Confucian school found at the
beginning of the ancient records of the Kojiki the names of
three deities who had come into existence and later disappeared.
They were called, the Divine-Ruler-of-the-August-Center-
of-Heaven, the High-August-Producing-Deity, and the Di-
vine-Producing-Deity. These three divine beings they recognized as the Japanese forms of the Chinese T'ien or Tao and its
two modes, the male Yang and the female Yin, from whose
interaction all the myriad existing things have sprung. The

three obscure deities had never had any vitality in the religion of Japan, but now philosophy exalted them as the "Three Deities of Creation," the starting point of the natural order of the universe. In the Buddhist systems, the highest rank was always reserved for the supreme, ineffable Buddha; all personal gods were only limited, local embodiments of the one true being. Neither of the philosophic groups ignored Amaterasu, but her glory was dimmed when she was reduced to the ranks among a crowd of other deities with a higher god above and beyond her.

By the fifteenth century scholars who were also priests, loyal to the ancient traditions, began to express resentment that the Japanese way of life and the native gods had been submerged under continental culture and foreign philosophies. The protest was just, yet the very men who made it, and pleaded for the restoration of the "Way of the Gods," were themselves products of the intellectual influences from the mainland. One of the most vigorous of the early loyalists, Urabe Kanetomo, spoke of deity in true Buddhist style, as an eternal, unknowable, formless, changeless spirit, the essence of all things. For him, however, this teaching was not Buddhist but pure Shinto. He announced that the usual interpretation of the native kami as local forms of Buddhist deities was truth in reverse. Actually, the Japanese gods were the originals and the Buddhist divinities their manifestations. The immanent divine spirit, embodied in Japan, had made it peculiarly the land of the gods. On this background the great Sun-goddess recovered her former splendor. As the founder of the empire and the ancestress of the Emperor she was given once more the highest rank among the gods.

The tides of patriotic and nationalistic fervor which rose in the eighteenth century and culminated a hundred years later in the breaking of the power of the Shogun and the restoration of authority to the Emperor, carried Amaterasu to the exalted place she now holds in the official life of Japan. The greatest scholar among the patriots of the restoration, Motoori (1730–1801), drew his inspiration from the ancient legends. With single-minded devotion he revivified the traditional myth that the great deity, Amaterasu-Omikami, established the Japanese state and sent her grandson from heaven to rule it. After him an unbroken line of divine descendants, their hearts constantly attuned to the will of the great goddess, are destined to rule the land forever. The power, prestige and glory of Japan flow from the divine founder and the divine Emperor.

From the eternal truth that the Mikado is the divine descendant of the gods, the tenet that Japan ranks far above all other countries is a natural consequence. No other nation is entitled to equality with her, and all are bound to do homage to the Japanese sovereign and pay tribute to him.[9]

Although Amaterasu ranks as a supreme goddess, she is peculiarly bound to the destiny of the Japanese state. The universal attributes with which other peoples have loaded down their gods do not appear in her character. She presides over the lesser deities, who care for the needs of the common people, and guards the welfare of the national life. Her wisdom and goodness are devoted to the interests of the Japanese as a united people, ruled by a divine sovereign. Worship of her is a phase of loyalty to the throne. In the official histories and text books of the schools she is presented as a lovable, generous founder and guardian of the state, whose careful forethought established the Japanese form of government under her divine descendants to endure through eternal ages. The great Sun-goddess belongs to Japan, and to other peoples only as they come within the orbit of Japanese destiny, to all mankind, perhaps, when the divine Emperor shall extend his dominion over the whole world.

The first stride of Amaterasu to wider sovereignty was given official recognition in July, 1940, when she was installed at the outposts of empire in Manchukuo. Attended by Japanese generals, Kang-te, the puppet emperor of the conquered land, dedicated a state shrine to her in the palace at Hsinking, to show that henceforth the spirit of the divine ancestress of the emperor of Japan will be the guide of the national life. To the military and economic bonds binding Manchukuo to the Japanese state is now added the bond of loyalty to the mighty Sun-goddess. Beyond this initial success far vistas beckon to Amaterasu with the promise of imperial power and glory if the territorial dreams of her worshippers can be realized.[10]

In order to make full use of Amaterasu as a symbol of patriotism and national loyalty, two forms of Shinto have been fostered in Japan. The official cult, conducted at state shrines, has been separated by decree from the area of religion. Toward this form of worship there may be no conscientious objection, for failure to do obeisance before the ancestress of the Emperor is classed as disloyalty to the nation. The religious freedom guaranteed by the constitution is not infringed in theory, for state Shinto may not be classed with Buddhism, Christianity, Mohammedanism, nor even the sectarian Shinto which is recognized as a religion. The Sun-goddess, under this state mantle, has won some singular triumphs over the foreign divinities who have dared to invade her Island Kingdom and the hearts of her subjects. The understanding deities of Buddhism would not be concerned, but the proud, intolerant "only" gods of Christianity and Islam must view with amazement the spectacle of adherents of their faiths bowing before Amaterasu. On August 13, 1937, a group of prominent Christians appeared at the shrine of the Sun-goddess at Ise and offered a prayer for the eternity and prosperity of the Emperor who is Manifest Deity; for the elevation of the national spirit and the exaltation of the national life, to the end that the sovereign may be glorified, and Japan, as the Land of the Gods, may become the standard for all other nations of the world; that the people of the nation may be prospered and blessed unto eighty generations and made to flourish like the multitudinous branches of the mulberry tree, and that they may be guarded with a guarding by day and night and be made prosperous and happy.[11]

Among the modern Shinto sects [12] there are several which continue the philosophic trends of pre-restoration times, when Buddhist and Confucian thought dominated the Japanese scene. There are many verbal variations of an ancient theme presenting the ultimate divine being as an indefinable, immanent, eternal presence, underlying the changing patterns of the actual world. This supreme deity is identified with one of the vague primeval figures of the old mythology, usually the first of the "Three Deities of Creation," who disappeared before the coming of Izanagi and Izanami. Shaped in the time-tested mold of speculative thought, God becomes the essence of all existence, the soul of all souls, manifest in many, yet one in all. Within this generous system any number of folk-gods may be accepted with tolerant understanding or devout belief. Some sects include the mythological figure of eight million kami; all groups give Amaterasu a place of special honor as the ancestress of the divine Emperor.

The Kurozumi sect has taken the final step in the exaltation of Amaterasu. For them she is not merely the Sun-goddess, supreme among the gods of Japan, but the Absolute Spirit whose presence is manifest in all the world and in all the events of time. She sustains the universe. From her light and her providential care all living things draw their nourishment and well-being. Health and beauty, truth and goodness flow from her. The many myriad deities and ancestral spirits are localized embodiments of her universal being. She has manifested herself in a special way in Japan as the head of the divine dynasty, but her spirit pervades all the world. In this philosophic dress,

Amaterasu might weather a storm bringing death to the other Japanese gods, or even disaster to the divinely governed state. In this form she has joined the company of vague, ineffable deities who will live until thought grows weary of rationalizing ideas inherited from primitive ages, or men have outgrown the weaknesses on which the gods grow strong.

The real Amaterasu, however, is not an abstract deity. She acquired her character and won her supremacy over the other gods in the historic development of the Japanese state. She made her early reputation as the Sun-goddess in the service of successful agricultural clans. As the deity of the victorious Yamato people who unified the empire, she became the ruler of the heavenly gods. When the men who made the myths used her recognized supremacy to buttress the authority of the ruling clan, and traced the lineage of the sovereign back to her, she acquired the special characteristics for which she has been best known and most highly revered. Her life now depends upon this special relationship to the Emperor and the divinely established state. Her service as a Sun-goddess and patron of rice culture has long been forgotten. The needs of the people in this life and in the hereafter are cared for by a competent company of native and foreign gods. If the Japanese nation is indeed "co-eternal with Heaven and Earth," and the imperial family continues to rule "through ages eternal," there will be no reason to doubt her divine efficiency.

Signs of danger to the life of the great goddess are beginning to appear, however, from another quarter. Scholarship has demonstrated that she was a Sun-goddess, and it is becoming more difficult for educated men in a scientific age to believe the theory of divine descent. Explanations are being offered to make the ancient myth more reasonable. Amaterasu is being interpreted as a human ancestress, a priestess of the Sun-goddess [13] who was possessed of her divinity while officiating at the shrine, or a real sovereign [14] of ancient times who was called Amaterasu, and whose career was connected with solar myths. If this thought prevails, the glorious Sun-goddess will be reduced to the level of humanity. Even as a human ancestress she might still receive worship in Japan, where all the war-dead become kami, but her former glory would be gone. Official education is striving to preserve the old myth, to build national pride and loyalty on belief in a divine land, a divine race and a divine Emperor directly descended from the radiant goddess. If the myth should fail, the usefulness of Amaterasu-Omikami would be ended; and oblivion feeds on useless gods.

Chapter IX

YAHWEH

Hear O Israel! the Lord our God, the Lord is one! [1]

WHEN Yahweh first emerged from the shadows that veil the period of prehistory he was the tribal god of a little group of semi-nomads in the unpromising lands of the Negeb, south of Palestine. There was nothing about him then to suggest that he would play a significant rôle in the cosmic drama. Every little segment of the moving mosaic of peoples seeking or defending a heritage in the lands east of the Mediterranean had its divine protector and provider. Yahweh was only one among many. In comparison with the great gods who watched the wars of empire in the Near East during the second millennium B.C., he was an unimportant figure. His fortune was made by a happy alliance with a federation of Semitic tribes who were destined to carve their hopes deep into the religious history of the world.

The land of Palestine knew many peoples before the Hebrews, and many gods before Yahweh. It was a highway of the ancient world over which passed restless hordes in quest of homelands and marching armies seeking the rewards of conquest and the glory of their kings. For thousands of years diverse ethnic stocks met and mingled their blood and their cultures in the land. The grasping arms of empire reached out over it from the Egyptian, Assyrian, Mitannian and Hittite thrones. At the beginning of the twentieth century B.C., the Hurrians poured in from the north to leave their mark on the mixture. In the eighteenth century the Hyksos, "Shepherd Kings," with their mixed multitude flowed through on their way to lordship in Egypt and came back as an ebb tide after the defeat of their dynasty. After 2000 B.C. there are occasional references to the Habiru who were later to become Yahweh's chosen people. They were small groups of wandering, nomad adventurers associated with the Hurrians and later with the Hyksos. The name of Yahweh had not yet found a place in the records of history.[2]

There was no lack of gods in Palestine during the second millennium B.C. Half a hundred names have been rescued from oblivion, and excavation may recover more, but many must be lost to memory forever. Each of the many tribes and cities had its own divine friends and protectors, but the great nature forces, important for people living from the soil, had the highest rank and widest power. El, the shining, sun-lit heaven was the greatest of the gods. A rival for the favor of farming folk was the great Ba'al of the storm, many-named, but best known as Hadad. His thundering voice was heard in the clouds; his weapon was the lightning and his great gift the fertilizing rain. These two gods, the all-ruling heaven and the storm rain, so often specialized as a War-god, were not peculiar to Palestine. Under different names they appear in the lists of gods from the shores of the Mediterranean, through the Near East, to India. The age-old battle of the seasons, summer dying before the attack of winter, to be revived again in the spring, was represented in the north by two gods—Môt, the season of crops, and Aleyn, winter and spring waters. As Môt died by the scythe at harvest time so Aleyn, god of the waters, perished with the coming of summer and its burning sun. With only changes of names this motif of the dying and rising gods persisted for two thousand years. Associated with the gods, and effective for success in war and agriculture were the goddesses, most famous of whom were Anath, Astarte and Ashera, wife of the great Ba'al, Hadad. All these gods died long ago, but when Yahweh came to claim his kingdom they were alive and powerful, beloved of the folk and firmly rooted in the cultural life.[3]

The northern tribes, who were later to be the more powerful part of Yahweh's people, were at home in Palestine centuries before his coming. As nomad immigrants, they began to filter into the land early in the second millennium B.C. The family of the great ancestral figure, Abraham, found a place in the wake of the Hurrian invasion in the nineteenth century. Some two centuries later other Hebrews shared the wanderings of the Hyksos. A powerful thrust led by Joshua, at the dawn of the fourteenth century, established rights of residence west of the Jordan. Under the name of Israel, the Hebrews were bound in alliance with other tribes of Canaan to defend their holdings and, during succeeding centuries, complete the conquest. Settled as farmers and cattle-raisers they advanced in wealth, power and culture. In addition to the services of their own tribal and ancestral deities, they gladly accepted the help of the gods of their new homeland who specialized in giving fertility to field and herd. The god represented in the form of a bull, perhaps the great Hadad, was especially popular with the Israelites. Immigrants from the south, wandering priests and seers, brought to the tribes of Israel glowing reports of the mighty deeds of Yahweh, but it was more than two centuries after their settlement in the north before he claimed them as his own.

Yahweh's original home was in the south.[4] His name, with its Arabic flavor, points to some forgotten migration from the farther south which brought him to the Negeb. There the tribe of Judah met him and was bound to him by bonds never to be broken. This tribe had a reputation for strength and aggressiveness.

Your brothers shall praise you, O Judah;
With your hand on the necks of your foes,
Your father's sons shall bow down to you.
A lion's whelp is Judah.[5]

Under the leadership of Judah the other tribes of the south
were united—Kenites, Simeonites, Calebites and Jeremeelites.
As his people grew in number and strength, the power and
importance of Yahweh were enlarged. It was with one of these
groups—the Kenites—that Moses found refuge in his flight
from Egypt. Brooding in discouragement over the plight of
his people, he saw the vision which convinced him that Yahweh could deliver his fellow tribesmen from their Egyptian
bondage. Moses' clansmen, the rescued Levites, became ardent
devotees and later priests of Yahweh. The Kenite, Jethro, probably expressed the conviction of all the tribes gathered to celebrate the return of Moses when he said, "Now I know that
Yahweh is greater than all other gods in that his power prevailed over them." [6]

Jethro's speech lights up the essential quality of Yahweh in
his early days. He was specialized from the beginning as a god
of power. In origin he was the storm, with wind, lightning
and thunder, the boisterous bringer of rain after heat and
drought. Storm-gods in some areas of the ancient world were
honored chiefly because they brought luxurious life to pasture
lands and growing crops, but very often they were transformed into gods of war. The mighty heavenly figure, with
awe-inspiring voice and terrible weapons, was an ideal leader
of armies. Yahweh must have been welcome in the Negeb as a
rain-giver but this phase of his nature was lost to sight in the
glorification of his strength and power. He was pictured as a
mountain-striding figure, appearing in fire and smoke, "his
lightning-bolts in his right hand," in whose presence the earth
trembled.

> O Yahweh when thou camest forth from Seir,
> When thou marchedst from the land of Edom,
> The earth quaked, the heavens also shook,
> The clouds, too, dripped water.
> The mountains rocked at the presence of Yahweh,
> At the presence of Yahweh, the God of Israel.[7]

The lightning was Yahweh's arrow, the thunder was his voice. He was El-Shaddai, the mountain god, exalted and mighty. By natural right he carried the titles "Man of War" and "God of Hosts." The fighting spirit of the tribe of Judah was reflected in Yahweh and reinforced by him. The southern tribes never forgot his victory over the Egyptians. He was their defender and deliverer, the terrible destroyer of their foes. In times of need, they could confidently cry to him,

> Arise, O Yahweh, that thy foes may be scattered,
> That those who hate thee may flee before thee.[8]

Time after time he came rushing from the cloud-gathering mountains of the south as a Storm-god to overwhelm their enemies with the torrential rain, hail, thunder and lightning. He had no rival in the art of war, nor as a ruthless destroyer of those who stood in the path of his people.

Yahweh began his march toward the mastery of Palestine early in the twelfth century. The federation of Judean tribes, inspired by Moses, moved northward to claim the land lying between the Negeb and the holdings of the tribes of Israel. Although these northern clans were old settlers and possessed an extensive territory, they were still ringed around with enemies. Many cultural and religious experiences separated them from the Judeans, but the two groups were drawn into an alliance by a common interest—the need for security and the desire to conquer the cities, fertile valleys and coastal plains still beyond their control. In that enterprise, the War-god of Judah played a central rôle.

Yahweh was an ideal divine leader for a people so long involved in warfare for the possession of their homeland. He met their need of a champion able to cut a path through hostile forces and to defend them against attack. They knew him as a god of ruthless power, terrible in his anger. He ruled his people with a firm hand and shared their attitudes toward the enemy. Within the clan he stood behind the social mores, and justice was administered in his name. He approved the tribal code which permitted deceit and dishonesty in dealing with the foe. To his loyal followers he was a friend to be trusted—and feared. His own southern people had had long experience and ample assurance of his kindly care. He was often angry with them, yet he loved them and could be depended upon to guard them jealously. Unlike so many gods of the early world, easily won to benevolence by priestly cunning, Yahweh kept a quality of reserve and sternness even toward his own, yet, at times, he could be persuaded to change his mind or stay his punishments by the plea of a favorite or by a pleasing offering. His ways were often unaccountable. Evil and good alike came from his hand. Vows, however rash, made to him had to be kept, regardless of the price in human suffering. The dark spirit that tortured Saul was his messenger. His holiness was fatal to Uzzah who touched the Ark, although the motive behind the act was entirely blameless. Saul broke faith with the Gibeonites, and the people of David's time atoned for the wrong in the anguish of three years of famine. In a burst of anger against Israel, he moved David to take a census of the people and then punished his obedience by sending three days of pestilence. Seventy thousand men died before Yahweh repented of the evil he had done.

The seers, who were his interpreters, found in these calamities signs of the god, austere and irresistible in power, who so often had come thundering from his dwelling place on the mountain heights to the help of Israel against her enemies. There was

comfort and security under the protecting leadership of a god
of awe-inspiring power. As an efficient War-god he dealt in
death and destruction. Such a champion could arouse courage,
confidence and loyalty in the hearts of those who fought under
his standard. Terror walked before him. The battle-hardened
Philistines were not afraid of Israel but the presence of Yahweh
on the field made them tremble.

> Their gods have come to them to the camp. . . . Alas for us!
> Who shall deliver us from the power of these majestic gods?
> These are the gods who struck down the Egyptians. . . .[9]

To men hedged about by hostility a god of power was essential. Yahweh justified his early reputation when David led his
people through stormy and war-scarred years to victory and
peace.

When Judah ruled all Palestine, Yahweh was enthroned as
Lord of the land. The local fertility figures were not disturbed
but the old high gods of heaven and storm were either merged
in him or thrust into the background. The northern tribes
learned to recognize in Yahweh the same God their fathers
had known under other names. Among the many deities, none
could compare in power and glory with the heavenly sovereign
of the united kingdom.

> Give unto Yahweh, ye gods,
> Give unto him glory and praise;
> Give unto Yahweh the glory due his name,
> Worship Yahweh in holy array.
>
> The voice of Yahweh peals across the waters——
> It is the God of glory thundering,
> Yahweh thundering over the mighty waters.
> The thunder of Yahweh is overpowering,
> The thunder of Yahweh is full of majesty,
> The thunder of Yahweh crashes down the cedars,

Yea, Yahweh crashes down the cedars of Lebanon,
Making Lebanon leap like a calf,
And Siryon like a wild ox.

The thunder of Yahweh hurls fiery bolts,
The thunder of Yahweh makes the desert tremble,
Yahweh makes the Desert of Kadesh tremble;
The thunder of Yahweh splits the oaks,
And strips the forest bare:
In his temple everything calls out, Glory!
Yahweh sits enthroned over the flood,
He is enthroned as King forever.[10]

On the field of battle, the supremacy of Yahweh was never
doubted. The first serious challenge to his status came when
his people began to learn and love the arts of peace. The
northern tribes had long ago learned from their Canaanite
neighbors that good crops and prosperity depended upon the
performance of the proper seasonal ceremonies; that the local
gods of the land, the Ba'alim, were the generous givers of the
goods of life for tillers of the soil. These deities were specialists
in agricultural fertility. Yahweh had no experience in farming. His glory had been won in the hard, rough life of the
desert days and the stormy years of strife. Thus he faced the
test of practical usefulness under changed conditions. The
attractiveness of the new culture and the growing desires of
the people weighted the scales on the side of the Ba'alim. In
such a battle for supremacy the god of the conquering people
must assume the duties of the native deities and so displace
them, or await a slow death from a disease always fatal to a
god—uselessness—as his people are captured by the gods of
the land who minister to the new cultural interests.

The early prophets played an important part in determining
the outcome of the divine conflict in Palestine. They were
fiercely loyal to Yahweh and represented him as hostile to all

rivals. With their voices echoing in the countryside there was
no danger that Israel would be allowed to forget him. At the
same time, the prophets slowed up the process of assimilation
of Yahweh to the culture of the land. They set their faces
against the new civilization and demanded devotion to the
simpler ideals of the nomadic life. They were supported by
groups like the Rechabites who remained stubbornly opposed
to settled agricultural living. Most of the people, however,
followed their practical interests and fell into the year rhythm
of farming folk with the seasonal ceremonies addressed to fertility gods. Thus they were compelled to combine two loyalties
—a recognition of Yahweh, their powerful champion in battle,
and a devotion to the Ba'alim as the source of immediate values.
The agricultural rites were accepted as necessary to guarantee
fertility and material wealth, yet at no time was there any
hesitation in acknowledging Yahweh as peculiarly Israel's God,
supreme in affairs of state, their leader and defender in all relations with other peoples.

In making use of the services of other gods who were better
qualified than he to meet their new needs, the people were
not conscious of any disloyalty to Yahweh. They had been
accustomed from of old to a plurality of deities. Yahweh was
now recognized as the owner of the land of Palestine, but he
was not yet intolerant of other, lesser gods. The *teraphim*,
images of the family or household divinities, were cherished in
the homes. The people were familiar with graven and molten
images of many gods in all the centers of worship, even in
connection with the cult of Yahweh. Solomon had built sanctuaries for the foreign deities, Chemosh and Melek. The menace
of the fertility gods, former owners of the land, did not seem
serious. In spite of the propaganda of the protesting prophets,
Yahweh was learning the arts of agricultural life and taking on
the pattern of the new culture. He was slowly replacing the
local gods and assuming their powers. Titles, like Ba'al and

Melek, belonging to them, were applied to him. Many of the
local sanctuaries of the Ba'alim passed into his possession. Even
the bull cult of the oldest tribe of the north was passing into
the control of Yahweh. By a natural process of assimilation he
was assuming responsibility for agricultural prosperity and
crowding out his rivals when political disaster checked his triumph in the north.

The rebellion of Jeroboam in the tenth century split the
northern tribes apart from the house of Judah. Saul had broken
his heart trying to weld these two peoples into one. After the
brief span of a hundred years, under David and his illustrious
son, they were willing to meet the future on different paths.
Jeroboam made the separation thorough. Not only did he break
the ties which bound the Israelites of the north to the throne
of David and Solomon, he led them back to their old religion,
away from the temple and Yahweh. The Levites who were in
the north were forced to go back to Judah and Jerusalem because Jeroboam refused to let them remain as priests of Yahweh in his domain.[11] He set up golden bulls at Dan and Bethel
and in this form restored the god of fertility Israel had known
for centuries. The old gods apparently came back to power
and Yahweh seemed to be forgotten. In reality conditions were
not as dark as they appeared to be. A gloomy prophet of a later
generation, lamenting his loneliness, could be assured that there
were thousands of loyal Yahweh devotees who had never
bowed the knee to Ba'al. The rebellion of Jeroboam was only a
temporary reverse for Yahweh, not a final defeat. Judah remained faithful. The prophets assumed the task of winning
Israel back to their God.

Elijah, early in the ninth century, was the most spectacular
champion of Yahweh's right to the northern kingdom. On two
major issues he daringly defied the ruling monarch in the name
of his God, careless of the sovereign's threats to his personal
safety. Although the scripture writers heaped abuse upon his

name, King Ahab was certainly friendly to Yahweh in the same manner that he recognized the value of the local gods and, as a wise statesman, made alliances with the gods of other nations. He was especially considerate of the Ba'al of Tyre, the god of his wife's people. Hundreds of official seers approved of his political wisdom but the spokesman of Yahweh was irreconcilable. When drought threatened the land with famine, Elijah made a dramatic challenge to the Ba'alim to match their might against the power of Yahweh, won a victory over the priests of Ba'al and vindicated the superiority of his God as a rain and fertility giver.

Not only was Yahweh jealous for his own status, but he was also unable to forgive a king's autocratic infringement of democratic rights. When Ahab, aided by his scheming queen, Jezebel, ruthlessly removed the owner of a coveted vineyard to increase the royal holdings, the voice of Elijah thundered disapproval. In this social crisis, involving injustice and a violation of the accepted mores of Israel, the resentment against Jezebel and her foreign Ba'al burst into flaming rebellion. The treacherous Jehu, driving to power through rivers of blood in his revolt against the family of Ahab, was able to enlist the Rechabites and the prophetic champions of Yahweh in support of his designs, because he identified his program with the warfare of Yahweh against the Ba'alim. Elisha's messenger anointed him for his blood-drenched campaign. Rebellion, deceit and slaughter were as nothing when weighed against the victory of Yahweh over the older, rival deities.

As the generations passed, the embattled prophets established their God as the supreme Ba'al of the land of Palestine. Gradually he assumed all the functions of the local fertility figures, adding the farming cults to his own. Yet Yahweh, as the conservatives knew him, was too austere to be associated with some of the essential, sensual rites of the new cult. Consequently the lure of the local deities long remained to trouble the peace of the prophets. When Yahweh condescended to take up the burden of farming, drove the Ba'alim from their altars and became himself the source of fertility, wealth and prosperity in the land, he gained unquestioned right to supremacy not only because of his victorious power, long known to Israel, but also because of his effective usefulness in their new cultural life. The first great test of adjustment and growth was successfully passed. Other gods had their recognized places in the sun, but from this time onward no god was able to match his might in Palestine nor, without his permission, to touch the tablets of destiny of his people. Yahweh ruled as Lord of the dual kingdoms of Israel and Judah.

After the destructive storm of Jehu's rebellion had passed, several generations of peace and prosperity permitted both Israel and Judah to test the social worth of their new civilization. The prophets, who kept their love for the simpler, democratic life of the past, saw their worst fears fulfilled. With the increase of wealth came sordid evils of social maladjustment—injustice, oppression of the poor, exploitation of the lowlier classes by officials and aristocrats. Love of luxury weakened the moral fibre of the wealthy, love of money led to corruption of the courts, perversion of justice and cruel indifference to the suffering of the dispossessed. The rich grew richer and the poor sank ever more deeply into wretchedness and frustration. Worst of all, the privileged classes attributed their wealth and prosperity to the favor of Yahweh because they had been careful in the correct performance of all required rites and sacrifices. This was the philosophy beneath the fertility cults which the Israelites had learned from the farming folk who knew the ways of the gods of the land. As the giver of agricultural fertility and prosperity, Yahweh was in danger of being drawn completely into the pattern of the Ba'alim. The old deities still lingered in the countryside. In many places Yahweh was only a new name for old familiar friends of the farmers.

Cults which shocked the early prophets continued, but under the new leadership of Israel's God. Although the official records ignore it, in at least one locality Yahweh, like all the other fertility figures, seems to have been provided with a wife, Anath.[12] Under the pressure of the cultural climate, he was in danger of being firmly bound to the soil of Palestine and reduced to the character of a local Ba'al whose favor was witnessed by his bounty and who could be managed by sacrificial technique.

Yahweh was rescued from this drift into oblivion by the great prophets of the eighth and seventh centuries.[13] Heirs of the wandering bands of Yahweh's spokesmen of earlier times, these men had a wide outlook and deep religious vision developed by the growth of the nation and the broadening of political horizons. Inspired individually to take up the prophetic task by the call of God, they were not bound by institutional traditions nor the conventions of the established priesthood. The prestige of their divine calling gave them access to the court and the private councils of the rulers. Since their burning words carried the authority of the will of Yahweh, even kings dared not challenge their freedom of speech.

These bold idealists were men immersed in the practical problems of the day. They watched the increase of injustice in social life, remembering Yahweh's relationship to the democratic tribal ideals of an earlier age. Jealousy for the God as they knew him burned like a flame in their souls. They could not close their hearts to the cry of the shepherdless poor at home, nor their eyes to the danger which threatened from beyond the border. The exploitation of the small land holders, the oppression of the poor, the arrogance and luxurious living of the rich, the smug complacency of the official classes in the presence of impending national disaster, moved them to passionate protest. The anger and anguish of the dispossessed flowed into eloquent words of warning, reinforced by the confident formula—

"Thus saith Yahweh." While the ruling classes in Israel basked in the warmth of prosperity, the prophets were aware of the oncoming shadow of doom behind which moved the irresistible might of Assyria. Wrestling with these issues, they transformed their God.

They stripped away all the entanglements of sacrificial ritualism woven around him by the Ba'al cults. In forthright words Yahweh spoke through Amos——

> I hate, I spurn your feasts,
> And I take no pleasure in your festal gatherings.
> Even though you offer me burnt-offerings,
> And your cereal-offerings, I will not accept them;
> And the thank-offerings of your fatted beasts I will not look upon.
> Take away from me the noise of your songs,
> And to the melody of your lyres I will not listen.
> But let justice roll down like waters,
> And righteousness like a perennial stream.[14]

The prophets could not but believe that Yahweh was concerned with justice, not sacrifice, with righteousness rather than ritual. They identified his will with the needful social ideals. He became a just and righteous God. In his name they hurled their condemnation against the licentious rich who sold the innocent for silver, and the needy for a pair of shoes; who trampled upon the heads of the poor and thrust aside the humble from the way; who crowded the lowly householder from his ancestral acres, and bribed judges in their own interests. The officials were so very careful in the performance of cult duty that they travelled from Dan to Beersheba lest some ceremony might be slighted. For the Ba'alim such service was essential; for Yahweh it was mere futility, since he desired mercy, not sacrifice, a listening heart not the fat of rams.

> With what shall I come before Yahweh,
> And bow myself before God most high?

Shall I come before him with burnt offerings,
With calves a year old?
Will Yahweh be pleased with thousands of rams,
With myriads of streams of oil?
Shall I give my first-born for my transgression,
The fruit of my body for the sin of my soul?
You have been told, O man, what is good,
And what Yahweh requires of you:
Only to do justice, and to love kindness,
And to walk humbly with your God.[15]

He sought only social values, actualized. The prophets made his meaning plain:

Cease to do evil, learn to do good;
Seek justice, restrain the oppressor:
Uphold the rights of the orphan, defend the cause of the widow! [16]

This was a very different Yahweh from the God of ruthless might whom the early prophets knew and again different from the fertility figures, lulled to social insensibility by the sensuous, sacrificial spells. The lightning of his fierce anger flamed against social evils. He was still a God of terrible power but also the embodiment of the moral attributes of the noblest, human ideal. Many gods of old were lost when, in similar social crises, they could not grow to the needful moral heights. They had no prophets so they died.

Even all Yahweh's splendid achievement of moral grandeur would not have been enough to save him, amid the storms of the following centuries, if his wise seers had not found a way to break the bonds which fettered him to the land of Palestine. Overwhelmed in the wars of empire, scores of gods have met their doom. Some of them are remembered still because their names are recorded on documents that have outlived them; others are gone, to be forever forgotten unless by chance the spade of the excavator turns up their names in some old

ruin. A god who loses his land and his people fades slowly from
the memory of men. Yahweh faced this threat for the first
time when the northern kingdom vanished from history in
721 B.C.

During the eighth century the prophets of Israel had
watched with apprehension the growing threat of Assyrian
power. They saw no escape from disaster, but they had a burning faith in Yahweh. If doom came to the people it could not
be through any weakness of their God but because they had
violated their trust, broken their covenant, turned away from
him to follow the false philosophy of fertility; because the
masters of Israel had turned their faces against the poor and the
land groaned under the burden of social evils.

> Israel is a spreading vine;
> His fruit renders him confident;
> The more his fruit increased,
> The more altars he made;
> The more prosperous his land became,
> The finer did he make his sacred pillars.
> Their heart is false; soon must they atone;
> Their altars shall be desecrated,
> And their sacred pillars destroyed.[17]

Therefore the long-awaited "Day of Yahweh" was to be a day
of darkness and desolation, not of gladness and light. The
harbingers of doom, the bearers of punishment were the peoples of foreign gods.

> O Assyria, rod of my anger,
> And staff of my fury!
> Against a godless nation I send him,
> And against the people of my wrath I charge him,
> To despoil them, and prey on them,
> And to trample them down like mire of the streets.[18]

Long and patiently Yahweh had pleaded for repentance and warned of the destruction to come—all to no avail. The King of Assyria flaunted his might as he marched to deal the death blow to Israel, but the prophets knew that Yahweh was commanding him, using him as the instrument of his purpose. Thus an unconquerable faith, interpreting an historic tragedy, lifted Yahweh to a position of authority on the world stage and gave him status above foreign gods, even while they were trampling upon his own people.

Instead of destroying Yahweh's prestige, the loss of the northern kingdom served rather to magnify his power and moral grandeur. At the same time it broke the first link of his bondage to the land.[19] As the first Isaiah contemplated the doom of Israel he dared to hope that whatever might befall the nation, Yahweh would always cherish the pious, non-political community of faithful ones. When, a century and a half later, Judah fell before the destructive might of Babylon, the pattern of faith, which had saved Yahweh in the earlier crisis, gave him complete emancipation from limitations to the boundaries of a political state. In this achievement the faith of the prophets was supported by other factors in Israel's experience. Yahweh had dwelt outside Palestine before he adopted them as his people. Long after the settlement in Canaan, he was consulted at his holy mountain in the south land. He had worshippers in other lands, and Elijah assumed that he had power in Syria. After 933 B.C., when Judah and Israel were separate and often at war, Yahweh, who claimed authority over both, transcended political boundaries. Moreover, he was the God of a people before he became the God of Canaan. When he rose in moral splendor above the ruins of his last earthly kingdom, he was prepared, as the God of a people, to begin his career as a God of the world.

From the beginning Israel had known Yahweh as a God of power. His might was magnified when he strode onto the international stage. Always jealous of his people he had never willingly shared their devotion with any foreign god. The legend of Moses on Sinai dramatized his sanction of the moral law. Sole master of Israel's destiny, righteous and powerful, he had been willing to let the tides of destruction overwhelm his experiment in nation building rather than tolerate desertion to other gods or disloyalty to human values. He loved his people and punished them. After this age of suffering, Israel never doubted that Yahweh was holy and righteous, a jealous guardian of the moral law.

The brief period of the Exile and the three centuries that followed were a time of severe testing for the people of Israel. The thread of their unity was unravelled into separate strands. Only a fraction of the population followed their conquerors unwillingly to Babylon. The larger part remained in the home land. Some fled to Egypt. From Palestine, toward all points of the compass, paths were luring ever larger numbers of Jews to the Mediterranean cities, to farther Europe, through the Near East on to the far-off Orient. Israel and Yahweh had already begun their cosmopolitan career.

The new conditions worked a significant change in Yahweh. He bowed to hear the cry of the lonely individual. When the enfoldment of national solidarity was stripped away from the people, and the temple with its great ceremonies was no more, the security which gathered everyone into a common destiny and responsibility was lost. Without the old familiar ways of communication with the august Yahweh whose concern had been not with individuals but with the ongoing nation, solitary souls were left to wander shepherdless. Ezekiel and Jeremiah met the need by lifting the common man to a place of personal responsibility to his God. While the wanderers sought consolation in glorious dreams, Yahweh took into his care the personal destinies of lowly folk.

During many generations, discouragement and hope alternated in the hearts of the faithful. The humiliation of the Exile was followed by a glowing enthusiasm when Cyrus seemed to be an agent of Israel's God. The great King, however, was no more favorable to the Jews than to his other subject peoples. Rejoicing at the return and the rebuilding of the temple ended in disillusionment, and the deep frustration of a conquered nation made restless by the memory of a splendid dream. The later Persian rulers were loyal to Ahura Mazda and little inclined to foster ambitions in the minds of the people of Yahweh. When Alexander the Great took the Jews under his protecting power, Israel's hope flamed up again.

As in earlier centuries, a faithful group of daring dreamers brought Yahweh triumphantly through this time of changing fortunes. Among the Babylonian exiles and in Palestine there were seers who stubbornly refused to accept defeat. Tearful lamentations over their desolate lot served only as a foil for their bold faith in the power of their God to save. Faith flowered out of frustration. To their unconquered spirits a "must be" seemed truer and more real than an "is." Although his nation was in servitude, Yahweh must be the greatest of the gods and he must be able to guarantee a future for Israel so glorious that all other deities would become mere nothings before him. The threat of other gods was very real. Yahweh had rivals not only in the great heaven gods, Zeus and Ahura Mazda, but also in the lesser local deities so comforting to the common man. Many in the Exile were captured by the glamorous gods of Babylon. The Jews who wandered to Egypt yielded to the ways of the land, worshipped Yahweh but also gods and goddesses as his companions. In Palestine the people turned to the friendly figures of the countryside, some with names as old as history and some newcomers—Hadad, Moloch, Atargatis and the Goddess of Fortune.[20] In this atmosphere of discouragement and frustration the later prophets molded the character of Yahweh in its classical form.

All limitations fell away from him. He became the one and only God of heaven and earth. He spread out the heavens as a tent to dwell in, gave the stars their names and guided their wanderings. Before him all the princes of the earth were as nothing. He watched in eternal calm the wind-blown dust of human generations. All other gods were merely empty names, helpless idols, powerless and futile to help their suppliants, but they who call upon Yahweh

> Shall renew their strength,
> They shall put forth wings like eagles,
> They shall run and not be weary,
> They shall walk and not faint.[21]

In their exaltation of Yahweh the prophets of this period gave to western culture one of its basic beliefs—that a divine plan undergirds the universe, that a divine purpose runs through time. With the far-seeing eyes of hope they saw the will of Yahweh as the thread of meaning on which all the events of history were strung. At the end will be the ideal Kingdom of a restored Israel. Yahweh will then make bare his almighty arm in the eyes of all the nations. His people are now afflicted and despised but they need not fear. Yahweh's love for Israel is beyond all human love. If he causes the faithful ones to pass through the fires of affliction, it is only that as God's suffering servant, they may bear the world's woe and manifest the greatness, goodness and holiness of Yahweh to all the earth and so draw all mankind to Israel's God. When his purpose is fulfilled through the faithfulness of his people, the day of Yahweh will break in splendor on a startled world. Then all nature will smile upon man. Justice and peace will dwell on the earth. From east and west, north and south, Yahweh will call the wanderers home to Zion. There they may sit secure in the shade of vine and fig tree with no one to make them afraid ever again.

Yahweh thus became master of the world's destiny, sole God, all-powerful and wise, holding the fates of all nations in his hands but giving a special place in the cosmic plan to his chosen people.

The wise and mighty Yahweh, sole ruler of the universe, throned in the celestial heights, was not left lonely in his heavenly splendor. He was surrounded by a radiant company of angels. The seers of Israel knew of old these messengers of the divine will who appeared on earth in human form. When they were brought into contact with Babylonian and Persian mythologies and envisioned the imposing majesty of earthly courts, they delighted to picture in imagination the glory of Yahweh's heavenly palace, the lofty throne and his innumerable celestial ministers in their graded ranks. The angelic retinue numbered many millions. They were ethereal beings, not immaterial, but of a fiery substance, blazing like light. Death could not touch them. Only the fiat of God could snap the thread of their immortal existence. This heavenly host, surrounding the throne, executed the divine will in the world. They regulated the heavenly bodies and the rhythm of nature. An angel of princely rank ruled the sea. Rain, dew, frost, snow, hail, thunder and lightning were in angelic control. Nations had their ambassadors in Yahweh's court. In the work of providence, revelation and punishment, the angels mediated the divine decrees. The pen of the recording angel set down indelibly the deeds of mortals. Silently among his companions moved the dark angel of death. As was natural in royal courts, there was often rivalry, as angelic ministers strove to influence their royal master to favor and forgive their beloved nations and individuals. It was a glorious company who served about the celestial throne.[22] They were dear to the hearts of the men who created them. Yahweh was drawn into intimate contact with earthly affairs by these human-like angelic messengers. If they threatened the unity of the one God of Israel, they humanized his transcendent majesty and suffused his decrees with grace and glamour.

After the almighty will of Yahweh, which controlled the course of world history, was extended to the care of every human life a problem emerged to threaten belief in his goodness and justice. Since the individual was directly responsible for his deeds it seemed reasonable that the wicked should suffer and that the good man should be the happy man. Life, however, presented a very different picture. The wicked were seen to flourish like the green bay tree while the man of virtue and moral integrity dragged out his days in pain and desolation. Job and his friends wrestled with this problem. The difficulty was more acute because the idea of resurrection had not yet emerged and it was not possible to justify the ways of Yahweh by balancing the scales in a better world to come. Satan was there, but he was not allowed to assume in full the rôle of his prototype, Ahriman, to relieve the good God from embarrassment. The answer dropped a veil of human humility between the secrets of the Almighty and the probing eyes of man's reason by asserting that Yahweh's knowledge was too high for human understanding. Since man cannot know he must trust. Faith, the good physician, furnished the medicine which gave surcease from pain and rest in glowing dreams. Many another god besides Yahweh has been rescued from the unsolved problem of evil by acknowledgement of man's ignorance and the wedding of resignation to hope.

When the stimulating atmosphere of Greek thought spread over the Near East, Yahweh faced the danger that has confronted the gods of all cultures when they have fallen into the hands of the philosophers. Unlike so many others he refused to be reduced to an abstraction. The practical sense of his people kept him vitally bound to a purposive, ongoing, historic process of which the goal was still unrealized. No timeless, ineffable abstraction could meet the needs of Israel's hope. Yet there was real danger, for a time, of a radical transformation of his nature which would have removed him from immediate contact with the human scene to a transcendent realm, shrouded in mystery, impenetrable by the power of man. The Palestinian and Alexandrian Apocrypha, the Septuagint translation of the scriptures and the Wisdom literature all toned down or eliminated the early vigorous imagery which pictured Yahweh with human form and qualities. Thought began to strip him of attributes, and to open a vast distance between him and lowly man. As the one transcendent being, dwelling in solitary splendor, responsible to himself alone, his essence never perfectly knowable, Yahweh was moving toward the formless realm of no return, but his anchorage in history would not let him go. That he was one and transcendent no one longer doubted, but he was also king of the heavens, creator, ruler and righteous judge, everywhere present, all wise, touching the earth by his providence in justice, mercy, loving kindness, long suffering and the forgiveness of sins. He was the Lord of heaven but he was at the same time the Father of his children.

The personal name, Yahweh, acquired a sanctity, a sacred power, so that only specially qualified individuals were permitted to pronounce it.[23] In reading the scriptures, Adonai, "Lord," was substituted for the sacred name. It was avoided in speech by the use of such expressions as God, the Almighty, the Most High, or the Holy One.

During the Hellenistic period, men of simple faith clung to the Yahweh of tradition with all his human qualities and his love for Israel, while the intellectuals continued to stress his ineffable transcendence and to tone down his meaningful attributes. When they had placed him on heights only attainable by pure thought, it was necessary to introduce a mediator. This service was performed by Wisdom, paralleling the Greek idea of the Logos. The Wisdom of God was no mere angel but the spirit of Yahweh himself, his companion in creation, the assessor at his throne, who brought God's personal presence into intimate relation with all the events of time. Thus the world was warmed by the radiant nearness of divine Wisdom, linking the earth and the awful, transcendent God. Although this mediating power was personal and in some manner distinct from God, the unity of Yahweh was so fiercely defended in Israel that there was never any danger of his falling into the Hellenistic or Christian pattern, with two persons in the one godhead.

What might have happened if Yahweh had been exposed to the full impact of Greek philosophy is illustrated by the picture of him presented by a devout Jew who was also immersed in the heritage of Athens. Philo of Alexandria was the first Jewish thinker to feel that the existence of God needed to be proved. For Philo the philosopher, God was the first cause, a self-determining mind, his essence forever beyond human understanding. He was without qualities, beyond all the conditions of space and time, incorporeal and transcendent. For Philo the Jew, Yahweh possessed all the attributes his Jewish heritage demanded—benevolence, perfection, omnipresent providential care, omniscience and goodness. Between the ultimately unknowable God and the world, he placed mediating divine powers who shared the mystery and wisdom of the Lord. Chief of these powers was the Logos, unbegotten, eternal Son of God, second in the divine hierarchy. If Judaism had followed the lead of Philo there would have been little to differentiate Yahweh from the God of the early Christians, but Israel's God remained safely guarded in the memory and hopes of his people. The first baptism in Greek thought touched him only lightly.

The needs of Israel demanded a purposeful God, concerned with the events of history, shepherding his chosen people through the insecurity and dangers of disappointing centuries. After the disillusion of the return to Palestine, the suffering and indignity of the period of Hellenization, the flickering out of the Maccabean hope, Yahweh's people searched the horizon, anxious for signs of the coming of his long-promised kingdom. If the flame of life-hunger had died in their hearts, their God might have become one of the company of vague, amorphous beings, without qualities, removed in quiescent perfection far from the troubled world of unfulfilled desires. Instead, he was clothed by practical religion with all the attributes useful and necessary for the realization of Israel's ideal.

It was not a philosopher's God in whose service Jesus of Nazareth lived and died. For him, as for the wise, teaching rabbis of the age, the Lord was a just and kindly Father of his earthly children, near at hand, watching over them with infinite tenderness. He was on the side of the poor and the oppressed. To the meek and lowly sufferers in a world of injustice he was friend and comforter. Holy and righteous, he welcomed with glad forgiveness all wandering ones who turned to him. To the faithful he held out the promise of a share in the coming kingdom of righteousness with all the joys of a happy earthly life. The heart hunger of a people found expression in this vision of Yahweh. Under the shelter of his love and power, they could wait patiently until hope flowered into perfect fulfillment.

But the waiting was long and the ways of the world were often cruel. Meanwhile, the chosen people found dignity, consolation and security in the sheltering protection of the Torah, the law of life by which they strove to be holy, even as God was holy. The Torah was supremely precious. It was preexistent, the daughter of the Lord, embodying the plan of the world. As the rabbis wove the vast web of the Talmud, elaborating, thread by thread, the pattern of the divine plan, Yahweh emerged from their meditations as a purposeful, personal being, wisely directing the flow of earthly events. Nothing escaped his knowledge. His providence extended everywhere

with the watchful care of a loving Father for his children. He
was not only the God of a nation; "I am Yahweh thy God"
meant that he was the God of every individual, man, woman
and child. He was the helper of the weak and suffering, healer
of the sick, liberator of captives, restorer of the dead. He
tempered justice with mercy in the forgiveness of sin. Like a
blanket of sunshine, his love and grace enfolded his people,
Israel. His all-seeing eye was upon them as he marshalled mankind toward his far-off goal.

Although they insisted upon the incorporeality of the Lord,
the rabbis often made him delightfully human and like themselves. He weeps every day. Every day he is angry, but only
for a fraction of a second. He prays to himself——

May it please me that my mercy may overcome my anger, that all
my attributes may be invested with compassion and that I may deal
with my children in the attribute of kindness and that out of regard
for them I may pass by judgement.[24]

During the first three hours of the day he studies the Torah——

The next three hours he judges the whole world and seeing that
it is liable to be destroyed, he rises from the chair of judgement and
sits down on the chair of mercy. The third three hours he supports
the whole world with food from the very largest creature to the
smallest one. And the last three hours he plays with Leviathan.[25]

Since disaster had fallen on Israel some felt that Yahweh would
not feel playful and so filled his last three hours with the task
of teaching the Torah to children. The Holy One of the
Talmud stooped to many human frailties. He defended himself against the charge of the nations that he had a father's
partiality toward Israel. He regretted creating certain things.
There could be no better evidence than these supposed lapses
of the great teachers, that the Lord was for them a real person, a lovable and effective God. When they were self-conscious

under the eye of philosophy, Yahweh became the transcendent ONE, holy, mighty, great and fearful, far beyond capture in the net of human attributes. As practical men, wrestling with the problems of living, they thrust through the veil of metaphysics into the presence of a personal God, whose wise and beneficent will ran through the world and whose love made pain and evil the servants of his purpose.

During the Middle Ages, Yahweh came face to face in rivalry with the God of Christianity and Allah of Islam. Neither of these deities offered a serious challenge to the Lord of Israel. Through the cultural enfoldment of the law and the antagonism of the other groups his people were doubly bound to him in devotion. Their dependence upon his protective care and their firm loyalty jealously guarded his status as the supreme, personal ruler of the world. But from this time onward, Yahweh was compelled to meet the menace of critical philosophic thought which, in all cultures, has reduced the gods to pale ghosts of their former selves. The first shock came through contact with the thought of the resurrected Greeks. In an earlier age, Yahweh had successfully evaded the danger because the contact with the superficial Hellenism in Palestine had served only to stimulate deeper devotion to the nobler ideals of Israel, and in Alexandria the great Philo had yielded nothing of his loyalty to Judaism in reconciling the truth of the Greeks with his own. Moreover, the main line of march of Yahweh's people turned aside from the climate of Hellenism. In medieval Europe, however, each of the three great rival religions was anxiously striving to prove its worth at the bar of reason. The ancient God of Israel was a magnificent person, exalted in heavenly splendor, familiar to the lowliest in his garment of attributes, drawn by the language of hope and affection into intimate contact with the homely, human problems of the folk life. As the living God of the masses, Yahweh was as real and knowable as Moses and the great sages through whom his will had been revealed. When the pervasive influence of the thought of ancient Greece spread around the Mediterranean, Jewish scholars began to be embarrassed by the robust deity so vividly portrayed in their tradition.

If the Jews had arrived at their idea of the one, transcendent God by a process of intellectual exercise in quest of a first cause, Yahweh would have been immediately reduced to an abstraction. But he was the efficient God of a people long before he acquired the function of creator and first cause of the world. He had achieved his character in the slow, historic development of Israel's hope. He was too intimately related to the desires and dreams of his people to be easily uprooted from the earthly scene. They knew him as an ever-present providence, champion of the social values of a human ideal. The perfect goal of their troubled pilgrimage through time was identified with the fulfillment of the divine will in history. The faithful who suffered and toiled for the glory of the world to come found their support and guarantee in him. The figure of Yahweh, clothed in the warm and colorful robes of rabbinical lore, refused to yield to the ethereal ideas of Greek philosophy. He was so inextricably enmeshed in Israel's will to live and to enjoy that even the intellectuals could not banish him to the rarefied realm of lost gods sacrificed on the altar of pure thought.

Thinkers followed the current mode of proving his existence which few had even thought to question. Maimonides, most brilliant intellect of them all, yielded to the fashion and stripped away all the positive attributes of the historic deity.[26] When reason had transformed his God into an unknowable essence of which neither unity nor existence could be affirmatively asserted, Maimonides allowed his heart to betray his head. The Lord continued to be, for him as for Israel of old, the creator and active ruler of the universe, whose will gave meaning to the events of time. In spite of the denial of attributes, he continued to pray to a personal God of wisdom and power who sorrowed in Israel's affliction and rejoiced in the happiness of his people. The fate of Israel was too precious and the conflicts of life too real to permit the retirement of Yahweh from active participation in the direction of human destiny.

Jewish Neo-Platonists, like the Aristotelians, had the intellectual hardihood to remove God in his essential being beyond the boundaries of human knowledge. To bridge the gulf thus artificially created they introduced the ladder of emanations. Both head and heart were satisfied since all that the Lord meant practically was retained in the mystical glow of the divine presence as the individual aspired toward the unknown. No god anywhere was so firmly bound to the task of carrying the burden of human needs and hopes as the deity of the mystical dreamers of the Kabbala. Yet they defined him intellectually as the Absolute, without attributes, will, intention, thought, word or deed, the unchanging ONE. Yahweh continued to be the religiously efficacious God of the fathers, although shrouded in the many veils of speculative drapery.

The mystical vision of Yahweh reached its culmination in the seventeenth century Hasidism. A wave of pietism, breaking through the restraining barriers of formal theology and cold legalism was sweeping over Europe. Both Christians and Jews were heart-hungry for security in the immediate presence of God. The rabbis had long ago developed the idea of divine immanence, but always on the background of transcendence. Baal Shem drew God completely within the cosmic process and made creation the continuous, ongoing manifestation of the divine existence. All nature and human life became radiant with the presence of God to the eyes of faith. Nature danced with joy. The observance of the law became a means of embodying the divine. Enfolded in the all-pervasive being of God, the individual could drop the shackels of formalism, laugh at care and tribulation, to find the safe refuge of the soul in the ineffable bliss of union with God. As Yahweh had stubbornly resisted being transformed into a formless First Cause by the philosophers, so now he refused to be submerged in the rosy colored mists of mystical emotion. The hosts of Israel saw him still as the transcendent, personal God, weaving on the loom of time the pattern of his wise and beneficent purpose.

Yahweh was only lightly touched by the chilly atmosphere of the mathematico-physical philosophies of the eighteenth century. But he bent graciously to the later thinkers who saw the divine presence moving through eons of evolution toward the realization of the ideal of humanity in a perfected society.

With the turn of the century and the spread of the Haskalah influence, Yahweh was suffused in the climate of a new world so enervating to all the ancient gods. The reduction of the age-old dualism left no supernatural, supernal realm in which purely spiritual beings might dwell. The effort to prove his existence was abandoned. The task of defending him from the well-stored armory of rabbinical learning was surrendered. Yet men needed him as much as ever in the maze of a swiftly changing world. To the manifold groups of the people of Israel, caught in the net of new problems, intellectual and social, Yahweh appeared in different forms. For those who dwelt in cultures still untroubled by the ferment of novelty and still tormented by Israel's ancient sorrow he was, as of old, the powerful guardian of a people's hope, a consoling providence and a Father in heaven. For those who went out eagerly to meet the new world in the sunlight of emancipation, he dropped the burdens of a special people, removed the marks that made him peculiarly Israel's God and became practically assimilated to the modernized, socialized God of Christianity. Between Yahweh detached from the cultural heritage of Judaism, and the Christian God freed from metaphysical trappings, there is only a verbal difference.[27]

Through all his life and all the vicissitudes of philosophic weather, Yahweh has stood for the noblest human values, a social ideal of perfected human happiness. Modern thinkers, intensely loyal to Judaism, who have lost the naïve faith of Israel's childhood and surrendered the metaphysical quest, feel the presence of their God in the moral ideals which lure mankind to ever nobler living. Yahweh is presented as the symbol of the soul of a people or the ground of the steady moral movement toward the ideal in the cosmic human process [28] or the symbol of the highest ideals for which men strive, the power that endorses what they believe ought to be and guarantees that it will be.[29]

The God of Israel has passed through many changes since that far-off time when a helpful phase of the upper heavens was emotionally charged with human qualities and personalized by the language of trust and hope. Into his developing personality were crowded all the rich experiences of a people. Through the centuries, the many attributes of his being were added as necessary for the solution of problems, the anchorage of hope, the sanction of social ideals, the guarantee of salvation. Thus he attained majestic proportions as the one, powerful, wise, good God of the universe, whose hand had molded all nature into beauty and order and was writing in deeds the epic of the human ages with Israel as the hero, in whose glorious future triumph all mankind will share.

Still, for the unquestioning multitude, Yahweh sits enthroned beyond the obscuring shadows of earthly existence, a comforting, loving presence, whose providence smooths the path of privation and pain, whose will gathers all the tangled threads of time into a meaningful pattern, who will, at last, actualize the dream of happiness in a kingdom of justice, brotherhood and peace. For many thoughtful men, however, who view the long vista of human history from the mountain heights of modern knowledge, Yahweh has become as nebulous as the lost gods who died when he was young. Robbed of his residence in the supernatural, relieved of his rôle as creator, divested of his human attributes, denied existence as a purposive person, he has become only a name, a symbol of an ideal hope—the hope that the universe will support man in the actualizing of his ideals.

Bearing the heavy responsibility for unfulfilled desires, he walked with his people through the frustrated ages to the dawn of today. Now, in the company of other great gods, he is transferring his burden to the reluctant shoulders of men. The time of divine tutelage is over for the children of earth. Yahweh may rest from his labors, to be remembered so long as man shall live, as the inspiring champion of Israel's hopes during the long centuries of a brave adventure in culture building.

CHAPTER X

THE CHRISTIAN GOD

I believe in God the Father Almighty,
    Maker of heaven and earth . . .
And in Jesus Christ his Son, our Lord . . .
And in the Holy Ghost.[1]

HE Mediterranean world is a graveyard of gods. Long before the records of history began, many generations of deities lived and died there. The spade of the modern excavator, probing deep into old ruins, reveals their long-forgotten names and tantalizing glimpses of their characters. When earlier culture builders yielded before the waves of hardier, hungrier folk, their gods too surrendered their sovereignty. But deities of culture do not die as men die. Their names may fade from memory but before they leave the stage they hand over their rôles to the gods who follow them. Behind the majestic figures of the Græco-Roman deities the eye of the historian may see the shadowy forms of the lost gods whose heirs they were.

When the early Christian missionaries began to preach the gospel of their Jewish Savior, the shores of the inland sea were the gathering place of a multitude of deities, embodying the cultural experiences of Egypt, Babylonia, Syria, Palestine, Asia Minor, Persia, Greece and Rome. In an atmosphere of tolerance and the interplay of cultures, the gods influenced each other in friendly rivalry. Each one held his place of honor for specific services rendered. The old deities of Greece and Rome were still active as patrons of cities, districts and families. Many hero gods who had proved their usefulness to man by cultural benefits were held in high esteem. Over the far-flung Roman Empire the majestic figure of the emperor towered like a god of order and peace. Everywhere in the Mediterranean area there were savior gods who had long outgrown their local origins as vegetation figures and assumed the rôle of redeemers from earthly tribulation and death. These deities had faced all the troubles that torment mankind and conquered them. They had gone down into the darkness of death and risen again, triumphant over man's last enemy. Consequently they could offer comfort, consolation and security to the lonely individual in this life and, beyond the grave, a blissful immortality.[2] In all the important cities, Yahweh of Israel was well known as a god of righteousness and power. Ahura Mazda of Iran stood on the eastern horizon, while Mithra, his Lord of Hosts, was following the Roman armies to all the borders of the Empire. Behind these many popular and personal gods, philosophers sought and found a principle of unity—an ultimate ONE, a first cause or an immanent divine logos.

The celestial population of spiritual beings was vividly real to men as time turned into the Christian era.[3] Even the skeptical Epicureans were willing to admit the reality of the gods—not those of the popular cults, but a celestial company exiled to an eternity of blissful quiescence in an interstellar heaven.

To this multitude of gods the early Christians added their Savior, the resurrected, heavenly Christ, associated with the jealous Yahweh of Israel. Neither they nor their gentile contemporaries realized that from their movement would emerge a new god to claim the lordship of the earth, before whose majesty all the elder, pagan deities would abandon their thrones, or linger in lowlier status to be christened as saints of the new religion.

Jesus had no thought of introducing a new god to the

world. He remained true to the God of his people Israel—the one, only Lord of heaven and earth, the all-wise, almighty creator and ruler of the world. He knew that as a supreme judge, Yahweh could be hard and severe, but at the same time kind and merciful. His forgiveness went out to meet the man who forgave his fellows and turned toward righteousness. All nature and all men were enfolded in his goodness and providence. His eye swept creation. Not a sparrow could fall to earth without his knowledge. He was not an absentee God, but a near-at-hand, personal presence, dealing directly with earthly affairs. His tender care was especially over those who were faithful to the ideal of the kingdom. He was a father ruling his household with authority; a generous master of his servants, but doing what he pleased with his own. His sovereign will, molding the centuries, gave security to the lowly lovers of righteousness patiently awaiting the coming of the Kingdom of God.

It was not the teaching of Jesus about God, but the teachings of Christians about Jesus that gave the Christian God the qualities which distinguished him from all the other gods of the Graeco-Roman world. Like Jesus himself, the early disciples and Jewish Christian churches recognized no God but Yahweh of Israel. If Christianity had remained within the boundaries of Judaism, interpreting Jesus as the Messiah whom God rescued from the realm of the dead, exalted to heaven and, on some fateful day, would send again in power to establish the perfect kingdom on earth, there would have been no need of a distinctive Christian God. But the new movement broke the boundaries of Judaism and won a spectacular triumph as a popular way of salvation in the gentile world.

When Paul carried the Gospel to the gentiles he did not dream of any threat of rivalry between his God and the Christ. For him, too, Yahweh was the one, almighty being,

creator and ruler of the whole world, a supreme and righteous judge whose will was absolute. Paul stressed, more than
Jesus did, the fatherhood and love of God. Christ, for him,
was a pre-existent, spiritual being, who came from heaven as
the Savior of mankind. He chose the neglected story of
Adam's fall as the starting point of his scheme of salvation. As
all mankind came under the power of sin and death by the
disobedience of the first man, so "through a man," the "last
Adam," Christ, "we have the raising of the dead." [4] Christ
was the son of the heavenly Father, and Christians who were
baptized and shared the Holy Spirit with him became also
sons of God. Paul did not call Jesus "God." [5] He was never
conscious of any disloyalty to Yahweh because of worship and
prayer devoted to Christ. The Savior was only one of the vast
celestial hierarchy around God's throne, especially endued
with the divine Spirit and commissioned with a special task.
After the completion of his world work he would deliver
the kingdom to God, that God might be all in all. It never
occurred to Paul that the exalted rank of the Savior of men
might require a new understanding of the ancient deity of
his people. Neither he nor his Jewish contemporaries could
have placed Jesus on an equality with God.

As the leadership of the churches passed from Jews to men
immersed in the religious ideas and patterns of Hellenistic
culture, the Messiah, Jesus, was advanced to the rank of deity.
Gentile Christians, attuned to the pervasive climate of polytheism, felt no hesitation in proclaiming as a new god their
Savior, Jesus Christ. The needs of salvation were fulfilled by
him. He had conquered sin and death and broken the bondage
of men to the demons. His resurrection linked him in function and prestige with the company of dying and rising gods
popular in the Mediterranean world. By the beginning of the
second century, Christ was worshipped as the real and efficient God of the Christian group. Belief in him as the divine

Lord and Savior was the only necessary test for entrance into the church.[6] The Fourth Gospel treated him as a god. Ignatius of Antioch repeatedly called him "The God." [7] In both east and west a brilliant galaxy of preachers and apologists—Justin, Tatian, Tertullian, Irenaeus, Origen—all professed that he was God.[8] Although the Christian Gnostics differed from other Christians in discarding the Old Testament and repudiating Yahweh, they were as devout and eager as any in proclaiming the true divinity of Jesus.

Christ was the healing, helping, serving deity of the new religion but, however exalted his divine rank might become, he could not be the sole God of the Christians. Not only had philosophy placed beyond all the personal savior gods an ultimate, unknown ONE, but in the cosmic background, bound to him by history, scripture and tradition, was the high, heaven God of the Jews. Thus the drift of a developing religion, blending the cultures of Greece and Israel, gave the Christians two gods. Of the two, Christ, the Savior, was more important for gentile Christians than Yahweh of Israel. It is probable that the lowly folk of the churches would have been quite content with the Lord Jesus Christ as an all-sufficient deity. Not only did the fact of his resurrection give them assurance of victory over death, as Paul had taught, but his incarnation touched human nature with divinity and guaranteed to all those united with him a divine immortality. It was enough for them that they had a divine Savior adequate to meet all the issues of life and to guarantee a happy hereafter.

> Thy pure image we worship,
> O good Lord, beseeching Thee,
> Pardon our failures.
> Christ, our God!
> Thou wast content in Thy good will
> To come in the flesh,

That thou mightest redeem those Thou hast made
From the bondage of the enemy.
Wherefore, thankfully we cry unto Thee,
Who fillest all with joy!
Our Savior, who didst appear
To save the world.[9]

At the same time they were not distressed by the inherited Yahweh, for among the many deities of the empire the addition of an extra divine being was not likely to trouble the common man. In the second century, however, Christianity attracted thinkers for whom the relationship of the two gods became a problem. Two interests were in conflict and neither of them could be surrendered. On the one hand, was the intellectual interest in monotheism, supported by Greek philosophy and the theological heritage of the Old Testament scriptures; on the other hand, was the desire for certainty of salvation, dependent upon the real deity of Christ. The Christian God took form under the necessity of preserving both interests.

There was a further difficulty in assigning the proper status to the Holy Spirit who, with Yahweh, was an inheritance from Judaism. His personality was not clearly defined but he was recognized as God's agent on earth before the coming of Christ and as the divine presence sent by Christ to dwell among men since his exaltation. In heaven, Christ was the son of the eternal Father, but on earth he was the son of the Holy Spirit by the Virgin Mary. Linked with the Father and Christ by ritual and scripture, the Holy Spirit was a logical candidate for the same divine rank.

The vague use of the terms "God," "Logos," "Spirit," might have avoided the differentiation of the divine functions into sharp personal distinctions. For thinkers of the Greek tradition the divine reason or Logos had served as a means of bridging the impassable chasm between the indefinable, transcendent God and the mundane scene of human life. When Christians identified Christ with the Logos, his career reached back into eternity as a mode of divine activity. Before all ages he was with the Father; at the beginning of time he acted as the divine agent in creation. He was the source of inspiration of prophets and sages. At last he took human form for man's salvation, died, rose from the dead and returned to the presence of the Father. This interpretation of divine manifestations might have been sufficiently vague to pass for monotheism had there not been another equally orthodox and traditional description of Jesus' relationship to God.

Ever since the time of Paul, Christ had been called the Son of God. The baptismal formula said, "Father, Son and Spirit." [10] God the Father and God the Son were definite and distinct persons. The term, "Son," seemed to imply that Christ was later in time and subordinate, thus challenging his power and usefulness as a guarantor of salvation. To say that he was begotten before all ages helped a little, but still did not make him eternal. Origen's phrase, "eternal generation," was a purely verbal solution and meaningless. Justin and Origen both spoke of Christ as a subordinate God. Justin classified the three divine persons according to rank—the Father, first, "The Son, who is truly God," second, and the prophetic Spirit, third.[11]

The confusion of language grew until by the close of the third century it became necessary to decide whether Christians believed in one God or three, and if one, to find a formula which would assert his unity and leave unchallenged the long established worship of three divine persons. The need of a united church to serve as a bond of unity and a source of spiritual reinforcement for the empire, moved Constantine to force the leaders of Christianity to a decision in the Council of Nicæa.

No educated Christian of the fourth century would have

admitted that he had more than one God, and yet scholars
highly placed in the church spoke of Christ as a second and
subordinate deity, while in popular practice the persons could
be as distinct as were the many manifestations of the Logos for
their polytheistic pagan neighbors. It was clear that the council must insist that the Christian God was one. The scriptures
were fixed and authoritative. They had established the doctrine of one, supreme God, the eternal Father, long before
men had dreamed of deifying Jesus. Yet Biblical scholars like
Paul of Samosata, who clung to the one God and interpreted
Jesus as a man especially endowed by the spirit of God, had
to be repudiated because the deity of Christ had become the
basis of assurance of human salvation. The Sabellians tried to
guard against polytheism by treating the three persons as
modes of the activity of undivided godhead. This solution,
carried through logically, led to the impossible conclusion that
the eternal God had suffered and died on the cross. Arius and
his brilliant friends were also interested in preserving the
unity of God. Like the Apostle Paul and thinkers of the second century, they found no difficulty in accepting the Son as
a heavenly being, similar in nature to the Father, begotten before all ages, but subordinate and not eternal. This view denied the real deity of Christ, reduced him to the rank of a
created being, and so destroyed his value as a Savior. It was
the union of the divine and human essences in him that guaranteed the salvation of human nature from corruption and
death. In monotheism the divine essence was limited to one
example; unless the Son was of that very essence, human nature was not infused with divinity and was doomed to death.
If Christ was a creature of time, and not of the same essence
as the Father, it was useless to say, "God became man that
man might become God." [12] The only formula which could
combine monotheism and the guarantee of eternal life for
man was, God is one essence in three persons. It was necessary

to say "three persons" rather than two because the Holy Spirit had to be included. From ancient times he had been recognized as a mode of God's manifestation. He was the Father of Jesus. Paul had spoken of him as the spiritual bond which united Christ and Christians as sons of God. So he joined the Father and Son to make the Christian God a Trinity.

The central value of a supreme and powerful God in any religion lies in the assurance of his ability to bring man safely to the goal of salvation. If Christ could have been the only God of the Christians all the essential values would have been preserved but the drift of cultures and the chances of history combined in the new religion the Jewish scriptures, with their ancient tradition of the one, supreme God and his Holy Spirit, Greek philosophy, and a Jewish Messiah who became a gentile Savior god, promising immortal blessedness. The Supreme Being of Christianity assumed the mantle of mystery as three in one because the only other choices were polytheism or futility as a gospel of salvation.

Many generations passed before the triune God was finally accepted by the whole Christian church. Men of intellectual integrity were sincerely troubled by what seemed to be a betrayal of the one, eternal God and the enthronement of three, under the cloak of an evasive and unscriptural formula. Peace came at last. The Trinity was established by authority and continued as a heritage of Christian truth so satisfactory to the metaphysical atmosphere of the East that the divine character remained fixed for the Greek Orthodox church until modern times. Even in the practical and politically minded West where God as a heavenly sovereign continued a developing career, the fact that the philosophic reasons for the trinitarian interpretation soon became meaningless did not, for centuries, interfere with verbal loyalty to the creedal statement.

And the Catholic Faith is this: That we worship one God in Trinity, and Trinity in Unity;

Neither confounding the Persons: nor dividing the Substance (essence).

For there is one Person of the Father: another of the Son: and another of the Holy Ghost.

But the Godhead of the Father, of the Son, and of the Holy Ghost is all one: the Glory equal, the Majesty coeternal.

Such as the Father is: such is the Son: and such is the Holy Ghost.

The Father uncreated: the Son uncreated: and the Holy Ghost uncreated.

The Father incomprehensible: the Son incomprehensible: and the Holy Ghost incomprehensible.

The Father eternal: the Son eternal: and the Holy Ghost eternal.

And yet there are not three eternals: but one eternal.

As also there are not three uncreated: nor three incomprehensibles, but one uncreated: and one incomprehensible.

So likewise the Father is Almighty: the Son Almighty: and the Holy Ghost Almighty.

And yet there are not three Almighties: but one Almighty.

So the Father is God: the Son is God: and the Holy Ghost is God.

And yet they are not three Gods: but one God. . . .[13]

When Rome, the imperial city, heir of a thousand brilliant years of Mediterranean culture, was captured by the barbarians, a chill of defeat struck to the heart of Christendom. Hope of a kingdom of God on earth faded. Supreme values took flight to the supernatural. A conviction of human frailty and futility, of the weakness of man's best strength and a deep sense of sin darkened the Christians' vision of the earthly scene. The drama of world history was vividly threaded with a single theme—the salvation of man from sin. The joy that the early church had felt in the assurance of the incarnation gave way to sombre emphasis on the crucifixion and the saving blood.

Draw nigh, and take the Body of the Lord,
And drink the holy Blood for you outpoured.

Saved by that Body, hallowed by that Blood,
Whereby refreshed, we render thanks to God.

Against that sacred Bread and holy Grail
The gates of hell itself cannot prevail.

Salvation's giver, Christ the only Son,
By that his cross and blood the victory won.[14]

More than ever before, the burden of human hopes was laid
upon the omnipotent arm of God. Failure and frustration
could not be accepted as final. With unconscious egotism, the
story of creation, from the beginning to the judgement day,
was read in terms of God's plan to save a select company of
souls from the general doom and lead them to eternal happiness. Members of the church were beneficiaries of the divine
will. Amid the ruins of empire, the church alone remained a
center of unity, a spiritual kingdom with an imperial head,
the representative on earth of the absolute Ruler in heaven.

As the warm sunlight of Hellenism faded from the west,
human life took on a sombre coloring. Hungry for security
and salvation, man surrendered the stage to God. For a thousand years the dominant thinkers of the Christian church
traced back every thread in the pattern of cosmic and social
events to the absolute will of their God. Augustine marked
the transition of the God of Christianity from the Greek era
to the Middle Ages. Under the influence of the Greek tradition, he defined God as the only reality, unchangeable, eternal,
the only real good, regarding whom our best science is nesci-
ence. He inherited a Trinity but the distinction of Persons
was not necessary for him. His God was one, and acted as one
under whatever name. "We say 'three Persons' not that it may

be so said, but that we may not keep silence." [15] All the qualities were applied equally to each of the persons without
distinction. When Augustine turned from the language of
philosophy to the more intelligible terminology of practical
religion his God was a personal being, an omnipotent monarch whose absolute will was the sustaining and guiding power
everywhere present in the universe. He it was who created the
world out of nothing and without the support of his will it
would fall away into non-existence. Whatever he willed, was.
The salvation of the elect was made as sure as the omnipotence
of God. He predestined some for eternal life, and by irresistible grace saved them. All others he foreordained to punishment and, by withholding his grace, allowed them to drift
to the doom the guilt of their sin deserved. Viewed as a heavenly sovereign, crowned with power and clothed with awful
dignity as a supreme judge, he was a God to be feared, but all
humble souls, who found refuge in the shelter of the church,
knew him as a God of love and grace. For them his omnipotence and irresistible will were no longer terrible but a sure
guarantee of salvation. From the beginning of time, God had
selected favored individuals from the peoples of the earth to
be members of his spiritual kingdom for, according to Augustine, the true religion had always been in the world but
was called Christianity only after the coming of Christ.[16]
Since that event the absolute God had chosen to channel the
divine grace as the means of salvation through the Christian
church.

Like the deities of all other religions, the God of Christianity had to face the threat of death as a useful God through
exaltation to the rarefied heights of thought by his philosophic
interpreters. Many of the divine friends of man who played
important rôles in the early world died of anemia under the
well-meant ministrations of metaphysics. Born in the primitive ages, they grew in moral grandeur and power as their

peoples advanced in culture, only to fall at last into the hands
of thinkers who robbed them of personality, purpose and
practical worth by refining them into pure but empty abstractions.

All religions have witnessed this interesting struggle between philosophic thought and the demand of practical religion for useful and worthful gods. Critical thinking, embarrassed by manlike deities molded by ages of human desire,
transformed them into pale and meaningless ghosts, far removed from any relation to human experience. Then reason
was compelled to build logical ladders into the unknown to
prove the bare existence of these abstract entities. Proved or
not, such deities were useless for religion. It was the qualities
acquired in earlier ages, when hope and desire were dominant
in dictating their characters, that made them valuable for
men. Scriptures and traditions pictured the gods with all desirable attributes and, because they had authority, they gave
the victory to faith over reason. Consequently, theologian
and layman alike kept the God they needed, a supreme benefactor, powerful, wise and good. Many times the Gods of Judaism, Islam and Christianity were rescued from the philosophic
death by scripture and tradition.

Throughout the medieval period the Christian God, under
the devoted attention of the theologians, had great difficulty
in retaining his vital personality. The active, vigorous God
who came striding through the scenes of Old Testament
drama, the mighty monarch on the heavenly throne of the
imperial period, was obscured by a screen of philosophic
thought. He faded into a vague presence looming dimly out
of the shadows of the unknowable. His existence had to be
proved and his character pieced together, line by line, with
the intellectual tools inherited from the Greeks. There was
never any doubt of the outcome, for the God who emerged
when the dialectical exercises were ended, was the familiar

figure of Christian tradition, whether he was reached by pure reason, or by reason plus mystic insight, or by reason plus revelation and faith. But the fire of simple, untroubled faith was often cooled by sophistication. Seen dimly through the glass of philosophy, God had an apologetic and artificial air. Enveloped in clouds of mystery, he appeared as a bodiless mosaic of attributes, patiently fitted together and fastened with the cement of logic.

If the thought of John Scotus Erigena, in the ninth century, had prevailed, the Christian God might have been so refined by reason as to lose all likeness to the personal, heavenly monarch of tradition. The Irish scholar lifted him so far above the reach of man's understanding that he became altogether unknowable. That he is, might be known but never *what* he is. The intellect is too feeble to grasp him and language too poor to describe him. Laudatory terms like wise, powerful, just and good fail to touch even the fringe of his unalterable perfection. He is all in all, the totality of being. The evolving, changing world is a manifestation of him. The soul of man is one with him, yet he is more than all the circumscribed universe—a limitless, simple reality, beyond personality and incomprehensible. Such glorification of God into meaninglessness was a familiar habit of high philosophy in Hinduism and Buddhism, but the Christian church refused to follow Erigena.

When feudalism was bringing order to the chaos of Europe, Anselm read the salvation theme of cosmic history in feudal terms. As a philosopher, he was forced to define his God as simple and indivisible, everywhere at all times yet beyond time and space, "the supreme essence, life, reason, salvation, righteousness, wisdom, truth, goodness, greatness, beauty, immortality, incorruptibility, immutability, blessedness, eternity, power and unity." [17] Anselm could not say that God was a good and wise being but only that he was goodness and wisdom. A God like this was far removed from the real, personal deity the early Christians knew but when Anselm dealt with the all-important problem of human salvation he brought his God back from the realm of pure thought to be a more comprehensible figure as the Supreme Overlord.[18] In feudalism, every rank in society had its honor demanding the proper satisfaction when injured. God's honor was infinite and required an infinite satisfaction for the injury incurred by man's sin. Man must pay but could not. Consequently, God became man in Christ and as the God-man gave his life to make full satisfaction to the divine honor for man. Since he had lived without sin, God had no claim upon him personally. As a reward for his submission to an undeserved death, he asked and received the gift of eternal life for the elect.

Anselm found the historic meaning of Christ in his death. The Fathers of an earlier age had stressed the incarnation. In the drama of salvation unfolding in history, churchmen saw the long labor of God as creator and savior ending in the eternal happiness of those selected from the general doom. The relation between the two divine persons, God the Creator and God the Savior, was explained in many ways, as the Christian deity came down the centuries, reflecting the values of the earthly social scene or changes in the intellectual climate.

From the late eleventh to the middle of the thirteenth century the Gods of the three great religions of Europe and the Near East were challenged by the thought of Aristotle. Competent scholars, who took the Greek thinker seriously, were no longer able to accept as true the description of God as personal, creator, providence and savior of men. These attributes were essential to Yahweh, Allah and the Christian God. Since it was not possible to ignore Aristotle in that age, theologians were compelled to demonstrate that their dogmas could be defended in the philosophic arena. This work was done for Islam by al-Ghazzali, for Judaism by Maimonides, for Christianity by Thomas Aquinas. The work of the Christian doctor was made easier because the Jewish theologian had shown the way. Aquinas was a great thinker but he was first of all a devout believer. He became the champion of his church against the heresies taking root in the sunlight of the new thought. His mind could handle the intellectual tools in masterly fashion to give his God philosophic dignity but he never dreamed of dropping any valuable divine attributes. As a clear thinker he was compelled to say that the real being of God was beyond the grasp of the human intellect so that we cannot know what it is and that nothing positive can be predicated of God.[19] Yet he did not leave him as a lifeless cipher suspended in the unknowable. Aquinas knew the nature of God by faith. The deity of scripture and history was more real to him than reasoning. The Creator God of the Old Testament was a vital person, comprehensible, possessing all the qualities valuable for the needs of men. The New Testament glorified a heroic Savior who walked the earth as a man and was enshrined in tradition as a member of the Godhead. There was no lack of color, vitality and character in the folk God of the scriptures. Not reason, but faith, filled out the picture of God for Aquinas.

> Hidden God, devoutly I adore Thee,
> Truly present underneath these veils:
> All my heart subdues itself before Thee,
> Since it all before Thee faints and fails.
>
> Not to sight or taste or touch be credit,
> Hearing only do we trust secure;
> I believe, for God the Son hath said it—
> Word of Truth that ever shall endure.[20]

Under the influence of philosophy Aquinas defined God as simple unity, Actus Purus, the first and final cause, eternal, changeless, passionless, loving himself as the most perfect, but after the process of intellectual proof and dialectical definition was over, the familiar God of Christian tradition was fully restored. His garment of attributes was neatly arranged and ordered; he was provided with a servicable shield against the attacks of heresy but little was added to his development.

Aristotle might well have been shocked by a god who was personal and a trinity, a creator of the world out of nothing, who was interested in human affairs and served man as providence, savior and guarantor of immortality. From Clement of Alexandria to Eckhart, theologians bowed their heads to the earth in humility before the unknowable God, but they lifted their hearts in appeal to a God they knew well—the supreme being molded by centuries of Christian history. Men like Eckhart might hope to scale the inaccessible heights to the unknown Godhead by a superrational flight of mystic insight. The God of practical religion was the supreme, heavenly monarch who had appeared on earth in human form. High on his celestial throne, holding the destiny of men in his hands, he was a being before whom the children of earth must needs walk humbly. With love and hatred, grace and wrath, he meted out forgiveness and damnation to men according to his will. His terrible anger burned against those who failed to make use of the means of grace and that great company who were doomed from birth to the eternal fires of hell. The realm of Satan was no figure of speech to the medieval mind. The devil and his innumerable host of torturing fiends were real. They had a recognized place in the cosmic scheme as the agents of God in the punishment of the damned.

The austerity of the Christian God during this period frightened simple and sensitive souls. Many, like Bernard of Clairvaux, turned to Christ who shared our human nature for consolation and guidance in the practical way of life——

Jesu, the very thought of Thee
With sweetness fills my breast;
But sweeter far Thy face to see,
And in Thy presence rest.

Nor voice can sing, nor heart can frame,
Nor can the memory find,
A sweeter sound than Thy blest Name,
O Savior of mankind!

O Hope of every contrite heart,
O Joy of all the meek,
To those who fall, how kind Thou art!
How good to those who seek! [21]

But Christ as the judge of the last assize seemed often as remote and severe as the high God himself.

Day of wrath! O Day of mourning!
See fulfilled the prophet's warning,
Heaven and earth in ashes burning!

O what fear man's bosom rendeth,
When from heaven the Judge descendeth,
On whose sentence all dependeth!

Wondrous sound the trumpet flingeth,
Through earth's sepulchers it ringeth,
All before the throne it bringeth.

Death is struck, and nature quaking,
All creation is awaking,
To its Judge an answer making! [22]

Lowly folk who did not dare to approach the heavenly presence made their appeal for help to the saints. They were a numerous company, many of them specialized in caring for some particular need. Some of the old pagan gods who had not been transformed into devils nor died of neglect lived on as saints of the church. The sainted Apostles, holy men and martyrs could be powerful advocates of needy humanity in the heavenly courts.

> O Christ, Thy guilty people spare!
> Lo, kneeling at Thy gracious throne,
> Thy Virgin-Mother pours her prayer,
> Imploring pardon for her own.

> Ye Angels, happy evermore!
> Who in your circles nine ascend,
> As ye have guarded us before,
> So still from harm our steps defend.

> Ye Prophets and Apostles high!
> Behold our penitential tears;
> And plead for us when death is nigh,
> And our all-searching Judge appears.

> Ye Martyrs all! a purple band,
> And Confessors, a white-robed train;
> Oh, call us to our native land,
> From this our exile back again.

> And ye, O choirs of Virgins chaste!
> Receive us to your seats on high;
> With Hermits whom the desert waste
> Sent up of old into the sky.[23]

Most helpful and best beloved of all was the Holy Virgin, Mary, the mother of God. She had a unique rank in heaven as the mother of Christ, the daughter of God and the spouse of the Holy Spirit.[24] Mary's motherhood gave her authority. She alone could stand with unveiled face in the presence of God to plead the cause of needy men. As Queen of Heaven she had royal powers and prerogatives. There was little likelihood that her Savior son would refuse her requests. "If you fear to find grace with God," said St. Bernard, "have confidence in finding grace with Mary." [25] Since the third century she has become ever dearer to her devotees. In Catholic circles her glory has grown brighter with the passing of time. Only God himself is worthy of worship higher than hers.

She alone can say to the Creator: Thou art my Child and I am Thy Mother. This is the reason why Christianity for nearly 2000 years has knelt at the feet of Mary and has asked for consolation in sorrow, help in need, health in sickness, strength in temptation, forgiveness of sin and a happy death, and has never asked in vain.[26]

By the close of the thirteenth century the character of God was established so firmly that it has remained unchanged for Roman Catholicism until today. The Heavenly Ruler of the west was no longer allowed to grow, as in olden times, in response to the lure of new cultural moods. While the tides of change transformed the world in thought, behavior and ideals, he dwelt apart, unaltered, behind the protecting walls of authority. Revealed in scriptures, defined by faith and rationalized by philosophy he had attained an imposing majesty as an absolute monarch, a Trinity, creator and ruler of the universe, holy, omniscient, omnipotent, infinite, a supreme personal being. His reason and will determined the direction and goal of world events. He predestined some men for salvation and others for eternal doom. He was a God to be feared, yet merciful and forgiving, furnishing grace and providential care for those who were candidates for salvation.

The four centuries which followed the Renaissance brought stirring changes to the cultural life of Europe, yet the God of orthodox Christianity remained almost unaffected. During this period new intellectual and social forces appeared which, in their maturity, were to rob him of his distinctive attributes, block the old sure ways of communion with him, break down the protecting wall of authority in the church, scripture and tradition, which had guarded him so long, and offer a long succession of gods of more modern pattern to take his place. A chasm was opened between the secular world, rapidly expanding through the increase of human knowledge, interests and power, and the realm of religion. For many generations, however, the God of the church was secure. Men began to glimpse alluring vistas of earthly joy and beauty which had been obscured by the narrow horizons of the Middle Ages, but leaders of the Renaissance were not in quest of a new God. The theologies of the Reformation challenged the authority of the church, rejected the Virgin and the Saints as mediators between the individual and the divine presence but acknowledged the authority of other creations of the church—the canon of scriptures, the early creeds and the traditional God.

The reformers magnified the austere and awful majesty of the heavenly king. They rejoiced in the eternal decrees by which divine predestination fixed the fates of men, for the salvation of elect souls was sure. Just as certainly vast multitudes were created to be eternally damned. In his early days Luther trembled before this terrible God and his threat of hell. After the assurance of salvation he basked in the beneficence of the divine nature.

> A mighty fortress is our God:
> A bulwark never failing;
> Our helper he amid the flood
> Of mortal ills prevailing.[27]

His God still surveyed the world with two faces—a stern face of wrath for sinners and a countenance radiant with grace and love for those on whom he had bestowed the precious gift of faith.

There was an element of subtle pride in the willingness of Reformation theologians to accept boldly God's inexorable predestination. Perhaps the rise of absolute monarchies in Europe made it natural to surrender human destiny to the will of an absolute ruler in the heavens. Elect souls were cozily content as beneficiaries of his majesty and power. The eternally damned did not write theologies. Religions have always made the plan of man's salvation the dominant design in the pattern of creation and, in spite of all human humility in the presence of gods, have unconsciously made them the all-sufficient servants of man in his quest for the unattained ideal. The glory of God was so emphasized by Zwingli, Bucer and Calvin that the human race seemed to sink into insignificance. At the same time, the total world program of this mighty God revolved around the fate of humble and helpless humanity. According to Zwingli, the good of man was the controlling motive of all divine activity.[28] The election of the saved and the reprobation of the damned were manifestations of the mercy and justice of the absolute king.

In the theology of Calvin, God attained the last sublime exaltation before the pervasive influences of science and democracy destroyed the old order in both earth and heaven. He was a personal being of ineffable majesty whose absolute will determined, in the silence of eternity, the vast panorama of earthly events now unfolding in the time span between creation and judgement. Every thread of meaning in the complex web of human history led back beyond the beginning to God's eternal decrees. The qualities universally necessary for a perfect God belonged to him—justice, love, goodness and wisdom—but they were overshadowed by his majesty, power and glory as the heavenly monarch. For his own glory he set the feet of men on the paths that led to heaven and the enjoyment of the divine presence or to hell and its eternal torment. He inscribed the fates of men for happiness or suffering not according to their personal merit or demerit but because he so willed. This hard quality in the absolute God added to the satisfaction of the saints and could trouble no one, for the book of eternal decrees was open only to the eye of God. All who chose to number themselves among the elect found dignity and security in the infallible enfoldment of the divine will. The great company of the doomed had an anæsthetic against despair in their unbelief. The Christian God, as Calvin knew him, was a practical and effective deity, a well-defined personal being whose irresistible will made all experiences of joy and sorrow, success and tragedy, glow with the warmth of the divine presence for those who could believe in him.

There is but one only living and true God, who is infinite in being and perfection, a most pure spirit, invisible, without body, parts, or passions, immutable, immense, eternal, incomprehensible, almighty, most wise, most holy, most free, most absolute, working all things according to the counsel of his own immutable and most righteous will, for his own glory; most loving, gracious, merciful, long-suffering, abundant in goodness and truth, forgiving iniquity, transgression and sin; the rewarder of them that diligently seek him; and withal most just and terrible in his judgements; hating all sin, and who will by no means clear the guilty.

God hath all life, glory, goodness, blessedness, in and of himself; and is alone in and unto himself all-sufficient, not standing in need of any creatures which he hath made, nor deriving any glory from them, but only manifesting his own glory in, by, unto, and upon them: he is the alone foundation of all being, of whom, through whom, and to whom are all things; and hath most sovereign dominion over them, to do by them, for them, or upon them whatsoever himself pleaseth. In his sight all things are open and manifest; his knowledge is infinite, infallible, and independent upon the creature; so as nothing is to him contingent or uncertain. He is most holy in all his counsels, in all his works, and in all his commands. To him is due from angels and men, and every other creature, whatsoever worship, service, or obedience, he is pleased to require of them.[29]

From the Reformation to the nineteenth century the God of the churches suffered little change. The lines of his character were firmly etched in orthodoxy. As the spread of democratic ideals mellowed the political and social climate, the austerity of the character of God was softened by a greater stress upon his grace and mercy. He became a loving father rather than an absolute king. Christ as the severe judge, enthroned with God in heaven, was gradually reclothed in the warm and lovable attributes of his human nature. Most of the trappings of the medieval, spiritual world fell away. The devil, as God's agent in punishing sinners, and his infernal torture chamber, were either explained away or quietly dropped. Practical Christians were beginning to see the unknown Father through an idealized image of the earthly Jesus, but the deity defined in the creeds was still formally accepted.

While the God of the churches was moving down the centuries from the age of the Renaissance within the protecting bounds of tradition, the cultural life of the western world was being transformed by forces which yielded a new understanding of the nature of the universe and of human nature, a new appreciation of man's powers and responsibilities, a widening of the horizons of thought, action, desire and dream. The slow-moving stream of social life, emerging from the lazy, century-long adjustments of the past, was tossed from problem to problem in the swift changes of the new age. The sciences, probing, with their searchlight of method, the heavens and the earth, plants, animals and man, flooded with illumination the winding paths of man's cultural pilgrimage. Theological structures which had had all the solidity of eternal truth became as unsubstantial as the stuff of dreams before that revealing light. Science, applied to materials, spawned machines, magnified the power of man, created industrialism, destroyed the securities of the past and challenged religion to find a new defense for human values. The bonds of authority which had been the main source of confident knowledge of the nature of God snapped one by one. The thinker, attuned to the currents of the secular world outside the church, was compelled to chart afresh the line of human destiny through a new earth under a new heaven. As a consequence there has been, since the dawn of the new age in the western world, a double history of God, on the one hand, the continuing God of orthodoxy and, on the other, a long series of substitutes for him as thinkers rationalized the inherited deity in relation to the new thought patterns and enlarged ideals of the passing generations in a changing world.

It was inevitable that the character of God should change as soon as he was exposed to the new intellectual climate without the protection of entrenched authorities. Christian theologians had always been frank in admitting that much of their belief regarding him could not be rationally proved. Some were willing to say that he was beyond the reach of reason, yet they remained untroubled so long as faith ushered them into the presence of God in all his historic splendor, fully authenticated by the authority of scripture and tradition. The humility which said, "I believe that I may understand," found faith in revelation, not in reason. Divine attributes that were sanctified by tradition resisted change. Thus God continued to be a Trinity for the church until modern times although the vital reason for the formula was outgrown after the fourth century. When God was made three in one, "Trinity" was the magic word which skirted the Scylla of polytheism and the Charybdis of denial of Christ's saving power. Augustine, who stood on the threshold of that creative period, found it empty of meaning. For him God was one. He did not like to say "Three Persons" and could not say "three somethings" (*tria quaedam*), yet he accepted the formula on authority and explained the three as memory, intelligence and love.[30] Anselm followed his interpretation but considered the mystery of the

Trinity really incomprehensible.[31] Abelard said, power, wisdom and goodness or love. Bernard of Clairvaux was perplexed but submissive. "The eternal and blessed Trinity I believe though I do not comprehend and I hold by faith what I cannot grasp with the mind." [32] Aquinas was able to make what seemed to him a rational demonstration of the existence of God and of many of his abstract qualities. He accepted the Trinity on the authority of revelation.[33] The Protestant reformers had no need of the formula. Luther was irritated by the term "Homoousion," and felt that the mathematical language of three in one was cold. He would have preferred to say simply, "God." [34] Calvin was willing to have such terms as "Trinity" and "Persons" buried out of sight if only it were agreed that the Father, Son and Spirit were one God and yet distinguished by some peculiar quality.[35] During the sixteenth century there were many criticisms of the Trinity by both Catholics and Protestants but only the Socinians abandoned the doctrine. It was authority that guarded the nature and character of the Christian God for believers. When this support failed, the deity of the creeds was no longer acceptable to thinkers immersed in the thought-forms and problems of the new age.

Yet there was no revolt from God. Philosophers and scientists alike were anxious still to believe in him. Judaism had impressed indelibly upon Christian culture the idea that through all the events of time was threaded the will of an eternal, all-wise, good and omnipotent, personal being. This fundamental of western thought was rarely challenged. Thinkers sought rather to modernize God. The celestial sovereign of historic Christianity belonged to a naïve, pre-scientific picture of the world. He was the heavenly director of an earthly drama in which man, with all his weakness and futility was the central figure. God set the stage in creation, decreed the plot, guided the action by revelation in prophet, Bible and church, and interposed on special occasions in providence and miracle. In a thrilling, pivotal scene he made a personal appearance as the God-man. At last, in the awful splendors of a final judgement, he was expected to bring the great drama to a close.

As science slowly extended its domain over the physical, biological and social realms, the familiar, human-like characteristics of God fell away and the lines of communication leading into his presence were broken one by one. While orthodoxy kept its correct theological phrases untainted, and anxious hearts, careless of creeds, prayed to a Father in heaven, the new climate of science and social change was gradually wearing away the substance of the traditional deity. It was a quiet process of erosion. When the earth lost its central place in the universe and assumed the lowlier rôle of a tiny planet swinging around the sun in the vastness of stellar space, the Biblical cosmology was undermined, and with it the imagery of heaven and hell, creation and judgement. The right of free criticism launched by the Reformers as a destructive weapon against the Roman Church could not be recalled. It respected no boundaries. With more subtle methods it went on unchecked to discredit the authority of supernatural revelation in scripture and tradition. The rule of law in the physical world made miracles worse than useless as evidence of divine activity. Faith in miracles was more difficult than faith in God. Then the proud claims of reason were challenged. It had been accepted, through the centuries of Christian history, as a trustworthy tool to demonstrate at least the existence of God and the reasonableness of revelation. Hume and Kant showed the futility and emptiness of all such rational proofs. By the end of the eighteenth century the religions of the non-Christian world were beginning to contribute their light toward a better understanding of Christianity. Knowledge of the religions of preliterate peoples destroyed the theory of the rationalists that all men have an innate idea of a supreme God as an original endowment of human nature. Historical interpretation of the scriptures and of the evolution of early Christianity restored his true humanity to the historical Jesus, revealed the process by which he was transformed into a God-man and traced the development of the doctrine of the Trinity as the outcome of a blend of cultures. Meanwhile, science enthroned change as king in the universe, from the invisible realm of the electron to the farthest sweep of stellar galaxies. The old world of eternal truths, fixed principles, and absolutes appeared as a process of ceaseless interaction and movement. All phases of culture, including religion and the gods, were seen to be creations of a life-process growing ever more complex. When at last the religious sciences began to unfold the natural history of religions, the Christian God took his place among the thousands of deities molded by the desires and needs of men. He was drawn completely within the bounds of the human, social process as the reflexion on the universe of man's longing for help and security. Thus the progressive development of the sciences furnished the insight into the history of the universe and man, which reduced the eternal, self-existent, personal God, enthroned in a supernatural, spiritual realm, to a symbol socially created, shaped by ages of cultural history, embodying man's faith that the universe will guarantee the ultimate victory of human ideals.

The change came slowly. Only as man's knowledge of the past spread from the physical and biological to the social and religious development of the race did the Christian God enter the twilight zone. During all the centuries he had moved on two levels—as the God of orthodox theology, nicely defined, decked out in all the attributes accumulated in the conflicts and triumphs of a historic religion, properly proved and accredited by authority; and as the limited, helpful, near-at-hand God of the folk, who were not careful of precise theological definitions but used their God in the simple, primeval way as the source of help, hope and consolation in time of trouble. Since the dawn of the modern age there has been a third level, apart from orthodoxy and above the unsophisticated plane of the folk, on which God assumed scores of different forms as he was adjusted to the ever-changing perspective of knowledge and ideals. Since the inexorable law which governs the gods is that they must change to keep abreast of the intellectual, moral and cultural growth of the people or die by neglect, the destiny of the Christian God is being worked out on this third level.

The early physical sciences had little effect on the character of God. The hand of orthodoxy was still heavy. In investigating the ways of nature, scientists felt that they were thinking the thoughts of God after him. Discovery of universal laws dominating a mechanistic, natural order served only to demonstrate the ancient faith in the rigid control of the divine will over the world. The men of science did, however, want to deal with a calculable, mathematico-scientific universe. God was placed in Sabbath calm outside his creation and excluded from interference with his work through miracle and special providence. His wisdom and power fixed the laws of nature and of human nature in the beginning so that he could dwell apart in his eternal, spiritual splendor as a spectator of the scenes of cosmic history until the time came for the final judgement. The effect of the first impact of science was not so much to change God as to render reference to him unnecessary for the understanding and control of the natural world.

While the rationalists thus banished God beyond the universe to leave the field free for science, there were others, toward the close of the eighteenth century, who found support in the revelations of science for a radiant religious optimism. For them God was not an absentee ruler but an immanent, creative presence in the world, marshalling all the events of time toward a perfect, final fulfillment. Herder saw history threaded with a golden chain of progress leading to the ideal of humanity, a harmony of reason, joy, freedom and love in a perfected society. Faith in the law of progress was not unlike the earlier trust in a divine purpose but the perspective was greatly changed. The vast spectacle of human cultures climbing adventurously through eons of time and change toward a far-off, splendid goal contrasted sharply with the older picture of a parochial world-stage bounded by creation and judgement on which God watched the performance of a pre-ordained drama of salvation. Wider vistas of knowledge, daring faith in human powers, roseate confidence in the future and bold assertion of the rights and worth of man marked the dawn of the nineteenth century. God was being drawn into the stream of flowing, temporal events. The gulf between the natural and supernatural was closed. Authority no longer stood at the horizon of human experience to open windows through which sure knowledge of the divine mysteries might enter. The shining wings of faith were folded. The quest for God in human experience and in the cosmic-human process began. The result was a great variety of gods with little resemblance to the sovereign Lord of Christian history.

Out of the German quest for certainty and security during the stormy, early years of the nineteenth century came God as the Absolute, ushered in amid the thunder of guns. Critical thought had discredited the old deity of the creeds. Weighted down with their burden of metaphysical tools, the intellectuals were seeking new social morale to overcome the failure of political hopes, a new avenue to the truth to replace the old authorities reduced to ruins by criticism, a sure refuge for spiritual values threatened by the arrogant advance of scientific method. Kant had shown the way to God by flight to a super-empirical self, free from the tyranny of science. Beginning with the functions of the finite and limited self, the moral will, feeling, aesthetic intuition, and thought, his followers climbed the ladder of dialectic to the Absolute Self. A long tradition of the western world, taking many forms in Neo-Platonism, Erigena, Eckhart, Spinoza, Boehme, assumed, in this new form, the dignity of a marvellous metaphysical edifice. Instead of a God dwelling in a supernatural realm, the whole universe was God manifested. Instead of man pathetically reaching out to find God, he was now one with God, the highest expression of the Absolute in time. God came to self-consciousness in man, found the highest social expression in the German state and the noblest religious manifestation in Christianity, the absolute religion. The needs of security, certainty of truth, personal dignity and worth were met, but the creators of the impersonal, purposeless, all-inclusive Absolute seemed to be atheistic to those who remembered the personal, heavenly sovereign of the past.

God had become a problem for the intellectuals. He had held his place as a living personality through the long centuries of Christian history, not because of rational demonstration of his existence and attributes, but because he was a phase of a primeval cultural pattern, developed and buttressed by unquestioned authority in scripture, church and tradition. When the authorities crumbled, thinkers were compelled either to abandon the traditional God or to transform him into a being better attuned to the intellectual and social climate of the new age. The Absolute of German idealism was only the herald of a long and colorful procession of Gods who were hardly more than ghosts of the older deity. God was a dominant idea of western culture, an inescapable fundamental, impossible to ignore. Philosophers and scientists did not discover God; they inherited the idea and rationalized it, each in his own manner. Through the many forms given to the Christian God during the last century, there was a thread of continuity. However vague and amorphous they might be by definition, they served, as gods have always served, to satisfy emotional needs and to guarantee the values of man's noblest ideal. In his multiple modern modes, God may be personal or impersonal, infinite or finite, perfect or growing, spiritual or material, transcendent or immanent, eternal or changing, static or purposeful, supernatural or natural, real or symbolic, all-powerful or struggling, according to the intellectual demands of his recreators and yet be used as though he were the God the fathers knew.

The modern world is vastly different from the one in which the Christian God acquired his orthodox character. It was inevitable that he should appear in a new form, but cultural change has come so swiftly and in so many areas of life that there is no longer any common agreement as to what God can or should be. The Gods offered by modern Christian thinkers are not only many, but multiform and often mutually contradictory. Some of them stand just outside the portals of orthodoxy. Many of them are too wraithlike to carry the weighty attributes of the historic world deities. At the end of the long line are wistful figures denuded of the essential qualities of deity, trying to feel at home in a purely naturalistic world. They range from the Absolute God and the "God forever beyond human comprehension" to the finite God and the God who is a symbol or an ideal. Some wear a full panoply of attributes, others have lost not only personality and purposiveness but also the age-old rôle of God as providence, comforter and guarantor of man's final salvation.

In spite of their multitude, these modern Gods fall into types according to their origin and the special interests of their creators. The qualities of the Christian God are most faithfully preserved by theologians who have projected the character of Jesus into the unknown, and picture God in his image. Others have made moral values central, frankly faced the fact of evil and arrived at some form of finite God, limited in power or wrestling with a recalcitrant element in his own nature, or struggling to achieve victory for the good in an unfinished universe. Many of the new Gods are scientific products arising from the effort to harmonize the god-idea with physical science, social science or the new religious sciences. Strangest of all is the new Absolute God of the Barthians, emerging from the frustration and despair of the post-war social bewilderment. The way back to orthodoxy was closed; the ghostly gods of the modernists seemed futile. Blind faith plunged into the unknown to find the needful security in an ineffable God.

A host of shadowy figures who bear the name of God are all that remains for thinkers of the once robust Christian deity, sovereign Lord of heaven and earth. In modern times he has been known as the Absolute, the World-Soul; [36] the Spirit of the Beloved Community; [37] the Grand Etre; [38] the Spiritual Nisus of an evolving universe; [39] the Unknowable; [40] the Totality of Life; [41] the Life Force; [42] a Christlike God; [43] the Common Will of Humanity; [44] an Eternal, Creative Good Will; [45] the Determiner of Destiny; [46] a conscious Person of perfect good will limited by the free choices of other persons and by restrictions within his own nature; [47] a Growing God; [48] a Cosmic Mathematician; [49] the Symbol of Highest Social Values; [50] the Principle of Concretion; [51] the Utterly Other; [52] That in the universe which yields the maximum of good when man enters into right relations with it; [53] the Totality of Personality producing Forces in the universe; [54] the Supreme Person of a World of Free Spirits; [55] an Eternal Cosmic Mind who suffers when matter makes his plans miscarry; [56] the Imagined Synthesis of Ideal Ends. [57]

In the bewilderment of this confusion of tongues the Christian God keeps a precarious hold upon the thought of the intellectuals. Meanwhile, Christianity as a living religion, has been turning with serious purpose during the last three decades toward the solution of the social problems of human living. If this practical movement should gather into itself the trained workers capable of leading it to success, and the values for which the Christian God has stood—love, justice, peace, security and consolation—can be realized in human relations, the layman will not be greatly troubled by the conflicting reports brought back by theologians and philosophers from their adventures into the unknown.

CHAPTER XI

ALLAH

There is no god but Allah;
Mohammed is the messenger of Allah.[1]

LLAH came late into the company of the great gods. His name and certain aspects of his character date back into remote antiquity, but only desert tribesmen knew that he was winning supremacy over the dying deities of Arabia until Mohammed rescued him from the obscurity of his homeland and prepared him for a rôle on the world stage.

In the sixth century A.D., the multitude of local gods, who had been friends of the Arab tribes through forgotten ages, were slowly fading into oblivion. They were originally fertility figures, heavenly nature powers, or values like Luck, Good-Fortune, Friendship, treated as divine forces.[2] Many of them had been neglected to death before the time of Mohammed. The memory of some was preserved on enduring stone and the names of others lingered in legends long after the gods were gone. In important centers the old deities still lived on, but above them was rising Allah, a more powerful being of universal sway.[3] The term Allah, a contraction of *al-ilāh* "the god," was enough to distinguish him from the local divinities with proper names.

The exaltation of Allah as the one god might have been achieved without any influences from outside Arabia. It was the custom of the tribes to refer to their own local deity as "the god" without using his name. Wandering tribes, using the common term for all their different gods, could easily have come to feel that behind the many names was the one god-head—Allah. The drift toward monotheism was, however, accelerated by outside pressure. The mighty gods of Judaism and Christianity stood at the border and cast their shadows over Arabia, while within the Hejaz the leaven of monotheism was spread by followers of both religions. Before these majestic foreign gods the ancient local deities of the Arabs could not stand, but Allah, unhampered by bondage to place and name, rose to meet them as an equal. Before Mohammed he was recognized as the Supreme Being, creator, giver of the rain of prosperity.[4] In his name all solemn oaths were sworn.[5] He was the one sure refuge in times of distress.[6] At Mecca the ancient fertility goddess, Allat, and her associates, Manat and al-Uzza, were regarded as his daughters.[7]

Conditions in Mecca gave little promise that Allah would grow into grandeur. The city was an important trading center, ruled by wealthy merchants, whose chief interest was in the mundane business of money-making. Even the Ka'aba, house of the god, and the religious fairs were esteemed by them primarily as a source of revenue and prestige. In this atmosphere Mohammed lived as an orphan child, and grew to manhood as one of the Meccan poor. Perhaps he remembered that his family had once been wealthy and powerful; certainly he was fired by ambition to rise above his lowly state and filled with resentment against the rich who were so callously indifferent to the sufferings of the people who had neither social status nor worldly goods. His brooding over social injustice blended with ideas, learned probably from Meccan Christians, of a divine judgement to come when the wicked dead would feed the fires of hell. Awed by the vision of a heavenly Judge, rewarding and punishing men for their deeds, he became convinced that God had called him to give warning of the coming doom. Raised to self-respecting dignity as a Warner divinely chosen, Mohammed made Allah the champion of the oppressed and the enemy of the social wrongs which had made his own youth a time of bitterness. Men who did not share their wealth with the orphan, the needy, the way-farer and the poor man whose lot was miserable, would feel the judgement of Allah. In the name of his god, Mohammed denounced the Meccan merchants——

> But ye honour not the orphan,
> Nor urge ye one another to feed the poor,
> And ye devour heritages, devouring greedily,
> And ye love riches with exceeding love.[8]

Allah, in this new rôle as judge, and in alliance with Mohammed, lost all the limitations of the past.

At first Mohammed called him "the Lord," using the name Allah hesitantly because of its association in Mecca with the three goddesses and perhaps also with the red carnelian image of Hubal in the Ka'aba. This phase passed swiftly as revelation gave him confidence in his own knowledge of "the God." Between Allah, growing under the molding mind of Mohammed, and the old god of Mecca a great gulf was opening. Mohammed had no doubt that his opponents were the ones deluded. He ridiculed the idea that God would have a wife and sons and daughters. Other gods were allowed no share in the world owned by Allah. The Meccans still assigned the Djinn to God as his associates; Mohammed made them his creatures, the servants of his will. Allah of the shrine and of Arabia was freed from all trammelings and exalted in lonely majesty to the heavenly throne as the one, all-powerful Lord, creator of the heavens and the earth.

Mohammed was convinced that he spoke the words of the same God who, in earlier ages, had revealed the truth of his "Book" to Jews and Christians. The ancient "Book" had descended upon his heart that it might be made known to his

countrymen in the "clear Arabic tongue." The Meccans were
not impressed. They smiled at his talk of resurrection and grew
angry at his threat of hell. When they asked for a sign of the
great Allah, Mohammed marvelled at their blindness in the
presence of his power and providence.

Verily God causeth the grain and the date stone to put forth: He
bringeth forth the living from the dead, and the dead from the
living! This is God! . . .

He causeth the dawn to appear, and hath ordained the night for
rest, and the sun and the moon for computing time! The ordinance
of the Mighty, the Wise!

And it is He who hath ordained the stars for you that ye may be
guided thereby in the darknesses of the land and of the sea! Clear have
we made our signs to men of knowledge.

And it is He who hath produced you from one man, and hath provided for you an abode and resting place! Clear have we made our
signs for men of insight.

And it is He who sendeth down rain from Heaven: and we bring
forth by it the buds of all the plants, and from them bring we forth
the green foliage, and the close growing grain, and palm trees with
sheaths of clustering dates, and gardens of grapes, and the olive and
the pomegranate, like and unlike. Look ye on their fruits when they
fruit and ripen. Truly herein are signs unto people who believe.[9]

When they still remained deaf to his warnings, Mohammed
found comfort for his failure by making the absolute will of
God the determiner of human destiny. The burden of responsibility for the fate of his people fell from his shoulders. "Now
have proofs that may be seen come to you from your Lord.
. . . I am not made a keeper over you." [10] "Verily God mis-
leadeth whom he will, and guideth whom he will." [11] "Whom
he pleaseth will he forgive, and whom he pleaseth will he punish; for God is All-powerful." [12]

During the years of Mohammed's Meccan ministry, Allah
became the one supreme God of heaven and earth, eternal,

omniscient, omnipotent, far removed in awful grandeur, yet "near to man as the vein of his neck," [13] a fearful avenger, yet forgiving and compassionate. He was the only guide for man, a victorious, self-sufficient sovereign, holding the arrows of human destiny firmly in his hand. He created Djinn and men for hell, yet the sunlight of his grace and mercy shone behind the storm clouds of his terrible power. Seated on his exalted throne in the high heavens, surrounded by angelic ministers, he ruled the universe without rivals or associates. Some of the angels worshipped him, some, like Gabriel, revealed his truth to man, others sped on wings of light to execute his will on earth. One of the original company, Iblis, too proud to humble himself before Adam, was banished from heaven and became the adversary of Allah, the tempter and deceiver of men.

In the hostile atmosphere of Mecca there was little prospect for either Mohammed or Allah. Fortunately Mohammed's reputation as a man of supernatural inspiration had reached Yathrib, later called Medina, "the city of the prophet." The tribes of the northern city were so weary of communal strife that they were willing to welcome Mohammed in the hope that he might find the formula of peace. There his sagacity, backed by timely revelations from Allah, soon made him master of all phases of the community life and Allah acquired the practical earthly support of economic, political, and military power.

After the prophet was firmly established at Medina and the bitter years of strife were drawing to a close, the narrow horizons of Arabia could no longer limit the earthly activities of the God of Islam. Mohammed had never doubted that the Lord who gave him revelations was the God known long before by Jews and Christians. The Torah, the Gospel and his own growing revelation, were all parts of the one, eternal Word. When the distinction between Judaism and Christianity became clear to him, and the truth of these older religions

conflicted with his own, Mohammed could only believe that
the others had falsified their scriptures. The Jews were stubbornly hostile to his message at Medina. Christians, who
thought that God had "begotten a son" and was "one of
three" he could not tolerate. The final break with the elder
faiths came, when victory crowned the Muslim arms in the
Arab homeland. The world program of Allah stood revealed.
In the earlier years, Mohammed thought of himself as the
messenger of God sent to save the Arabs, one of a long line
which included Adam, Noah, Abraham, Moses and Jesus. Now
he was the "Seal of the Prophets," [14] an apostle with a mission
to all mankind. As the shadows of death drew near to him the
armies of Arabia were waiting to break down the border barriers and spread the glory and dominion of Allah in a vast
crescent around the old Mediterranean world. Before the God
of Mohammed it was only meet that all the earth should bow.

God! There is no God but he: the Living, the Eternal. Nor slumber
seizeth him, nor sleep; his, whatsoever is in the heavens and whatsoever is in the earth. Who is he that can intercede with him but by his
own permission? He knoweth what hath been before them and what
shall be after them: yet naught of his knowledge shall they grasp,
save what he willeth. His throne reacheth over the heavens and the
earth, and the upholding of both burdeneth him not; and he is the
High, the Great.[15]

When Allah began his triumphant march to world dominion, the voice of his prophet was already stilled in death, but
the teaching of Mohammed, gathered together in the sacred
Koran, remained as a shield of authority to protect his God
from too radical transformation through contact with the
older cultures. The sudden rolling back of the horizon was no
immediate shock to Allah. His people knew him as the one
God of the earth long before they carried his banners over the
borders of the homeland. The tasks of empire, however,

brought problems unknown to the tribal life of Arabia, for which the Koran made no provision. New ways of living and swiftly expanding desires made it necessary to put new content into the will of Allah. He came from the relatively simple culture of Arabia to rule an empire which stretched in a vast sweeping crescent from Syria through Egypt to Spain, from the Mediterranean eastward to the portals of India. Some of these lands had been mellowed by the sunlight of culture thousands of years before the victory shout of Islam startled a drowsing world. Deep under buried cities or wind-blown through old ruins was the dust of the doers and dreamers who lit the fires of civilization in the dawn ages. In these lands had dwelt the ancient gods, proud and boastful, who had sanctioned man's early efforts to weave cultural values into an ordered society. They were long dead and lost in oblivion, yielding their thrones to a younger generation of gods, more exclusive and arrogant, the world-challenging deities of Israel, Iran and Christianity. Over this vast domain was spread a colorful covering of thought forms, interwoven by the drift of many cultures through a score of centuries, in which were blended Greek, Jewish, Christian, Gnostic, Manichaean, Zoroastrian and Buddhist influences. No one of these intellectual heritages was dominant everywhere, but each gave its distinctive coloring to the fundamental pattern in some area of the Muslim world. In the effort to preserve his dignity and supremacy in the midst of these challenging cultural forces Allah was buffeted by the winds of change.

As he set out to administer his world kingdom, the God of Mohammed, as the faithful knew him, was a real person with characteristics like their own but on a nobler and vaster scale. It was no shadowy figure that watched over men from the heavenly throne. Allah had a body with hands and feet, eyes and ears. He was austere and terrible as became a god who held the reins of world destiny in his hands, but to the Muslim, yielding himself to the divine will, he was merciful, compassionate and of boundless generosity. Like all lowly folk everywhere, the worshippers of Allah could think of God only in terms of their hopes and needs.

Allah was plunged into the campaign for human salvation and world mastery with no prophet to interpret his will and to lay down the lines of strategy. The guiding hand of Mohammed had been removed suddenly without provision for leadership, legislation or administrative machinery. The "last prophet" of God could hardly have a successor, but necessity led the religious-political community to find a formula for earthly guidance in the selection of Vicars of the Apostle of God—the Califs. In plotting the path through new situations and new problems, the spirit of Mohammed hovered over his successors as they sought guidance from his former acts and decisions in meeting the emerging needs.

In the *Sunna*—the Tradition which cherished the memory of Mohammed's sayings and deeds and served as an authority second only to the revealed Koran—Allah appears as a delightfully human person. He balances various parts of the universe on the fingers of one hand and shouts, "I am the King, where are the Kings of earth?" [16] When hell begins to fill up he packs it down with his foot until hell cries out, "Enough, enough." [17] The last man to enter paradise will win this undeserved reward because God will be moved to laughter by his outrageous presumption upon the divine good nature.[18] The eagerness of Allah to forgive and save is an oft-repeated refrain in the Tradition. If a man lost his camel in the desert, searched for it in vain until he fell asleep through utter weariness and then, at his awakening, found his camel at his side with water and provisions in its mouth, the joy that man would feel is not equal to that Allah feels when a believer repents. He sends his messengers searching through hell to rescue anyone who has in his heart faith even as much as a grain of mustard seed. Over Allah's throne are written the words, "My mercy will overcome my anger." [19] Desire and faith thus mellowed the character of the God who since the earliest Meccan days had awed men by the terrors of doom. Although his inscrutable will fixed the fates of men for the alluring joys of paradise, or the flaming fires of hell, the anxious heart hoped that repentance and submission might weight the scales on the side of mercy. Allah of the Tradition was always transcendent, aloof as a majestic sovereign, but he kept his useful, human qualities. The corrosive intellectual atmosphere of Hellenism did not dim his vivid personality for the compilers of the lore handed down by the companions of the prophet.

The rich, colorful character of Allah and his intimate linking with the human scene are apparent in the ninety-nine "most excellent titles," given to him in the Koran and invested with magic power in the Tradition.[20] The names clothed him with the useful and desirable qualities essential to a god who was the guarantor of human hopes. Many of them were attributes of majesty, extolling his grandeur, exaltation, power and glory. Some expanded his knowledge to omniscience as the hearer, seer, knower, witness, from whose all-seeing eye nothing in heaven or earth was hidden. Social values found support in names which embodied the qualities of justice, righteousness, holiness and truth. Nearer to the needs of the lowly folk were the titles which expressed his boundless liberality and generosity as patron, provider, providence and giver of bread. Fearful and anxious before the awful master of destiny, Muslims tugged at the sleeve of fate with names describing Allah as merciful, forgiving, compassionate, patient and long-suffering. All the titles were meaningful because, under the cloak of reverence, they daringly placed responsibility upon Allah for meeting the many needs of men. Every approved form of human desire clamoring for fulfillment found an answer in some phase of the divine nature.

The Muslim, praying for help, could select the special name suitable for each situation to release the limitless resources of divine beneficence.

Allah, of the beautiful names, had won his place as a masterful world god, efficient and useful, bound by the strong cords of human heart-hunger to the toiling, hoping, suffering pilgrims on the path to paradise. The theologians had not yet begun to worry about saving him from the philosophers. His attributes bore the stamp of their social origin. The names had an earthy flavor. They meant that Allah could be trusted to satisfy the homely, physical desires for food, health, wealth, security and freedom from suffering and fear, the wider social desires for knowledge, power, victory, justice and peace, the personal desires for honor, affection, relief of sorrow, forgiveness, and a safe passage through the grave to the heaven of bliss. When all the qualities involved in the names of Allah are assembled they make a robe of royalty worthy to be worn by a god molded by human hearts to champion the hopes of man.

The name "Father," so precious to Jews and Christians in appealing to their gods, was denied to Allah. When he took the leadership of the local deities in the early days, the Meccan goddesses were given rank as his daughters. Mohammed scoffed at the idea of a god having daughters when he might as easily have sons. The austere Allah of his vision, maker of heaven and earth, who brought things into existence by the creative word, could have no need of begetting either sons or daughters. When Mohammed found that the Christians called Jesus the Son of God, and from some confused legend learned that Yahweh of Israel had a son, Ozair, he denounced the doctrine as untrue and unworthy of the supreme God of the world. Tradition was faithful to the word of the prophet, until in the wars of empire and philosophy, it was too late to talk of a Father God in Islam.

One law governs the life of the gods through all their development and change. They must guarantee the values of the highest ideal of the perfect life for man. While the centuries drift lazily over an untroubled world, their task is easy; but in ages of conflict when cultures meet and mingle, giving rise to new desires and problems, the gods often find themselves in perplexing situations. Rival intellectual and social interests strive to enlist the divine support. Where there is a company of gods, they may vary in character and share responsibility for the diverse ideals and programs. But a solitary God, like Allah, must bear the burden alone. In the effort to be still the one God and yet yield to the pull of new interests, he seemed, for a time, to be touched by the sickness of split personality, bewildered in the effort to choose the new character which would equip him to meet, with divine dignity and usefulness, the altered cultural conditions.

The problem for Allah was especially difficult. He was in face to face contact with other great gods, each claiming world sovereignty—Yahweh, Ahura Mazda and the God of Christianity. They were at home in the lands which he invaded and often put him on the defensive as his character was matched with theirs. Still more troublesome was the intellectual climate which sapped the vitality of all gods with human qualities. For several centuries Allah of the Arabian folk-religion was engaged in a struggle with philosophers, and was in danger of losing his original character in spite of his protecting cloak of Tradition.

Empire also brought more practical issues than the conflict of ideas to trouble the peace of Allah. The complex culture created new desires which clamored for the support of the divine will. The solution of problems totally foreign to the simple life of Arabia called for an enlargement of the functions of Allah and a new interpretation of his nature. The empire builders, driving to practical goals across the interests and desires of the faithful followers of a plainer desert ideal, used divine predestination to justify their success. They gloried in the absolute will of God. On the other hand, the frustrated and dispossessed, thrust aside by the masters of power, insisted that God must be ruled by the law of goodness, leave freedom to the human will and hold men, even rulers, to responsibility for their deeds. The revelations of Allah in the Koran were sufficiently diverse to give support to either position. Moreover, converts to Islam could not divorce themselves from their various cultural heritages and worshipped, not Allah of Arabia and the Tradition, but an Allah seen through the thought-screens of their own inherited ideas. Torn by these complex and divergent influences, many generations passed before the character of Allah was set in its orthodox mold.

The God of Mohammed had come out of his homeland a clear-cut, forthright figure, humanly familiar as an Arab sheik sketched on a canvas of cosmic proportions. Tradition had softened and deepened his original qualities as new needs arose. By the "beautiful names" the believer could confidently lay hold upon some phase of the divine nature in any time of trouble, or to ease the pain of unfulfilled desire. During the first two centuries of his imperial career, like all the other efficient folk gods, Allah was a comprehensible person, splendid enough to hold the helm of the universe, but also an interested spectator of the earthly scene, and near enough to hear the call of men. When Muslims bowed before his grandeur and might, and compensated for their weakness by extolling his mercy, forgiveness and generosity, they bore witness to the maturity of Allah as a practically effective god. The lowly folk were content to trust his ability to provide for the needs of their earthly pilgrimage, and to guarantee perfect blessedness in the future. They troubled not at all to understand him.

The intellectuals, however, from their first contact with the thought of Syria, were haunted by the ghosts of ancient Greek philosophers, suggesting subtle doubts regarding the existence and nature of this all-too-human deity.[21] Sustained by the hopes and needs of a people, Allah had grown to greatness, unquestioned and uncriticized. Now he was plunged into the fires of philosophic thought and forced to defend his personal qualities against the refining influences of his intellectual friends. When thinkers followed the arguments of the Greeks to demonstrate his existence they found at the end of the ladder of logic, not the familiar Allah of faith, rich in qualities, but a vague, disembodied First Cause quite useless for the needs of religion and life. In the effort to find a rational basis for the valuable characteristics of God so dear to Islam, the intellect was baffled. Scepticism and agnosticism followed close on the footsteps of reason. In the hands of the philosophers Allah might have died of anemia. To have passed the test of critical thought at the cost of being transformed into a pale abstraction would have marked him with the malady from which no god recovers—uselessness. Fortunately he was too securely protected by the authority of the prophet, the Koran, and Tradition, to depend upon the dubious support of philosophy for his continued life and influence in the world. In the choice between revelation and reason, the stern needs of living weighted the balance toward faith in a God endowed with all desirable qualities.

Like the other great gods of the world, Allah was clothed by faith with every characteristic needful for the fulfillment of the desires of his people. His many useful attributes were accepted without question but in the intellectual and social climate of the empire thought labored long to find a satisfactory definition of his unity and absolute will. The unity of Allah demanded defense at all costs. Since the days of Mohammed it had been a distinctive quality of the god of Islam. In the atmosphere of Greek thought with its essences and universals, the eternal attributes of Allah seemed to threaten his unity. Thinkers feared that they might assume separate existences in their own right and so complicate the godhead with a multiplicity of eternal beings. Other gods gave warning. The attributes of Ahura Mazda of Iran had long ago attained independent existence as celestial, personal figures. The unity of the Christian God had been shattered by what Muslim thinkers saw as the personalizing of attributes of the original ONE. There was a vast expenditure of energy in quest of a formula which would leave the saving value of the attributes untouched, and yet preserve the divine unity. As self-styled champions of unity, the Mutazilites denied the existence of any eternal attribute of the deity. Only the essence of Allah could be eternal. It was incorrect to say that God has attributes, or that the attributes are phases of his nature. The accurate statement would be that Allah is omniscient as to his essence, or God is a being who knows by means of a knowledge which he himself is. These were the saving words—a subtle verbal solution of an insoluble intellectual problem.

The orthodox followers of tradition were not so anxious about distinctions. They were content to guard the divine unity by saying that the attributes are eternally inherent in the essence of Allah, without separation or change. No one doubted the efficacy of the characteristics of Allah for human needs. Through the long battle of words he remained for practical religion the old familiar god, thoroughly competent to hold the reins of destiny, to shepherd the faithful to blessedness and to plunge the infidel into the ultimate torments of hell, according to his choice and decree.

At the very beginning of his world career, Allah was recognized as a god of absolute will. He was fate in personal form. Only the greatest theologians in other religions, following the logic of theism through to its goal, have seen that to believe in one, absolute god means to embrace determinism. Not logic but the facts of history gave Muslims their absolute Allah. His desert origin and the atmosphere of conflict in his early career made him from his earliest days more autocratic than the other great gods. Mohammed had needed a strong deity who could impose his steely purposes upon the events of time. He had found comfort in times of discouragement in the faith that all things happen according to the divine decree. Tradition followed him. But thinkers in contact with older cultures were troubled by this implacable destiny fixed by the will of Allah. The Gods of Judaism and Christianity had a gentler quality. Grace, goodness and justice were more prominent in their characters. Moreover, the social conscience demanded recognition of human free will and responsibility as a basis for moral living. The rationalists challenged the absolute will of Allah in the interest of justice and moral responsibility. They could not believe that he would will evil as well as good, nor that men could be condemned to suffering here and hereafter without responsibility for their deeds. Exalting the goodness of Allah, they insisted that he willed all things according to goodness and justice. Some even asserted that he not only would not, but could not, will anything but the good for his creatures. This was a brave attempt to relieve Allah from responsibility for evil and transfer the burden to the evil purposes of men.

The traditional view of God, however, was too firmly rooted. Orthodoxy refused to put any limitations upon the divine will. It must be absolutely free. There could be no necessity upon God even to do justice. As the creator of all things he was the supreme master. Man could have no claim against him. He determined the fate of every individual from birth to death and beyond. No man had power to do any deed except as God willed. Both good and evil came from him. The devious paths men travel, leading at last to paradise or hell, were all charted by the divine decree. Some thinkers were so

thorough in their glorification of Allah as absolute will that
they denied all law in the universe, all causality in the natural
and social realms, to load upon him the tiresome task of re-
arranging every atom of the universe every second, so that
the world was a new creation from the hand of God with
every passing moment. If there seemed to be regularity and
continuity in events, it was because Allah chose to create in
that way. Rarely has any people made a god so absolute as the
God of Islam. The seeds were in the Koran, and found fertile
soil in the Muslim social structure. Autocratic princes whose
wills and whims could not be effectively challenged by their
subjects furnished an earthly pattern for the majestic Allah
on the throne of heaven.

Muslims learned to rejoice in Allah as the stern master of
destiny. They knew his many ideal qualities and trusted him
to give comfort and security to those who needed his help
in times of distress. As fate, he wrote a final "Kismet" only
upon the past. No man knew the fashion of the future. Faith
and hope could still appeal for tomorrow's happiness to the
God of inexorable will. The doors of destiny stood open for
unfulfilled desire. At the same time there was a quieting assurance in knowing that the deeds of every day were fixed by
divine decree. It gave courage in times of danger, release from
the gnawing of remorse, freedom from anxiety in frustration,
calm resignation in privation, peace in sorrow and pride in
successful achievement. The will of Allah not only gave certainty that all that is, is right, but touched with divine depth
the commonplaces of daily living.

Old gods, whose prophets have made them living realities
in the service of their people, live on through long ages without great change in the hearts of the unlettered masses. Untroubled by philosophic doubts, the lowly believers can only
be shaken in their faith by tragic disorder in their routine of
daily living. Even against this invitation to doubt his good-

ness or his power, Allah had a protection in the fundamental doctrine of his all-wise will governing human destiny. Without trying to understand the reason for their fate, the people could use their god as a shield against the fears and tribulations of every day. For meditative minds, however, cultural experience during the ninth and tenth centuries did serious damage to Allah as a consoling and effective, working god. He seemed to be withdrawn as an inscrutable being, far from contact with human hearts and the call of earthly needs. It was not so much the veiling mists of metaphysics that obscured him. Theologians, in their studied efforts to make him intellectually respectable, had toned down the vitality of the homely, heavenly champion of Mohammed with eyes and hands, "his body firmly settled on his throne." Moreover, the times were often troubled. The fickleness of princes, tyranny and intolerance in high places, sudden shifts of fortune, the ruthlessness of warring sects, noisy conflict over the divine nature, made more needful a door of refuge into the comforting presence of God.

Many intellectuals, to escape bewilderment, turned longing eyes backward to the security of the faith of earlier days. Al-Ash'ari (d. 935) gave form to that trend. He restored the Allah of the Koran and Tradition, but with a difference. All the human imagery which made him so vividly real as the heavenly friend of the faithful must be true of him, but the meaning of the words could not be the human meaning. He had a face, two hands and eyes, for the Koran so described him, yet no man could know their form. All terms which express perfection may be applied to him, but in a different and higher sense. Thus Al-Ash'ari presented Allah as a comprehensible god to the naïve multitude and guarded him against the attack of the skeptic; preserved the literal descriptions of the scriptures and saved them from being stumbling-blocks to thought. Sheltered under the shadow of authority, he defied the philosophers and kept the ancient Allah, the one, eternal being, creator and sustainer of the world, who was omnipotent and omniscient. Allah knew not only what men do but what they will to do, not only what happens but how what does not happen would have happened, if it had happened.[22] All the myriad threads of life's intricate patterns flow into place under the direction of his will. Good and evil, bitter and sweet, help and hurt come to man according to Allah's predestination. No man is independent in his deeds. God wills that some shall believe, and graciously guides them and cares for them. He wills that others shall not believe and leads them astray. As the absolute sovereign over his creatures he decrees what pleases him. If he should bring all men to paradise there would be no injustice. If he sent them all to hell, he could not be accused of wrong-doing. The creator and absolute Lord of the universe may do what he wills with his own.

Allah, of the rigid decrees, in this orthodox dress was an effective god for both the ignorant man and the intellectual. In naïve simplicity he could be visualized as a majestic personal being, with human characteristics, possessing knowledge, power, life, will, hearing, sight and speech. All the qualities which Allah had acquired in the development of Islam were retained. At the same time thinkers knew that their god was more, and less, than the Allah of the common people. The philosophic bath had washed out, for them, the clear and human meaning of his attributes. None of the descriptive terms could be taken in a literal sense. But since they were sure that philosophic truth and religious truth must be one, they could accept the traditional words as faint flashes of insight into the nature of God who, in his true being, was beyond the grasp of understanding. While the man of simple faith made his plea to a real and comprehensible Allah, the intellectual peered beyond this simple figure, sending his heart and mind in quest of the unknown.

Against God ruling as fate, however, the social conscience found voice in the repeated protests of philosophers and rationalists. For them the power and sovereignty of Allah were not so important as his justice. Blind faith might find a drugged peace in complete surrender to almighty power but a god of justice, who gave men freedom and imposed responsibility upon them for moral living, seemed to be necessary if individuals were to be held socially accountable for their actions. The Mutazilites were willing to attribute to divine predestination experiences of trial and deliverance, adversity and prosperity, sickness and health, death and life, but not moral good and evil, virtue and vice. Over against the texts of the Koran which supported the doctrine of divine decrees, they set the passages which stressed human responsibility. They appealed to reason for support—to no avail. Reason may often destroy a deity, or at best refine and mellow his acquired qualities, but the character of a god is drawn from deeper, social sources. The absolute Allah of al-Ash'ari was perfectly acceptable to the autocratic rulers, the dominant law schools, the defenders of tradition and the popular masses blindly following their religious leaders. Through tragic and tempestuous centuries, Muslims learned how to reap the full reward of comfort and consolation from their god of the eternal decrees. Enfolded in the strong arms of destiny, hearts hungering for divine help could commit their sorrows and failures, distress and poverty to the divine will with calm peace and resignation.

Some members of the far-flung and divergent empire of Allah were not content under the autocratic rule of the heavenly king depicted by orthodoxy. In spite of his many beautiful names which bound him to human needs, they found an austere and forbidding quality in his personality. The master of the terrors of hell, whose inscrutable will fixed the fates of men forever, was awe-inspiring, and far removed.

The desire to draw Allah into more consoling communion
with the heart of man had been growing in Islam since the
eighth century. The Muslim masses, who did not probe into
the nature of God, followed the formula of faith and hoped
that the Lord of heaven would deal more wisely and gener-
ously with them than the lords of earth, but many thoughtful
men were troubled. In them there was a conflict between the
head which could not find the god they sought, and the heart
which hungered for the peace of secure enfoldment. The supreme emotional value of a god lies in the feeling of safe at-
homeness in his presence, in his nearness to the call for help
and guidance. Yet from the eighth to the eleventh century,
there had been a persistent tendency, under the double pressure
of reason and orthodoxy, to thrust Allah into heights so remote that only thought could reach him. Rationalism was
reducing him to a vague being, without any emotional appeal.
As an eternal First Cause, he not only failed to stir the deeps
of devotion but seemed to be far-removed from any possible
concern with human troubles. Even theology had been so
anxious to defend his unity, and so careful to dehumanize
his attributes that the vast difference between God and man
chilled the hope of fellowship with him for all but blind believers, untroubled by the spark of thought.

The influence of Neo-Platonism or of Aristotle in Neo-
platonic dress led some Muslim thinkers to seek security
through the union of the soul with God. Ibn-Sina labored to
demonstrate the intimate relation between the human soul
and the first cause of all. The Brethren of Purity identified
Allah with the Primal Absolute Cause. From this original
source came by emanation, first the active intelligence and
then the abstract soul which is embodied in the multitudes
of human individuals. Man, therefore, is a spark of the divine
fire. He remembers his homeland and is ever questing, by
discipline, by noble living, by mental toil to find the way

back to bliss and perfection in the source from which he sprang. Thus, intellectually the vast gulf between God and man was bridged, and relationship with Allah, even as a vague First Cause, took on an emotional glow.

Following the lead of emotion, the Sufi mystics completely closed the chasm between the human and the divine. They turned their backs upon reason, made a formal bow to orthodoxy to find in the deep experience of the heart a path into the presence of God——

> Whoso seeks God and takes the intellect for guide,
> God drives him forth, in vain distraction to abide;
> With wild confusion He confounds his inmost heart,
> So that, distraught, he cries, "I know not if Thou art." [23]

For them, all life was radiant with the splendor of the divine presence. Allah was no longer the far-off, inscrutable Lord of the universe separated from man by the obscuring veils of difference. He was the lover, the friend, the beloved. His perfection found expression in love and beauty. He was the soul of all souls. When the self was completely surrendered, and only the thought of God filled the heart, all the veils of separation fell away and the Sufi became intoxicated with the ecstasy of being lost in the divine unity. Learning was accounted folly, reason a shackle, the dull formalism of the law a crutch for the spiritually lame. The boundaries between religions became meaningless, all creeds indifferent, for only the heart held the mystery of the meaning of Allah——

> Cross and Christians, from end to end,
> I surveyed: He was not on the cross.
> I went to the idol-temple, to the ancient pagoda;
> No trace was visible there. . . .
>
> I bent the reins of search to the Ka'ba:
> He was not in that resort of old and young. . . .

I gazed into my heart:
There I saw Him: He was nowhere else.[24]

———

Oh heart, we have searched from end to end:
    I saw in thee naught save the Beloved.
Call me not infidel, O heart, if I say,
    Thou thyself art He.[25]

———

I am He whom I love, and He whom I love is I.
We are two spirits dwelling in one body.
If thou seest me, thou seest Him;
And if thou seest Him, thou seest us both.[26]

Thus the Sufis made the final and most daring flight of religious faith—identifying the life of man with the manifestation in time of the life of Allah. Instead of the old formula of faith, "There is no God but Allah," the mystic said, "There is nothing but Allah." At one stroke the anxious quest for salvation, the weary toil of man's earthly pilgrimage, the fears and sorrows of life's lonely way vanished. There was no longer need to search the sacred books for evidence of God's interest in man's well-being. There was no more need of prayer to span the vast expanse to the throne of God. No longer need man lift eyes filled with awe and hope to an unseen being in an unknown spiritual realm. The obliterating unity of Allah included man. The omnipresent will of Allah enfolded all things, and cradled the resigned heart in blissful security and peace. All actions are God's, for God is all.

In the market, in the cloister—only God I saw.
In the valley and on the mountain—only God I saw.
Him I have seen beside me oft in tribulation;
In favor and in fortune—only God I saw.
In prayer and fasting, in praise and contemplation,
In the religion of the Prophet—only God I saw.
Neither soul nor body, accident nor substance,

Qualities nor causes—only God I saw.
I oped mine eyes and by the light of his face around me
In all the eye discovered—only God I saw.
Like a candle I was melting in his fire;
Amid the flames outflashing—only God I saw.
Myself with mine own eyes I saw most clearly,
But when I looked with God's eyes—only God I saw.
I passed away into nothingness, I vanished,
And lo, I was the All-living—only God I saw.[27]

While the mystics found the joy and peace of intimate union with Allah, they made no attempt to obliterate the characteristics of the historic personal god, or to transform him into an impersonal Absolute. When they said, "The being of all things is God: there is nothing except Him," or, "I am God," they did not mean what the Buddhist or Hindu means when he speaks of the unity of man and God. The union with Allah of the Muslim mystic was not an incarnation of God in man, nor an infusion of the divine essence, nor a union of the divine and human natures, nor a displacement of the human attributes by the divine. It was an act of identification with God by complete surrender. Allah kept his royal and majestic state. For the Sufis he was still clothed in all the qualities of tradition. The essential thing for the mystics as for orthodox Islam was the absolute will of Allah. Since all the events of time and all the acts of man are the manifestation of the divine will, the individual is lost in God when he realizes that all he is and does, is only an expression of the being and doing of Allah. Man is nothing, because God is all. Man is everything because he is safely included in the absolute will of God. The Sufis sang of wine and drunkenness, of love and ecstasy because these symbols could best express a joyous self-surrender in humble devotion, as well as the care-free calm and exalted pride of embodying the divine will.

At the close of the eleventh century, Allah had a brilliant

champion in the greatest of Muslim theologians, al-Ghazzali.
With the heart of a mystic and the head of a philosopher, he
mediated between the poetic pantheism of the Sufis and the
cold intellectualism of orthodoxy. The efforts of the philosophers to find and define Allah, he felt, led only to material-
ism and a denial of any God of value to man. He turned back
from his wanderings in the waste lands of philosophy to
revelation, the Koran and Tradition. His god is the living,
personal Allah of faith with all his characteristic qualities,
but seen through the mystic vision of Ghazzali he appears
nobler and more attractive. All the crudities of the earlier days
are gone, and the aloofness of the austere, transcendent unity
is lost in the omnipresence of a purely spiritual being. Allah
is the one, only, living god, creator and lord of the worlds,
visible and invisible, all-wise, all-powerful, just and good. He
sees and hears, but not with eyes and ears. He seizes and creates
but not with hand or instrument, for his qualities are not the
qualities of men. Through the ages he has spoken to mankind, in the Torah, the Gospel and the Psalms. The Koran is
his eternal word. His knowledge embraces everything. Not a
leaf falls but he knows it. "He knows the creeping of the
black ant upon the rugged rock in a dark night and he per-
ceives the movement of the mote in the midst of the air." [28]
By his will the heavens and the earth were created out of nothing, by his will they are guided, and in the last solemn hour
of time they will pass away at his command. "There does not
come about in the world, seen or unseen, little or much, small
or great, good or evil, advantage or disadvantage, faith or unbelief, knowledge or ignorance, success or loss, increase or
diminution, obedience or rebellion except by his will. What he
wills is, and what he wills not is not." [29] Eternal and unchanging, the shuttle of his wise will weaves the lives of men into
the pattern dictated by divine justice. His mercy is over those
who believe. Not one will be left in the fires of hell who has

in his heart the weight of a single grain of faith. His glory suffuses everything. His presence is everywhere. The unveiled eyes of prophets and mystics see him in nature, but best of all in their own hearts.

By the beginning of the twelfth century the character of Allah had crystallized into a lasting pattern. The threat of metaphysics which had troubled him for four centuries was overcome. The virile god of tradition won his way back to the leadership of Islam. During the period of philosophic criticism there were times when he seemed to be fading into a formless figure—a mere verbal abstraction. In the effort to make him intellectually acceptable, reason had tried to push him into the unknown, and to tone down the warm human qualities which made him valuable as a folk god. As a First Cause, or an eternal, necessary being, touching man's abode beneath the moon only through a series of emanations, he would have been useless as a god of the lowly people and he could not have held his place for long in the hearts even of philosophers. Reason was providing a dignified burial for the richly endowed, personal Allah, weaving his shroud of subtle, obscuring words; but a god who has been vividly alive for the imagination of a people through stirring centuries does not take death and dissolution gracefully—even a gentle death under the scalpel of thought. Some intellectuals did indeed follow their thinking through to skepticism or agnosticism. In the struggle between faith and philosophy, however, the prestige of Mohammed, the Koran and Tradition, the orthodox law schools and the needs of the people were on the side of Allah against the philosophers. The greatest philosopher of Islam, Ibn Rushd (Averroes), recognized the danger of the conflict and offered the formula for a treaty of peace. He separated the domain of faith from the domain of thought and set up "no trespassing" signs between them. With Allah safely secluded in the realm of faith, philosophy could travel its own high road without affecting him in any way. Reason might refuse to report any knowledge of Allah; yet the lowliest and most ignorant Muslims knew him. He had come to them as all gods come to men, not as a creation of pure thought, but as a gift of the uncriticized past, acquiring distinctive character in the experience of Mohammed, hallowed and enshrined in the vivid imagery of Tradition. It was enough that he was available by faith as a powerful heavenly person, a helper, guide and guardian amid life's sorrows, perplexities and fears.

After the thirteenth century, Allah was untroubled by any challenge to change for five hundred years. His contact with Greek thought had left its marks upon him. Intimate interaction with the God of Christianity had emphasized his unity and mellowed some of the sterner qualities of his early days. The shock of the Crusades left him unaffected. Political tyrannies, justifying the accomplished fact on the basis of divine decrees, had served only to etch more deeply the inexorable quality of his absolute will. When Islam surrendered the torch of intellectual leadership in the thirteenth century and the glory of Bagdad was buried under the Tartar hordes, there were few thinkers who cared or dared to question the Allah of faith. The religious leaders of the masses withdrew from the dangerous adventure of thought to find shelter behind the tested defences of orthodoxy.

The Allah who emerged from the Middle Ages to await the coming of the modern world was a supreme, personal god, creator, ruler, Lord of heaven and earth, with the seven essential qualities of power, life, knowledge, will, hearing, seeing, speaking. The holy book, the Koran, uncreated and eternal, held its place of paramount importance because it was Allah's word, a key to the rich treasure house of divine truth. Qualities which trailed Allah from Arabia through the winding ways of Tradition still clung to him. He was called proud and awful, mighty and majestic, merciful and compassionate, great and generous, but the qualities which ever held the central place in his character were his unity and his absolute will. As the one, alone, single sovereign, Allah inscribed the pages of the book of destiny for individuals, nations and the world, according to his inscrutable purpose.

During the last two centuries, the ancient rivals of Allah for world dominion, the Gods of Israel and of Christianity, have been changing their medieval costumes to assume forms more acceptable to the fashion of an age of science and social idealism. Allah has been awakened to the need of adjustment only during the last fifty years. His character as the one, absolute master of human destiny had been so firmly fixed, so hardened in the fires of controversy, that he was unaffected by the long era of frustration during which Islam was elbowed from its high place in world politics. His will justified events and fostered a mood of quiet acceptance and resignation. To the unthinking masses, who used their god instead of questioning him, his almighty power and wisdom gave courage and hardihood in tragedy, anæsthesia against sorrow, and peace in the darkest hours. For the wise and ignorant alike, Allah bore the burden of responsibility for the ordering of the world plan.

The Muslim peoples, however, are no longer content with things as they are. The forces which are transforming all old cultures have broken through the protective covering of orthodoxy in Islam. Among Muslims, spread over three continents, with vastly varied cultural conditions, the leaven of modernism has worked with different degrees of effectiveness. There came a feeling of resentment of the political and economic backwardness of the Muslim states, a growing revolt against the complacent, orthodox leaders and a desire for a new education, modern scientific knowledge and the fruits of applied science. The spirit of social reform which had made all other peoples restive in the presence of old evils during the nineteenth century at last captured the intellectuals of Islam. They began to search for justification in the Koran for their vision of a modernized Muslim world and man's responsibility for creating it.

Allah was not caught in the first wave of change. Movements in Africa and Arabia which sought to save Islam by a return to the primitive simplicity of the religion of the prophet were content with the Allah of the common people. The greatest leader of Egyptian reform at the close of last century, Sheik Muhammed Abdou,[30] left all the traditional characteristics of Allah intact. For him, the God of Islam was eternal, without beginning and without end, unique in his existence and perfection, powerful, living, knowing, willing, hearing, speaking, seeing. At first glance one seems to see the ancient Allah, unchanged, standing at the threshold of the new age. But there is a difference, for Sheik Abdou repudiated the fatalism of the divine decrees, made man share responsibility for making a good world, and claimed the support of the divine will for the values of his vision of a new social order. This is the prophet's way of changing his god. Because he is perfect, his purposes must point toward the realization of the noblest ideal. Thus, by the very loyalty of his interpreter, Allah is being modernized to be practically useful to the builders of a new world.

Like all the great personal gods who have survived until modern times, Allah is losing the characteristics which marked him indelibly as the god of a special group. The struggles, hopes and fears of the Muslim people gave him the distinctive qualities so carefully cherished and so passionately defended in the historic past. For modern thinkers the rivalries of the gods are over. The world has grown too small. Intellectual and cultural influences overflow all boundaries. Internationalism and democratic social idealism are replacing the old, defensive nationalism in the modern religious ideal. The gods tend to blend into one. As he appears in the liberal literature of the post-war period, Allah can scarcely be distinguished from the God of the Christian liberals. He is no longer the austere monarch ruling the world with autocratic will. Justice, beauty, forgiveness and love find a larger place in his character, as becomes the god of an age reaching out prayerfully toward an ideal of democratic internationalism.

In the modern world, Allah faces new forms of philosophy, grounded on the findings of science, more threatening than was the thought of ancient Greece. Signs of the dissolution of his old self are beginning to appear. He is being removed from his transcendent separateness as a supreme Person to become the immanent spiritual reality of the evolving, cosmic process. In one attempt at reconstruction of Muslim thinking,[31] he is interpreted as the Absolute Ego, including in his being the whole of reality. The life of Allah thus finds expression in self-revelation, which is the ongoing creative process of the universe. His creative energy is in the mechanical movement of the atoms of matter and on a higher level, in the free movement of thought in the human ego. He is one with his creation. The countless varieties of living forms reveal the infinite wealth of his being. Out of the many levels of selves, from the material to the human, there is emerging, in man, the capacity for conscious participation in the creative life of God. Thus the world is reaching the point of intelligent self-guidance, which may reveal the ultimate nature of God in the final triumph of goodness. Meanwhile, Allah is self-limited because he has chosen finite egos to be participators in his life, power and freedom. All the old attributes of Allah find a new meaning in this interpretation of the universe as the self-revelation of the life of God.

The interest of the new philosophy is not in defending the Supernatural Being who carried the burden of human hopes

through the historic ages, but in the facts of modern knowledge, and the intellectual and social problems of man's life
in the new age. If the ancient God cannot be retained, the
heart of man, even as philosopher, will persuade his intellect
to find a way to preserve the values of god by some process
of recreation of the divine image. But when men become im-
patient with the slow grinding of the mills of God, confident
of their new powers, and desperately serious in the task of
making the old vision of a good world come true, they are
likely to lose interest in preserving either the old God of
autocratic will, or his modernized philosophic image. For one
Muslim group, at least, Allah has lost meaning in this way.
"The belief in a Supreme Being ruling the universe according to his whim not only shows vast credulity, but it results
in a sad weakening of the human spirit which it condemns to
hopeless futility." [32]

Allah still lives on—but not as the clear, well-defined personality of the olden days. The Muslim masses may cherish
and give him life into the indefinite future, but thinkers are
leading him along the path that ends in a surrender of the
divine functions into human hands. When man at last assumes responsibility for the creation of the values he desires
and finds the plastic stuff of reality yielding readily to his
molding intelligence and will, some day he will look up from
his work, surprised to find that God has taken the opportunity
to disappear.

CHAPTER XII

THE TWILIGHT OF THE GODS

Whether there be gods or no gods,
Man is, and man's task.

OW long can the gods endure the conditions
of our modern world? In every land, they are
challenged by the restless intellectual and social forces transforming all phases of traditional
cultures. They cannot be tomorrow what they
were in the less complex ages in which their characters were
formed. Already change has laid hold upon them testing their
worth for the new world. The little gods of the little people
are dying with no defenders to stay the hand of death. Long
and well they answered the call of the lowly folk who hardly
dared to bring their private troubles to the mighty deities
who ruled the universe. For ages the smiling tolerance of
the officials in church and state protected these folk divinities
until the enervating intellectual climate and swift social
change of the modern age dried up the springs of their vitality. Now the great gods face the test, for the ancient rule
still stands, however it may be veiled beneath the show of
reverence, worship and prayer—a god lives by his value to
man.

If the shadows of night are gathering about the gods our
world has known, the only novelty in the event for cosmic
history will be the manner of their passing. Many generations of divine beings before them arose from lowly origins,
lived through their bright eon of glory and vanished.

Weighted with honor and empire, they were majestic figures to the peoples who praised them as almighty and eternal. They speak to us now only from their tombs. Yet some of them reached an age not yet attained by any of the gods we know. Others, Hittite, Hyksos, Greek and Roman deities, rose to power with splendid promise, played out their rôles with meteoric swiftness and were gone after little more than a millennium.

The lives of the gods have been relatively short as man now counts cosmic time. If this story had been written three thousand years ago a very different list of divine names would have appeared as the greatest deities of the world. Of the gods in our record only Yahweh, Ahura Mazda and Shangti (T'ien) were active at that time and the historian might well have passed them by as minor figures. He could hardly have guessed that they would attain the nobility of character and wide dominion that has won them world renown. Two thousand years ago, the Christian God was still in the womb of the future, Amaterasu-Omikami was no more than a local, tribal deity, and the dawn of the career of Allah still five centuries away. To man, of few years, the gods seem to be immortal. Man's life is fragile as the flowers of the grass; a god spans the centuries, sharing the enduring strength of a people, a nation, a culture. Yet these things too are infected with mortality, and gods bound to them rarely survive their destruction.

No generation of deities ever contemplated a stranger world than that in which the great living gods await the hour of destiny. They are crowded together on a planet which the mind and might of man have narrowed to a neighborhood. Their peoples are entangled in a network of forces that cross all boundaries of creed, color and culture. The conflicting wills of men, reinforced with superhuman power, have been able once more to make a shambles of the earth and to challenge the values of justice, love and peace which the gods have ever been expected to undergird and guarantee. Modern men have been willing to free them from many tasks performed in ancient times, only to claim more anxiously than before their support for social ideals. Ormazd, Yahweh, Amaterasu, Allah or the Triune God of the Christians—which one of these supreme personal deities holds the secret of the future? Brahman, the ineffable, and the timeless Buddha never assumed any responsibility for the world's creation, nor ever taught men to hope that a divine purpose threaded the earthly round of pain and sorrow. In pity they touched with healing fingers the tortured victims of lust, ignorance and illusion, but their great gift was escape to the bliss eternal. If modern man must find a formula for the good life on earth these impersonal, timeless, purposeless gods are of no avail. They were molded by men who aimed at the realization of divinity, not the perfection of man.

What of the personal gods? Can Amaterasu fulfill the faith of her people and bring, through her divine descendants on the throne of Japan, the era of peace and happiness to all the earth? Will Yahweh make good his promise of long ago to establish the kingdom of righteousness, justice and peace among men? Does Allah, of the eternal decrees, survey the modern scene with poised assurance that all events are marching in obedience to his all-wise, all-powerful will? Is the mighty champion of Zarathustra's faith perhaps preparing the last terrible battle against the powers of darkness which will usher in the reign of goodness in an earth made new? And the Christian God, all-wise, all-good, all-powerful like the others—is he still master of the world plan? Is he leading the peoples by divers paths through toil and terror, hope and anguish to the age of love and brotherhood of which his earliest followers dreamed? There is no answer to such questions. Confucius said it and Mencius repeated it—"Heaven does not say anything."

History gives no assurance that the gods in whom any particular generation believes will continue to be the divine rulers of the future. The actors in the sublime drama of the ages have changed too often. Our intellectual climate may become so different from that in which the historic deities were at home that it will be ever more difficult to find a place in the universe for any one of them. If they must live only as wistful ghosts behind the abstract phrases of philosophy, the gods with full-formed characters, whom the people loved and trusted, will be no more.

Another danger arises from changes in social structure directed by selfish men who care not at all that the gods are guarantors of justice, and do not even trouble to follow the ancient pattern and identify their purposes with the divine will. For them and for their victims, the gods are as though they were not. It is difficult now to conceal from even the most ignorant that groups with sufficient strength and intelligence may make what they will of the world. Gods who may be ignored by the powers that dictate good and evil for the millions forfeit their age-old rights. If men should become convinced that their heavenly protectors have surrendered control of this life, they may also learn to dispense with divine consolation in their sorrows and seek more realistic remedies for earthly ills. There would only remain the divine promise of happiness in another life. Multitudes in many lands would still want their gods to fulfill that promise.

In ancient times gods fell when their empires crumbled before conquering hosts who took over in the name of their own deities. The same process has been quietly at work in the last few centuries through the territorial spread of the domin-- ion of the Christian God. The power and prestige of his peoples, the material and cultural values associated with him, have crowded many old folk deities into obscurity and won millions from allegiance to their ancestral gods. At the dawn of the twentieth century it would have seemed fantastic to suggest that brute conquest might return to the earth to displace the divinities of nations in the modern world. Then it would have seemed more reasonable to believe that the gods would be outgrown through the advance of knowledge and the enrichment of culture, or that their vivid personalities would be refined away by thought. Christians expected that the scores of Oriental deities, if not their own, would vanish in the white light of deeper understanding. Now the pillars of the temples and the foundations of the old order tremble under the impact of new and terrifying forces. Modern conquerors have improved on their predecessors in the use of destructive might, but their chief threat lies in their mastery of the techniques for destroying established beliefs and attitudes by conditioning the mind of youth to the ideas and loyalties which support the new order. To this subtle weapon the gods are peculiarly vulnerable, for every one of them belongs to a historic tradition and draws his strength from the institutions which foster faith in him. If, in the Orient and in the West, old cultures must bow in obedience to new masters with strange gods or no god at all, a future historian may record how mighty deities, who still claimed world sovereignty at the beginning of the twentieth century, surrendered their thrones as silently and as finally as did their predecessors thousands of years ago.

Gods do not die easily. They may be displaced, reduced to inferior rank, lose caste with the ruling and intellectual classes, but a survey of the ages leaves a vivid impression of their amazing hold on life. The gods of Greece and Rome were safe in the faith and affection of the people for centuries after the intellectuals had outgrown them. The deities who have shepherded the lowly folk of India and China were not discouraged because thinkers two thousand years ago ceased to believe in them. Even the active intolerance of the Christian God could not destroy all the old Mediterranean and North European divinities. Some of them are alive today as beneficent saints of the church.

Deities who are useful, live as long as men have faith in them. For one in need, faith has never been difficult, since all our gods, great and small, are spirits, and mankind has been conditioned since primitive times to believe in the existence of spiritual beings from whom help may come. They are not visible and tangible. What reality they have in their varied personal characters was given to them through the centuries by the clamoring desires of men. They are handed down from generation to generation as part of the cultural heritage. Often a divine reputation for valuable service may be transmitted as sacred lore from remote ages. The mighty gods of the modern world are alive today because each of them bears the qualities which identify him with a distinct tradition. He is, therefore, able to stir the hearts of his people as they remember the wisdom, power and goodness manifested in his work for their deliverance. Not "God" nor the god of a foreign scripture and tradition, but the "God of our fathers" is the living god of faith for each of the religions. Only one deadly enemy lies in wait for the gods—the cultural change which undermines the tradition and institutions which foster faith in their ability to serve and save. With emotion, desire and faith as a triple shield, divine spiritual beings may elude indefinitely the arrows of critical thought. Reason did not create them, nor can reason either prove or disprove their existence. It would be extremely difficult to prove the nonexistence of an unseen being dwelling in the unknown.

In all high cultures, the mind of man has wrestled with his heart over the gods. They were firmly entrenched in the rhythmic routine of living long before thought turned speculative eyes upon them. The experiences of early man which gave the gods their start were on a deeper level than the rational. Nature forces which helped him in his hungerings were humanized by emotion and, like himself, endowed with souls by his fateful, primeval imagination. Men of the prehistoric ages made the pattern of deity. If the gods had remained what they were in the beginning, they would have played no significant rôle in history. But some of them magnificently outgrew their origins. Through them the universe was enlisted in the fight for human values. As supreme rulers of heaven and earth, they transformed the cruel face of actuality with a smile that promised future good. All-wise and all-good, they were trusted to support with their power the noblest hopes and highest ideals, the moral values and unrealized wishes of the heroic folk who were conquering their way through a troubled world, refusing to accept frustration of their desires. Each people read the events of history as a revelation of the character of its god and endowed him with the qualities necessary to give assurance of the kind of life visualized as ideal. Sometimes he served as sanction of the established social code, and always as the guarantor of salvation, the realization of the vision of perfect happiness. The ideal phase of the human adventure was embodied in these majestic deities who could be so perfectly what man was not, but only hoped to be. The qualities he would like to possess, the bliss he would like to enjoy, and what he would like to be—these things were eternally realized in the gods. Long before philosophers came to trouble them, they had become pure spiritual beings on this grand scale with only an occasional epithet, some ancient song or a legend of the long ago to keep alive the memory of their origin in some real and visible phase of nature.

The supreme deities all acquired their characters in history. They were not discovered by thought probing the secrets of the universe. It was man's desire for a good life, rich in material and social values, that gave his gods the qualities of justice, love, goodness, power, mercy and anger against wrong doing. The sacred scriptures of the religions display in vivid and pathetic episodes how human needs determined the distinctive personal qualities of each of the gods. Ahura Mazda took form in the anguish of Zarathustra's struggle. Yahweh responded to the needs of Moses and the prophets. Mohammed found the Allah he needed to solve his problems. To give authority to the Yamato rulers of early Japan, Amaterasu issued to her divine grandson the heavenly edict. Later official interpreters spoke of the scriptures as the revelation of God to man. In reality they reveal the kind of god man needed at critical points in his social history. The human situation was reflected on the heavens and the god of each people answered the call. The environing universe was made friendly, values needful for noble living acquired cosmic support through the characters given to the gods. The creative power in this process flowed from the heart, from desire, hope and faith, not from the mind.

The time came, however, in every culture, early in the Orient, later in the West, when the intellect could no longer accept the gods of tradition as the final reality of the universe and set up beyond them in the unknown an original, impersonal power. The reasons for the flight beyond the personal gods varied with the cultures, and thinkers in widely separated parts of the world and in different centuries followed different paths to the goal. Some of the causes underlying their intellectual unrest were doubt of the existence of the gods, mystical experiences of ecstasy, inability to reconcile the rule of a personal deity with the cruel fact of evil, the æsthetic desire for a tidy universe, the quest for a reality beyond all taint of the limitation and change of personal existence. Out of this philosophic labor were born strange deities with no family resemblance to the historic gods who had grown up with the people and earned their right to devotion by their records of service. They were called the attributeless Brahman, the Dharmakaya, the spiritual Absolute, the Tao, the Idea of the Good, the Unmoved Mover, the Logos, *Ens Realissimum,* the First Cause, the deep Sea of Being of which worlds and generations are merely the sunlit waves of transient existence. Almost without exception they could only be defined by such negative terms as impersonal, timeless, unknowable, changeless, purposeless and without desire. Not only were they beyond the grasp of man's understanding, they were unaffected by the desire and anguish, the good and evil of the everyday human world.

If the verdict of intellect on the ultimate deity had been taken at face value the world would have been virtually godless many centuries ago. Enthronement of the unknown, impersonal ONE would have cut the roots of belief in the historic gods whose real value to men was in their possession of the very qualities denied to the abstract deity of thought. This vague colorless being, by definition, could never be useful as a god. If it was impersonal, what relationship could it have to the social problems of personal beings? If it was timeless, action had no meaning, and the pathetic struggle of men for values in a changing world became mere illusion, the dream play of shadows. If it was purposeless, how could it have any interest in man's battle for the victory of good over evil and his passionate prayers for help? If it was unknowable, what light for human guidance could ever break through the obscuring veils?

How could the thinkers of past ages take seriously the abstract, ghostly deity without qualities? More important, how could the old gods live on after they had been so brusquely thrust aside by the leaders of thought? The answer is simple. The religious philosopher was conditioned by his culture to belief in a divine, spiritual power ruling the world from the unseen. He had a god, or gods, on his hands, entrenched in popu-

lar faith and hoary with antiquity. Moreover he often felt as
deep an emotional need of divine help as the less intellectual
folk who inherited their gods and accepted them uncritically.
Without this conditioning he might have followed the thread
of thought to a first cause or an ultimate unity, but he would
never have discovered the attributes that made the popular
gods lovable. In reality his philosophic ultimate was the shadowy reflection on the unknown of the god who shepherded his
youthful years. His heart reached out to it as though it still
possessed the qualities his mind denied. Only rarely did thinkers
break free from the pull of tradition, deny the gods and surrender their help. It sometimes happened in transition periods
of loss of faith. The Charvakas of India and intellectuals in
China did it more than two thousand years ago but the Greek
Epicureans were so impressed by the universal belief in the
gods that they kept them in their system, at the same time in-
sisting that they were useless for human purposes.

The familiar, friendly, popular gods are the only divine
friends man has trusted. They became what they are because, century after century, the people read into the smiling-
frowning face of the universe the hope that "good will be the
final goal of ill" and that behind the frustration and waste of
transient existence were power, wisdom and goodness working
for ideals men held dear. If these gods die from the human
heart the divine drama is over. The denatured deity of the intellect may be ignored for it has never had any meaning except
that surreptitiously borrowed from the historic gods. The personal deities of India's folk tradition served as broken lights of
the ineffable Brahman. Maimonides and Aquinas, awed by
Aristotle, admitted that no positive qualities could be assigned
to the Unmoved Mover, the First Cause, the *Actus Purus,* but
took the acts attributed to God in Jewish and Christian history
as revelations of him and assumed that the characteristics of
the well-known deity, molded by historic experience, pointed

toward the nature of the Being thought could not define. In Islam, al-Ghazzali, after years of wandering in the maze of philosophy, boldly asserted that God must have the qualities assigned to Allah in the sacred Koran. The historic gods are the only ones that have worthful meaning for man, and the revelation of history is that they were born of nature's response to human needs and grew to magnificent proportions with man's expanding hopes. Each one of the great gods enshrined in the hearts of the people of the modern world has his own unbroken life-story of development from primitive beginnings to his present status as a richly endowed supreme God of the universe. All are different and all are alike. They bear the stamp of their cultures, but each of them has the qualities essential to guarantee ultimate happiness for man. The thought of past ages could not destroy them because the thinker, like his unlettered fellows, needed the salvation they could bring. The undying fire of human desire kept the altars of the gods alight. The conclusion is clear; if the gods of the people perish there is no god beyond.

Yet it has been said repeatedly during twenty-five centuries, by men who could no longer believe in the divine figures of the folk, and, more recently, by some who have viewed the changing deities of history, that all these represent merely ideas of God; behind and beyond them is the true unchanging divine reality. Under the form of faith, this statement carries a deadly agnosticism. All we have ever had, all we can ever have are ideas of God. The crucial problem for the believers in a god behind the changing gods is whether the ideas are truthworthy, whether they point to a real deity who ever remains hidden. There have been tens of thousands of ideas of God, endlessly varied and contradictory. Are they to be understood as the pathetic blunderings of men trying to find a being who watches their ignorant groping from serene, celestial heights? Gods must be accepted as real to be effective. No Moslem or Christian of past centuries could have maintained his faith, if he had not known that the god revealed to him in his scriptures was the true God. If all the past ideas have been faulty or only partly true, which one of the modern gods best embodies the nature of the god behind the veil? Who will say, except the devout Muslim, that Allah is more real than Ormazd? And how shall the Christian convince the son of Islam that his triune deity is truer to reality than Allah? Each religion stubbornly retains the essential qualities of its own god. Even mystical experience, which transcends the intellect in its flight to the hidden god, has found only the deity described in the mystic's own religious tradition. It would be startling news if he came back to report a meeting with a god whose qualities belong to another cultural coloring. The life-stories of the supreme gods show that the qualities men most highly esteem and the powers needful to guarantee human values belong to them all. Are these common characteristics, perhaps, a revelation of the nature of the god beyond man's ken? If this conjecture were accepted as true, the traditional gods, without their distinguishing marks would be denatured, with a lamentable loss of emotional value and there would remain only another idea of God, faulty like the rest. All roads return to the folk deities. The god ideas of the past came neither by a grudging revelation from an incomprehensible god, nor a blind questing after him through time. In the long ages of his way-faring, man found his gods in nature's friendly phases, transformed them into mighty masters of the universe and molded them to meet his needs. Each of the great gods bore the standard of a people's hopes through time. Faith gave them reality. If these gods are not real, faith in a veiled being who can never be truly known will not save God for the world.

Mankind has been conditioned for untold thousands of years to the presence of gods. In ancient times, in some cultures, helpful deities were familiar companions in the routine

of daily living and active participants in all the great ceremonies of state. In ages of frustration, the all-powerful, personal gods took the center of the stage for some peoples. Then
dependence on God became so deeply entrenched that men lost
faith in human nature and all its works, abased themselves
before the Mighty Master of Destiny, extolled his goodness,
love and measureless grace, expecting from his hands the free
gift of salvation. The Zoroastrian scorned this easy way, called
for work and struggle against evil, and, as a soldier fighting for
the good, was vividly aware of the presence of his divine leader,
Ahura Mazda. The cultures which molded the attitudes of mankind were suffused with a divine presence. Recognition of God
in some form became a human habit. In the strange light of
this new age, in the noise and strife of this new world of man's
making, the gods become vague and unreal, but the habit remains. Many a modern man would be startled by the recognition of how little God means to him in his daily life and would
probably be angered by a sudden Nietzschean announcement
that God is dead.

The old habit of belief is fostered by highly placed individuals who are worried by the tides of change eroding the foundations of the established order. Like Cicero and Hsun-tzu,
two thousand years ago, they are not ardent believers themselves, but think belief is good for the masses and makes for
social stability. The habit is fed by institutions with a vested
interest in God. No priest has ever since been so unashamed
in identifying his own well-being with the worship of the
gods as the Brāhman of three thousand years ago, yet all religions record the stubborn conservatism of the official priestly
class. Israel knew the struggle between the priest and prophet.
So did Iran. In modern times the intellectual has joined forces
with the prophet in the cause of faith, the one to bring belief
in God abreast of modern knowledge, the other to make belief
in God mean devotion to social values. In this new form, the

age-old habit of believing is transformed into an earthy pattern of behaving. At the last, however, the surest hold the gods have upon their peoples today is also the oldest. It is anchored in the unfulfilled desires of men. Brute fact tramples the flowers of hope, now as always. In times of overwhelming sorrow, of black despair, in the night of death, the heart would gladly reach out to find the comforting hand of God. But who can tell us surely what and where he is? Does he still stand "within the shadows, keeping watch"? Sense knows not, reason knows not, science knows not, only faith lifts the standard emblazoned with the device—"Must Be."

The gods live by faith. Today it is a cultured faith; a faith tempered in the fires of experience, not the bold faith which made the historic gods robust and omni-competent. It does not come before God, as in primitive times, with a market-basket, asking for dinner. It has become too sophisticated to expect that the almighty arm will be bared to avenge our wrongs and give victory over our enemies. Outside of official circles, it is a little shamefaced about asking something for nothing, even the gift of free grace. Only in Japan does it retain the old confidence in the divine selection of a chosen people. Awed by the vastness of stellar galaxies, it falters to affirm that man is the darling of the universe and that the whole scheme of things is stage setting for his epic experience. Modern faith is modest. The heaven-scaling wings that ranged to bring back answers to earth's unceasing requests are folded. It is a faith for crises, when human wisdom fails and all the achievements of man's hand and brain are of no avail. After he has walked as far as eyes can see the path, toiled until strength is gone, when he is lost in a maze of problems which only become more tangled as he tugs at the threads, when he feels his utter futility before the overwhelming forces arrayed against him, then faith takes flight again to whatever worthful form may be left of the god his fathers knew.

Wisely, men might remember that the gods have kept their thrones because they served the human cause. In the beginning, men, battling for bare existence, expected them to provide the material goods of life. In higher cultures they were enlisted in support of the social values which gave joy, dignity and nobility to the human adventure. Prophets brought their gods thundering from the heights to stem the tide of injustice, to rescue the afflicted, to strike down the wicked oppressors of the poor. The almighty power and irresistible will of the god were terrible only to the evil-doer. To the champions of the lowly, suffering children of men, they gave assurance that the good would at last prevail. The moral values which make life lovely did not have their origin in the gods. Love of kindness and honor, devotion to justice and right, self-sacrifice for causes dear to man, aspiration toward goodness and nobility have never depended upon the gods for their hold upon the heart of man. They flowered out of human experience as men tried to learn the art of living happily together. A god who had earned the right to be trusted by his people was clothed with the most perfect qualities and in return put his power behind the human code and ideal.

No deity could maintain his existence in the modern world who stood in the path of the realization of social values. As the record shows, all the gods of the world have been socialized. Whatever other over-beliefs may cling to them, they now embody the social ideal. No longer may the god of absolute will give eternal happiness to his favorites and eternal damnation to others for his own glory. Few, in the modern world, would find use for a god, dwelling in quiescent bliss in a spiritual realm, indifferent to earthly affairs. Once world-weary men sought release from frustration by mystic union with such divine absolutes, but a sober responsibility for creating the good society weighs heavily upon the hearts of religious men today. If God is, he must mean success for that task. Even if the lifting of the veils of mystery should reveal, behind the friendly gods man has shaped by his desires, an inexorable power with no concern for man's puny planning, the children of earth, like Prometheus, would defy its might and still try to build out a little sunlit valley of happiness in their sequestered nook of space, until time tolled the closing of man's day.

Only one more word remains to be said. More important than faith in God is devotion to the human ideals of which he has become the symbol. Too long the strong gods have been made to bear the burden. Wistfully man has watched for the day of divine action to dawn and ever healed the hurt of disappointment with more passionate faith. Hopes hung in the heavens are of no avail. What the gods have been expected to do, and have failed to do through the ages, man must find the courage and intelligence to do for himself. More needful than faith in God is faith that man can give love, justice, peace and all his beloved moral values embodiment in human relations. Denial of this faith is the only real atheism. Without it, belief in all the galaxies of gods is mere futility. With it, and the practice that flows from it, man need not mourn the passing of the gods.

NOTES

CHAPTER I

THE BIRTH OF THE GODS

[1] Hesiod *Theogony*, 105–107.

[2] Prodicus of Chian. "The sun and moon, rivers and fountains, and in general whatever furthers our life were deemed gods by the men of old times on account of the profit received from them, as the Egyptians deify the Nile. And on this account, bread was worshipped as Demeter, wine as Dionysos, fire as Hephaistos and in short, every useful thing." As quoted in Sextus Empiricus, "Adversus mathematicos," viii, *Opera quae extant* (Geneva, 1621), p. 311.

[3] Euhemerus, see Lactantius, "Divinarum institutionum," i, *Opera Omnia* (Zweibrücken, 1784), pp. 38 ff.

[4] Critias, as quoted in Sextus Empiricus, *op. cit.*, pp. 318–319.

[5] Justin, "Apologia pro Christianis" i, 66; ii, 5, *Patrologia Graeca*, VI, cols. 430, 451–454; also Tatian, "Oratio adversos Graecos," *op. cit.*, cols. 822–827.

[6] P. D. Huet, *Demonstratio Evangelica* (Amsterdam, 1680), pp. 99 ff.; Samuel Bochart, *Geographia Sacra* (4th ed.; Lyons, 1707).

[7] Charles de Brosses, *Du culte des dieux fétiches* (Paris, 1760).

[8] N. S. Bergier, *L'origine des dieux du paganisme* (Paris, 1767), I, Part I, 3, Part II, 75.

[9] Notably Sanchuniathon, Prodicus of Chian, Diodorus Siculus, Banier, duPuis, Fourmont, Heyne, Hume.

[10] Herbert Spencer, *Principles of Sociology* (New York, 1877); Edward B. Tyler, *Primitive Culture* (London, 1871).

[11] Albert Réville, *Prolegomena of the History of Religions*, trans. A. S. Squire (London, 1884).

[12] Émile Durkheim, *The Elementary Forms of the Religious Life*, trans. J. W. Swain (New York, n.d.).

[13] R. R. Marett, *The Threshold of Religion* (2d ed.; New York, 1914).

[14] Wilhelm Schmidt, *Der Ursprung des Gottesidee* (Münster, i.W., 1912–   ) 6 Vols. to date.

[15] Rigveda I, 113:7.

CHAPTER II

HOW THE GODS CHANGE

[1] Don Marquis, *Dreams and Dust* (New York, 1915), p. 105.

CHAPTER III

THE GODS WHO DIED

[1] Don Marquis, *Dreams and Dust* (New York, 1915), p. 103.

[2] On Babylonian and Assyrian religion, see, Morris Jastrow, *Aspects of Religious Belief and Practice in Babylonia and Assyria* (New York, 1911).

[3] Jastrow, *op. cit.*, p. 35.

[4] George Foot Moore, *History of Religions* (New York, 1925), I, 235–236.

[5] On Elam, see, George C. Cameron, *History of Early Iran* (Chicago, 1938).

[6] On Egyptian origins, see, Kurt Sethe, *Urgeschichte und Älteste Religion der Ägypter* (Leipzig, 1930); for history of the gods, J. H. Breasted, *Development of Religion and Thought in Ancient Egypt* (New York, 1912).

[7] Breasted, *op. cit.*, pp. 324, 326.

[8] On Greek origins, see, Martin P. Nilsson, *The Minoan-Mycenaean Religion* (Lund, 1927); on Greek survivals, J. C. Lawson, *Modern Greek Folklore and Ancient Greek Religion* (Cambridge, 1910).

[9] On Roman origins, see, Franz Altheim, *A History of Roman Religion* trans. Harold Mattingly (London, 1938); for history, W. W. Fowler, *The Religious Experience of the Roman People* (London, 1911).

[10] On Teutonic religion, see, P. D. Chantepie de la Saussaye, *The Religion of the Teutons*, trans. Bert J. Vos (Boston, 1902).

CHAPTER IV

AHURA MAZDA

[1] The Ahuna Vairya, the most effective formula of orthodox Zoroastrianism, used constantly in worship through the centuries. Scholars have never been able to agree upon a translation. English versions vary from:—"The will of the Lord is the law of holiness: the riches of Vohu Manah shall be given to him who works in this world for Mazdah, and wields according to the will of Ahura the power he gave him to relieve the poor" (Darmesteter) to—"Even as he (Zarathustra) is the Lord for us to choose, so is he the Judge according to Right, he that bringeth the life-works of Good Thought unto Mazdah, and (so) the Dominion unto Ahura, even he whom they made shepherd for the poor" (Bartholomae and Moulton).

[2] P. v. Bradke, *Dyâus Asura, Ahura Mazdâ und die Asuras* (Halle, 1885), p. 80.

[3] A. A. Macdonell, *Vedic Mythology* (Strassburg, 1897), pp. 43–46.

[4] See Rigveda I, 24, 25; II, 28; V, 62, 63, 85; VI, 67; VII, 60, 61, 64–66, 86–89; VIII, 41, 42. Trans. R. T. H. Griffith (Benares 1896–97).

[5] Rigveda VIII, 41: 10.

[6] Rigveda V, 85: 6.

[7] Atharvaveda IV, 16: 1–5.

[8] Rigveda VII, 66: 13.

[9] Rigveda V, 66: 1.

[10] Rigveda I, 25: 20.

[11] H. S. Nyberg, "Die Religionen des Alten Iran" (Ger. Trans. H. H. Schaeder, *Mitteilungen der vorderasiatisch-aegyptischen Gesellschaft.* Leipzig, 1938), XLIII, pp. 330–332.

[12] The place and date given to Zarathustra and his movement have varied from Western Medea to India, and from 6000 B.C. to the 1st cent. A.D. Orthodox tradition among the Parsees makes Zarathustra a Medean and places the beginning of his mission 258 years before the time of Alexander. The material on this topic is summarized in A. V. W. Jackson, *Zoroaster, the Prophet of Ancient Iran* (New York, 1899), pp. 150–225; and Nyberg, *op. cit.*, pp. 44–45. The present treatment follows Nyberg as to place. Available data, giving due weight to Vedic material, seem to demand a date for Zarathustra not later than the close of the 2nd millennium B.C.

[13] Yasna 32: 9–15; 48: 10.

[14] Yasna 33: 4.

[15] Most satisfactory English translation in, J. H. Moulton, *Early Zoroastrianism* (London, 1913), pp. 343–390.

[16] Nyberg, *op. cit.*, p. 263.

[17] Yasna 30: 3.

[18] Yasna 45: 2.

[19] Yasna 30: 9; 31: 4; 33: 8.

[20] Nyberg, *op. cit.*, pp. 260 ff.

[21] *Ibid.*, pp. 233–327.

[22] Yast 19: 16. Trans. J. Darmesteter, *Sacred Books of the East*, XXIII, 290.

[23] Yasna 36: 1–4.

[24] *History*, Bk. I, 131.

[25] Trans. in R. G. Kent, "The Recently Published Old Persian Inscriptions," *Journal of the American Oriental Society*, LI, 199.

[26] Yast 10: 123; 15: 2; 5: 17.

[27] Yasna 1: 1–4. Trans. in G. F. Moore, op. cit., I, 380.

[28] Yasna 19: 5–6.

[29] Yast 1: 1–3.

[30] Cow's urine.

[31] Sacred twigs.

[32] Yasna 62: 1–11; Vendidad 18: 18–27.

[33] Bundahis 30: 19 ff. Trans. E. W. West, *Sacred Books of the East*, V, 6.

[34] See the treatment of this question in H. S. Nyberg, "Cosmogonie et Cosmologie Mazdéenes," *Journal Asiatique*, CCXIX, 56, 106–107.

[35] Dinkard, Bk. IX, chap. 30: 4.

[36] Menuk-i Khrat, 8: 17–19, 21.

[37] Yast 10.

[38] Sad Dar, Chap. iv.

[39] Bundahis 1: 14.

[40] *Ibid.*, 2: 10–11.

[41] Mardan-farukh, "Sikand-Gûmânik Vigar" *Sacred Books of the East*, XXIV, 117–251.

[42] M. N. Dhalla, *History of Zoroastrianism* (New York, 1938), p. 443.

[43] D. P. Sanjana.

[44] P. A. Wadia, *Zoroastrianism and Our Spiritual Heritage* (Bombay, 1923).

[45] M. N. Dhalla, *Our Perfecting World* (New York, 1930), p. 9–10.

Chapter V

THE GODS OF INDIA

[1] The Savitri, the most sacred verse of the Vedas. Rigveda III, 62: 10.

[2] Atharvaveda IV, 16: 2–5. Trans. A. Kaegi, *The Rigveda* (Boston, 1886).

[3] Rigveda II, 21: 6.

[4] Rigveda III, 34: 11.

[5] Rigveda X, 124: 5.

[6] Atharvaveda XIII, 3: 13.

[7] Rigveda I, 164: 46.

[8] Rigveda X, 129: 6–7.

[9] Rigveda IV, 24: 10.

[10] Satapatha Brahmana 2.2.2: 6. Trans. J. Eggeling, *Sacred Books of the East*, XII, 309.

[11] Chandogya Upanishad 7.25.2. Trans. F. M. Müller, *Sacred Books of the East*, I, 124.

[12] *Ibid.*, 3, 14: 1, 3–4.

[13] Mahabharata 3.271.47.

[14] *Ibid.*, 3.189.5 ff.

[15] Brahmajala Sutra 2.5. Trans. T. W. Rhys Davids, *Sacred Books of the Buddhists*, II, 31.

[16] "Bhuridatta-Jataka" 8.208, *The Jataka*, Ed. E. B. Cowell (Cambridge, 1907) VI, 110.

[17] An illuminating treatment of the origins of the two popular gods, Vishnu and Śiva is, Sir R. G. Bhandarkar, "Vaisnavism, Saivism, and minor Religious Systems," *Grundriss der Indo-Arischen Philologie und Altertumskunde* (1913), III, pt. 6.

[18] Katha Upanishad 1.3.9. Trans. F. M. Müller, *Sacred Books of the East*, XV, 13.

[19] Mahabharata 3.189.27 ff.

[20] See, Sir John Marshall, *Mohenjo-daro and the Indus Civilization* (London, 1931), 3 vols.; also, Ernest Mackay, *The Indus Civilization* (London, 1935).

[21] Rigveda VII, 21: 5.

[22] Rigveda I, 114: 8.

[23] Atharvaveda XI, 2: 1–31; XV, 5: 1–7.

[24] Śvetaśvatara Upanishad 6.11.

[25] Visnu Purana, Bk. I, chap. 22. Trans. H. H. Wilson (London, 1864).

[26] Mahabharata 12.344.

[27] *Songs of Kabir*, trans. R. Tagore (New York, 1916), p. 82. By permission of The Macmillan Company, publishers.

[28] *The Ramayana of Tulsi Das*, trans. F. S. Growse (Cawnpore, 1891), II, 169.

[29] Nicol Macnicol, *Psalms of Maratha Saints* (London, 1919), p. 73.

[30] Tiru-Mular, quoted in J. Estlin Carpenter, *Theism in Medieval India* (London, 1921), p. 353.

[31] Dayanand Saraswati, *Satyarth Prakash*, trans. Durga Prasad (Lahore, 1908), p. 542.

[32] *Sādhanā* (New York, 1913), p. 107.

[33] *Gitanjali* (New York, 1930), p. 9. By permission of The Macmillan Company, publishers.

[34] *Ibid.*, p. 64.

[35] J. C. Ghose, *The Positive Religion* (Bhowanipur, n.d.).

CHAPTER VI

BUDDHAS AND BODHISATTVAS

[1] The Buddhist devotional confession, from *Khuddaka-Patha*, i.

[2] On early Buddhism see: T. W. Rhys Davids, *Buddhism* (New York, 1896); C. A. F. Rhys Davids, *Outlines of Buddhism* (London, 1934); for an historical study of the spread of Buddhism and its modern form, an excellent work is J. B. Pratt, *The Pilgrimage of Buddhism* (New York, 1928).

[3] T. W. Rhys Davids, *Early Buddhism* (Chicago, 1908), pp. 72–73.

[4] *Majjhima Nikaya*, i, 487.

[5] *Sutta Nipata*, Bk. I, sutta 8. Trans. Lord Chalmers, *Buddha's Teachings* (Cambridge, 1932), pp. 37, 39.

[6] An excellent story of this development is in E. J. Thomas, *The History of Buddhist Thought* (London, 1933); see also, Paul Oltramare, "La Histoire des idées Théosophiques dans l'Inde," *La Theosophie Buddhique* (Paris, 1923); for Buddhist cosmology see, W. M. McGovern, *A Manual of Buddhist Philosophy* (London, 1923).

[7] *Majjhima Nikaya*, i, 69–70.

[8] *Lalita Vistara*, Chap. vii, trans. P. E. Foucaux (Paris, 1892), I, 79; see the parallel stories in E. J. Thomas, *The Life of Buddha as Legend and History* (London, 1927), pp. 31–33.

[9] *Dhammapada*, 165. Trans. A. J. Edmunds.

[10] *Digha Nikaya*, ii, 88.

[11] *Suvarnaprabhasa-Sutra*, Chap. xxvi. Trans. D. T. Suzuki.

[12] *Saddharma-Pundarika*, Chap. xv.

[13] *Ibid.*, Chaps. i and xi.

[14] Hendrik Kern, *Manual of Indian Buddhism* (Strassburg, 1896), p. 66, n. 2.

[15] *The Larger Sukhavati-Vyuha*, Chap. xvi.

[16] For illustrations, with descriptive commentary on these Mahayana deities, see, Alice Getty, *The Gods of Northern Buddhism* (Oxford, 1914).

[17] J. J. M. DeGroot, *Le Code du Mahayana en Chine* (Amsterdam, 1893), pp. 16–17.

[18] K. L. Reichelt, *Truth and Tradition in Chinese Buddhism* (Shanghai, 1928), pp. 181–182.

[19] The most complete study of Tibetan Buddhism is, L. L. Waddell, *The Buddhism of Tibet* (London, 1895); see also, Sir Charles Bell, *The Religion of Tibet* (Oxford, 1931).

[20] Waddell, *op. cit.*, p. 435.

[21] For the Japanese phase of Buddhism see, Sir Charles Eliot, *Japanese Buddhism* (London, 1935).

[22] Quoted in, J. Hackin and others, *Asiatic Mythology* (New York, n.d.), p. 30.

[23] Dai-o (1235–1308), trans. in D. T. Suzuki, *Manual of Zen Buddhism* (Kyoto, 1935), p. 175.

[24] T'ai Hsu, *Lectures in Buddhism* (Paris, 1928), p. 48.

[25] Lakshmi Narasu, "Is Buddhism a Religion?" *The Buddhist Annual of Ceylon* (1927), III, 71.

[26] Dhammapada, 160.

CHAPTER VII

THE GODS OF CHINA

[1] *Tao-Te-Ching*, Chap. xxv. Trans. Ch'u Ta-Kao.

[2] See, Herrlee G. Creel, *Studies in Early Chinese Culture* (Baltimore, 1937), pp. 49–95.

[3] The best work on the earliest Chinese culture is H. G. Creel, *The Birth of China* (London, 1936).

[4] See, Wang Chih-hsin, "The Religious Experience of the Chinese People," *Chinese Recorder* (1927), LVIII, 192–207; L. C. Hopkins, "Pictographic Reconnaissances, being Discoveries, Recoveries and Conjectural Raids in Archaic Chinese Writing," *Journal of the Royal Asiatic Society of Great Britain and Ireland* (1917), pp. 773–813.

[5] From an article still unpublished, "A New Theory of the Origin of T'ien, 'Heaven.'"

[6] From the *Kou Yü*, quoted in Fung Yu-lan, *A History of Chinese Philosophy*, trans. Derk Bodde (Peiping, 1937), p. 39.

[7] *The Chinese Classics*, trans. James Legge (London, 1871), III, 283, IV, 340.

[8] *Ibid.*, IV, 448, 505.

[9] *Ibid.*, p. 523.

[10] *Ibid.*, pp. 582–583.

[11] *Ibid.*, p. 348, cf. 325–326.

[12] From a sage of the sixth century B.C., quoted by Fung, *op. cit.*, p. 68.

[13] *Lun Yü*, Bk. iii, 12.

[14] *Ibid.*, Bk. vi, 20.

[15] Mo-tzu, Chap. xxvi, Yi-pao Mei, *The Ethical and Political Works of Motse* (London, 1929), p. 138.

[16] *Ibid.*, pp. 135–136, 151.

[17] *Ibid.*, p. 145.

[18] *Tao-Te-Ching*, Chap. xxv.

[19] *Ibid.*, Chap. XLII.

[20] *Ibid.*, Chap. xxxvii.

[21] *Ibid.*, Chap. v.

[22] Chuang-tzu, Chap. xxiv. H. A. Giles, *Chuang Tzu, Mystic, Moralist, and Social Reformer* (London, 1926), pp. 333–334.

[23] *Ibid.*, p. 23.

[24] *Ibid.*, p. 31.

[25] *Ibid.*, p. 158.

[26] *Ibid.*, p. 82.

[27] *Lü-Shih Ch'un Ch'iu*, Chap. xiii, 1.

28 *Chung Yung*, Chap. i, 1–2, Chap. xx, 18; *Mencius*, Bk. IV, pt. i, chap. xii, 1–3.

29 *Huai Nan Tzu*, trans. Evan Morgan, *Tao, the Great Luminant* (London, 1933), p. 11.

30 *The Works of Hsuntze*, trans. Homer H. Dubs (London, 1928), p. 301.

31 *Ibid.*, pp. 173–174.

32 *Ibid.*

33 *Ibid.*, p. 181.

34 *Ibid.*, p. 183.

35 Han-fei-tzu quoted by Fung, *op. cit.*, p. 177.

36 Tung Chung-shu, Address to the Emperor Wu Ti, Quoted by J. K. Shryock, *The State Cult of Confucius* (New York, 1932), p. 56.

37 *Lun Heng*, Bk. 3, Chap. v., trans. Alfred Forke, "Selected Essays of the Philosopher Wang Ch'ung," *Mitteilungen des Seminars für orientalische Sprachen* (Berlin, 1906–07), IX, 181–399, X, 1–172.

38 *Ibid.*, Bk. 18, Chap. i.

39 *The Philosophy of Human Nature*, trans. J. Percy Bruce (London, 1922), p. 147.

40 *The Philosophy of Wang Yang-ming*, trans. F. G. Henke (Chicago, 1916), p. 52.

41 *Ibid.*, p. 83.

42 *Lun Heng*, Bk. 25, Chap. iv.

43 *Ibid.*

44 *Mencius*, Bk. VII, pt. ii, chap. xiv, 4.

45 J. Hackin and others, *Asiatic Mythology* (New York, n.d.), pp. 266–267; see also, Lewis Hodous, "The Pearly Emperor," *Chinese Recorder*, L, 749–759.

46 See, Edouard Chavannes, *Le T'ai Chan* (Paris, 1910).

47 *Ibid.*, p. 438, n. 2.

48 *Shryock, op. cit.*, p. 190.

CHAPTER VIII

AMATERASU-OMIKAMI

1 The "most sacred Imperial Edict," *Nihongi*, Bk. II, 16.

2 C. W. Bishop, *The Historical Geography of Early Japan*, Smithsonian Institution Report, 1925, pp. 552–553.

3 *Nihongi*, Bk. I, 11, 12. Trans. W. G. Aston (New York, 1924).

4 *Kojiki*, I, xi. Trans. B. H. Chamberlain, *Transactions of the Asiatic Society of Japan*. Suppl. to Vol. X.

5 *Ibid.*, I, xvi.

6 *Ibid.*

7 *Nihongi*, Bk. III, 3.

8 Genchi Kato, *A Study of Shinto, the Religion of the Japanese Nation* (Tokyo, 1926), p. 145.

9 Sir Ernest Satow, "The Revival of Pure Shinto," *Transactions of the Asiatic Society of Japan*, Reprints (Dec. 1927), II, 177.

10 The account of the dedication of the shrine to Amaterasu in Manchukuo and a translation of the Emperor's rescript is in *Japan Advertiser*, July 16, 1940.

[11] Iwasaburo Okino, *The Shrine Problem* (Jinja Mondai) (Tokyo, 1939), p. 149. Digest and trans. by D. C. Holtom.

[12] On Shinto, and especially the sects, the best work is D. C. Holton, *The National Faith of Japan* (London, 1937).

[13] Nobuhiro Matsumoto, *Essai sur la mythologie japonaise* (Paris, 1928), pp. 71–80.

[14] Genchi Kato, *op. cit.*, pp. 53–54.

CHAPTER IX

YAHWEH

[1] The Shema, Deut. 6: 4.

[2] For an argument for the presence of Yahweh in North Palestine, in early times see, Julius Lewy, "Influences Hurrites sur Israel," *Revue des Études Semitiques* (1938), pp. 49–75.

[3] A view of some of these recovered gods may be found in J. W. Jack, *The Ras Shamra Tablets* (Edinburgh, 1935).

[4] For the general interpretation of the early history of Yahweh I am indebted to Theophile J. Meek, *Hebrew Origins* (New York, 1936).

[5] Gen. 49: 8. O. T. quotations from *The Bible, an American Translation* (Chicago, 1935).

[6] Exod. 18: 11.

[7] Judg. 5: 4–5.

[8] Num. 10: 35–36.

[9] I Sam. 4: 7–8.

[10] Ps. 29: 1–10 trans. Moses Buttenwieser, *The Psalms* (Chicago, 1938), p. 148. The name "Yahweh" has been retained in the text where Professor Buttenwieser translates "Lord."

[11] II Chron. 11: 13–14.

[12] For a discussion of Anath see, Albert Vincent, *La Religion des Judéo-Araméens d'Éléphantine* (Paris, 1937), pp. 622–653.

[13] An excellent treatment of the prophetic period is, J. M. P. Smith, *The Prophets and Their Times* (Chicago, 1925).

[14] Amos 5: 21–24.

[15] Mic. 6: 6–8.

[16] Isa. 1: 17.

[17] Hos. 10: 1–2.

[18] Isa. 10: 5–6.

[19] J. M. P. Smith, "The Effect of the Disruption on the Hebrew Thought of God," *American Journal of Semitic Languages and Literature*, XXXII, 261–269.

[20] S. A. Cook, "The Inauguration of Judaism," *Cambridge Ancient History*, VI, 180, 189–90.

[21] Isa. 40: 31.

[22] Ludwig Blau, "Angelology," *The Jewish Encyclopedia*, I, 583–589.

[23] "The four letters may be mentioned or heard only by holy men whose ears and tongues are purified by wisdom and by no others in any place whatsoever." Philo, *Life of Moses*, iii, 11.

24 *Berachoth*, Folio vii, col. 1.

25 "Tract Abuda Zara" *New Edition of the Babylonian Talmud*, Ed. and trans. Michael L. Rodkinson, X, 5.

26 *Guide of the Perplexed*, trans. M. Friedländer (London, 1885), Vol. I, Chap. 58.

27 The God of Reform Judaism is of this type. See, Abba Hillel Silver, *Religion in a Changing World* (New York, 1930).

28 Hermann Cohen, "Religion und Sittlichkeit," *Jahrbuch für jüdische Geschichte und Literatur* (Berlin, 1907), X, 98–171.

29 Mordecai M. Kaplan, *The Meaning of God in Modern Jewish Religion* (New York, 1937), pp. 323–324.

CHAPTER X

THE CHRISTIAN GOD

1 From the Apostles' Creed.

2 H. R. Willoughby, *Pagan Regeneration* (Chicago, 1929).

3 S. J. Case, *Experience with the Supernatural in Early Christian Times* (New York, 1929).

4 I Cor. 15: 45 & 21.

5 Rom. 9: 5 seems to be an exception, but see Goodspeed's translation, and the discussion in A. C. McGiffert, *The God of the Early Christians* (New York, 1924), pp. 22–29.

6 Acts 16: 31.

7 *Epistle to the Ephesians*, Chap. xv; *Epistle to the Romans*, Chap. vi.

8 S. J. Case, *Jesus Through the Centuries* (Chicago, 1932), p. 151.

9 An anonymous early Greek hymn, from, Mrs. Rundle Charles, *Te Deum Laudamus* (New York, 1899), p. 40.

10 Matt. 28: 19.

11 Justin, *Apologia*, 1.13.

12 Athanasius, *De Incarnatione Verbi Dei* 54.

13 The so-called Athanasian Creed. Phillip Schaff, *The Creeds of Christendom* (New York, 1919), II, 66–67. By permission of Harper and Brothers, publishers.

14 Anonymous communion hymn (c. 6th cent.), in, Stephen A. Hurlbut, *Hortus Conclusus* (Washington, D.C., 1931), pt. 4, p. 11.

15 *De Trinitate* 5.9.

16 *Retractionum* 1.13.3.

17 *De Divinitatis essentia Monologium*, Chap. xvi.

18 *Cur Deus Homo*.

19 *Summa Theologica* Pt. iii, q. 1. art. 2, cf. *Summa Contra Gentiles* Bk. i., Chap. 14.

20 By St. Thomas Aquinas, trans. in, Matthew Britt, *Hymns of the Breviary and Missal* (New York, 1922), pp. 190–191.

21 Britt, *op. cit.*, p. 109.

22 Hurlbut, *op. cit.*, pt. 9, p. 13.

23 Ascribed to Rabanus Maurus, in, Britt, *op. cit.*, pp. 312–313.

24 Rt. Rev. Msgr. Pohle, *Mariology* (St. Louis, 1926), p. 19.

[25] Fr. Kilian J. Hennrich, *Our Blessed Lady* (Paterson, N.J., 1938), p. 23.

[26] *Ibid.*, p. 37.

[27] Trans. by Frederick H. Hodge (1853).

[28] *De Providentia Dei*, Chap. iv.

[29] The Westminster Confession of Faith, Schaff, *op. cit.*, III, 606–607.

[30] *De Trinitate* 5.9–10.

[31] *De Divinitatis essentia Monologium*, Conclusion.

[32] *Sermo* 76.6.

[33] *Summa Contra Gentiles*, Bk. i, chap. 3.

[34] *Confutatio Lutheriana* (Erlanger ed.), V, 505–506. Later he was reconciled to the term as true to Scripture and useful against heretics, see, Julius Köstlin, *The Theology of Luther* (Philadelphia, 1897), II, 268–269.

[35] *Institutes*, Bk. I, chap. xiii, 4–5.

[36] The Panpsychists, e. g. Samuel Butler.

[37] Josiah Royce.

[38] August Comte.

[39] Conwy L. Morgan.

[40] Herbert Spencer.

[41] Ralph Barton Perry.

[42] Henri L. Bergson.

[43] Bishop F. J. McConnell.

[44] H. A. Overstreet.

[45] Eugene W. Lyman.

[46] James B. Pratt.

[47] E. S. Brightman.

[48] William James.

[49] Sir James Jeans.

[50] E. S. Ames.

[51] Alfred N. Whitehead.

[52] Karl Barth.

[53] H. N. Wieman.

[54] Shailer Mathews.

[55] F. C. S. Schiller.

[56] John E. Boodin.

[57] John Dewey.

CHAPTER XI

ALLAH

[1] The first of the fundamental pillars of Islam, the confession of faith, in El Bokhari, *Les Traditions Islamiques*, trans. O. Houdas & W. Marcais (Paris, 1903), I, 12.

[2] Theodor Nöldeke, "Arabs (Ancient)," *Encyclopedia of Religion and Ethics*, I, 661 ff.

[3] Discussion of the origins of Allah, from different points of view, may be found in Julius Wellhausen, *Reste arabischen Heidentumes* (Berlin, 1897) and D. B. Macdonald, "Allah," *Encyclopaedia of Islam*, I, 302.

4 *Koran*, Sura 29: 61 f. Trans. J. M. Rodwell.

5 S. 6: 109, 16: 40, 35: 40.

6 S. 10: 23, 29: 65, 31: 31.

7 S. 16: 59 f.

8 S. 89: 18–21.

9 S. 6: 96–100.

10 S. 6: 104.

11 S. 35: 9, 13: 27, 74: 34.

12 S. 2: 284.

13 S. 50: 15.

14 S. 33: 40.

15 S. 2: 255.

16 El Bokhari, IV, 300, cf. 592.

17 *Ibid.*, p. 609.

18 *Ibid.*, pp. 314–15, 599–600.

19 *Ibid.*, pp. 588, 595.

20 The ninety-nine names are, the Merciful, the Compassionate, the King, the Most Holy, the Tranquil, the Faithful, the Protector, the Victorious, the Mighty, the Self-exalted, the Creator, the Maker, the Former, the Forgiver, the Wrathful, the Giver, the Cherisher, the Conqueror, the Knower, the Seizer, the Expander, the Depresser, the Exalter, the Strengthener, the Disgracer, the Hearer, the Seer, the Ruler, the Just, the Benignant, the Informer, the Great, the Pardoner, the Rewarder, the High, the Great, the Rememberer, the Powerful, the Satisfier, the Glorious, the Kind, the Guardian, the Answerer, the All-embracing, the Wise, the All-loving, the Glorious, the Provider, the Strong, the Firm, the Friend, the Praiseworthy, the Beginner, the Reckoner, the Restorer, the Life-giver, the Destroyer, the Living, the Self-subsisting, the Finder, the Glorious, the Unique, the Eternal, the Powerful, the Prevailing, the Leader, the Finisher, the First, the Eternal, the Everlasting, the Innermost, the Revealer, the Governor, the Pure, the Propitious, the Remitter, the Avenger, the Merciful, the King of the Kingdom, Lord of Glory and Honor, the Equitable, the Assembler, the Rich, the Enricher, the Possessor, the Prohibitor, the Afflicter, the Benefactor, the Light, the Guide, the Creator, the Observer, the Inheritor, the Director, the Patient, the Mild. Quoted from, E. M. Wherry, *A Comprehensive Commentary on the Quran* (Boston, 1884), II, 242.

21 On the schools of Muslim thought see, T. J. de Boer, *The History of Philosophy in Islam*, trans. Edward R. Jones (London, 1903); Duncan B. Macdonald, *Development of Muslim Theology, Jurisprudence and Constitutional Theory* (New York, 1903); and Baron Carra de Vaux, *Les Penseurs de L'Islam* (Paris, 1923), Vol. IV.

22 From a short creed by al-Ashari, in, Macdonald, *op. cit.*, p. 299.

23 A verse attributed to Mansur Hallaj, in *The Doctrine of the Sufis*, trans. from Arabic by A. J. Arberry (Cambridge, 1935), p. 47.

24 Quoted in R. P. Masani, *The Conference of the Birds* (Oxford, 1924), pp. 11–12.

25 *Ibid.*, p. 12.

26 Mansur Hallaj, trans. in R. A. Nicholson, *Studies in Islamic Mysticism* (Cambridge, 1921), p. 80.

27 Baba Kuhi of Shiraz, trans. in R. A. Nicholson, *The Mystics of Islam* (London, 1914), p. 59.

[28] From the *Ihya* of al-Ghazzali, trans. in Macdonald, *op. cit.*, p. 302.

[29] *Ibid.*, pp. 302–303.

[30] *Rissalat al Tawhid*, Ed. with introduction by B. Michel (Paris, 1927). On Sheik Abdou see, C. C. Adams, *Islam and Modernism in Egypt* (London, 1933), pp. 18–176.

[31] Sir Mohammed Iqbal, *The Reconstruction of Religious Thought in Islam* (London, 1934), pp. 59–89.

[32] Section 15 of the foundation principles of the Turkish journal, *Idjtihad*.

INDEX

Absolute, the: Adi-Buddha as, 139, 142, 154; Amaterasu as, 211; Brahman as, 99-104, 110, 115-116, 119, 120, 121, 124; Christian God as, 279-280, 281; Dharmakaya as, 138, 142, 148, 152; of philosophy, 26-27, 322-323; relation of, to personal gods of India, 102, 110, 115; Śiva as, 110; Tao as, 148, 178 ff.; T'ien as, 184; Vairocana as, 148, 211; Vajradhara as, 154; Vishnu as, 107, 110, 117; Yahweh as, 246.

Adad, 34.

Adi-Buddha, 139, 142, 154.

Adityas, 58, 59.

Agni, 90, 91, 95, 157, 161.

Ahriman: 75, 76, 87, 239; creator of evil, 83; perverse thought of man, 85; problem for theologians, 81-85. *See also*, Angra Mainyu.

Ahuna Vairya, 57, 72, 332 note 1 of Chap. IV.

Ahura Mazda: 25, 31, 36, 58-87, 172, 236, 251, 294, 315, 316, 321, 325, 326; and other Ahuras, 66, 67; and problem of evil, 21-22, 64, 66, 71-72; blended with Auramazda, 69; creator of good, 71, 81; drift toward omnipotence, 80-84; flight to India, 84; influence of other gods on, 78, 80, 81, 83, 86; in the modern world, 84-88; molded by Zarathustra, 20, 63-67; relation of, to Dyaus and Varuna, 58, 66, 92; relation of, to other Amesha Spentas, 65, 68-69, 78-79.

Akhnaton, 41-42.

Akshobya, 139.

Alemona, 53.

Aleyn, 219.

Allah: 20, 21, 24, 264, 284-313, 315,

316, 321, 324, 325; absolute will of, 287, 295-299; and problem of evil, 298; as Fate, 297, 302; as First Cause, 296, 303; as heavenly judge, 285; before Mohammed, 284, 285; characteristics of, 287-288, 290-291, 309-310; determinism of, 298-300; empire and, 289-290, 294-295; in Iran, 80, 81, 83-84; in the modern world, 312-313; in the Sunna, 291-292; influence of other gods on, 24-25, 285, 290, 294, 310; molded by Mohammed, 285-289; mysticism and, 304-306; ninety-nine names of, 292-293, 341 note 20; of orthodoxy, 301-302, 308, 309-310; philosophy and, 296, 303, 307-308; supreme God of heaven and earth, 286; unity of, 296-297.

Amaterasu-Omikami: 199-217, 315, 316, 321; as Absolute Spirit, 215; as Dharmakaya, 211; bound to Japanese state, 213, 216; Christian prayers to, 214-215; claim of, to world dominion, 213-214; conflicts of, with Susa-no-Wo, 200-202, 204-206; identified with Vairocana, 159, 211; Imperial ancestress, 199, 207, 208, 212, 213, 216; in the modern world, 216-217; influenced by Buddhism, 211-212; patroness of agriculture, 207; Sun-goddess, 200, 202, 204, 205, 215-217; supremacy of, 206-207, 213; symbol of Japanese patriotism, 214.

Ameretat, 65, 68.

Amesha Spentas, 68-69, 70, 72, 78-79.

Amida, 158, 160. *See* Amitabha.

Amitabha: 139, 140, 143-144, 145, 147; Buddhafield of, 144, 152; free grace of, 144; in China, 149; in